P9-DXF-991

PSYCHOSIS AND POWER

James M. Glass

PSYCHOSIS

Threats to Democracy

AND POWER

in the Self and the Group

Cornell University Press · *Ithaca and London*

First published 1995 by Cornell University Press.

Library of Congress Cataloging-in-Publication Data

Glass, James M.
Psychosis and power : threats to democracy in the self and the group / James M. Glass.
p. cm.
Includes bibliographical references and index.
ISBN 0-8014-3037-2 (alk. paper)
1. Psychoses—Social aspects. 2. Despotism—Psychological aspects. 3. Democracy—Psychological aspects. 4. Toleration. 5. Projection (Psychology) 6. Power (Social sciences)—Psychological aspects. 7. Consensus (Social sciences)—Psychological aspects. 8. Control (Psychology)—Political aspects. I. Title.
RC512.G53 1995
616.89—dc20 94-35314

Printed in the United States of America

⊗ The paper in this book meets the minimum requirements of the American National Standard for Information Sciences—Permanence of Paper for Printed Library Materials, ANSI Z39.48-1984.

For Maria Klement, Roger Lewin, and Clarence Schulz

Thus, they love their delusions as they love themselves.

SIGMUND FREUD

The academic philosophic background and the realistic foreground of psychoanalytical experience approach each other; but recognition of the one by the other does not occur as often or as fruitfully as one might expect.

WILFRED BION

Could cosmopolitanism as moral imperative be the secular form of that bond bringing together families, languages, and states that religion claimed to be? Something beyond religion: the belief that individuals are fulfilled if and only if the entire species achieves the practice of rights for everyone, everywhere.

JULIA KRISTEVA

CONTENTS

ACKNOWLEDGMENTS

I AM grateful to the patients and staff of the Sheppard and Enoch Pratt Hospital in Towson, Maryland. My debt to this remarkable institution is spelled out in some detail in the Afterword to this book. During the course of my research, countless patients, nurses, mental health workers, psychotherapists, occupational, dance, and art therapists made available to me their impressions, thoughts, expertise, knowledge, and guidance. It is difficult to imagine an environment more dedicated to ameliorating horrifying emotional anguish than the Sheppard-Pratt of the 1970s and 1980s. But more on that in the Afterword.

It is impossible to thank all the staff members who over the years generously gave of their time, but I do want to acknowledge the cooperation and support of Drs. Rachel Hamilton, Charles Peters, Miles Quaytman, and Gerald Whitmarsh, and on the nursing staff Rosalie Alsop, Jane Cole, Jane Goldsborough, and Robert Hurvich. Joan Lewin and Cristy Bergland, the dance and art therapists, provided important and revealing insights. Drs. Maria Klement, Roger Lewin, and Clarence Schulz gave me advice, direction, and instruction; without their strong command of clinical literature and practice, I would have been lost in the often confusing and emotionally draining patient narratives. These gifted therapists enabled me to make some philosophic and political sense of the language and histories of individuals suffering disabling emotional and psychological dislocation.

I am grateful for the conceptual and editorial advice of Fred Alford, Roger Haydon, and Linda Zerilli. The manuscript benefited enormously from their participation in its various stages of development. I thank Fred Dallmayr, Jean Elshtain, Jane Flax, Sy Rubenfeld, Michael Weinstein, and Victor Wolfenstein for their reflection and comments on specific chapters and arguments. I also thank my typist Flora Paoli, whose skill continually brought my various revisions into sharper focus.

My wife, Cyndi, and my children gave me patience, warmth, concern, and laughter. I will always cherish the interruptions, the moments of connection and love.

And finally, to the patients who shared with me their thoughts and feelings, I say thank you. I leave the hospital wards with great respect for these individuals and great sorrow for what they have had to endure, the private terrors that consumed their lives, ruined their relationships, and destroyed happiness, pleasure, and even laughter, their fight to transcend this suffering, to recover life and the sense of possibility. It is a heroic struggle, sometimes won but, tragically, too often lost.

JAMES M. GLASS

College Park, Maryland

INTRODUCTION

PATIENTS in hospitals like Sheppard and Enoch Pratt, which at one time offered long-term refuge and asylum from what R. D. Laing called the prevailing winds of opinion and belief, revealed a form of knowing and being which told very special stories about the self, its operations, history, and projections. Within those stories lay an experience of pain, vivid images of the havoc emotional anguish works on the body and its senses, messages about desire and will inscribed in the self as hallucination and delusion, and the self's projection of these messages onto a larger public space. It is this kind of knowledge about the self which is philosophy, literally the *doing* of philosophy. This peculiar peripatetics perhaps has something in common with the philosophy

The Sheppard and Enoch Pratt Hospital in Towson, Maryland, is a nonprofit, private, multiservice psychiatric hospital. It was founded by Quakers at the turn of the century and has long had a reputation for humane, caring treatment and for respecting the rights and dignity of its patients. During the years of my research the hospital offered a variety of therapeutic services, including psychotherapy, dance, art, and occupational therapy. In addition its staff was trained to listen to and to "be with" the expressions of the inner self. While medications were used at the hospital, they were but one element of a comprehensive treatment approach. Both therapists (psychiatrists, psychologists, social workers) and staff (nurses and mental health workers) paid particularly close attention to relationships, their content and development, and their impact on the life of the unit. I will have more to say about this in the following chapters.

practiced by Heraclitus and the other pre-Socratics. Walking with the other in a wilderness of meaning and being, constructing and deconstructing images, finding and losing languages—such activity may at certain junctures yield evanescent revelations that soon fall away into the timeless, unreachable spaces of the self.

Thinking about and listening to these languages became, for me, a journey from lived experience to speculation, from the clinical reality of distorted images, wrecked lives, and hallucinatory terrors back to theoretical argument about more abstract and public or political concerns. Much of the research for this book was done in an office in Windy Brae, one of the oldest buildings on the grounds of the Sheppard and Enoch Pratt Hospital. Parts of the horseshoe-shaped building had been renovated a few years earlier. One wing housed administrative and financial offices, and the half moon at the top of the horseshoe had been turned into a modern, well-furnished lobby area. But the wing where my office was located remained pretty much as it had been when the building was constructed in the 1920s.

The upper floors of this three-story building were mostly empty but for an itinerant researcher or two. A consultant to the hospital from time to time used one of the rooms for interviews. A division of a Baltimore social services agency held meetings with clients. In the basement, at least for a time, Sheppard operated a day hospital, a sort of custodial operation and social hall where day patients could meet and try to relax or participate in the many organized activities.

Windy Brae, situated on top of a small hill, overlooked the grounds of the hospital and a nearby grove of rather imposing pines, maples, and oaks. In the rooms of my wing, each with its own closet, basin, and window, patients long ago had lived, slept, and suffered, but no patients had been housed there for many years. Now, the building, long past its prime, waited for the renovation that would turn it into a modern office complex for therapists connected with Sheppard. The unchanged physical structure, it seemed to me anyway, held melancholy secrets: stark bricks, concrete, mortar, tiles memorialized a collective past. Lamentations were carved into a legacy of stone.

In its current incarnation, the building—certainly my wing of it—seemed ancient. The dull, flat, white paint was peeling. The worn and dreary rooms were tiny cubicles, just large enough for the bed, desk, and reading chair they would once have contained. The hallways were narrow and ill lit, paved with the familiar linoleum squares. At the end of each corridor was a large bathroom, with its bank of toilets, chipped enamel sinks, and a couple of showers. The place had the aura of an old Sidney Greenstreet movie. Yet, the building also seemed comfortingly permanent. The red-brick walls, thickly laid with plaster, were so solid that even a sledge hammer couldn't penetrate. The double-hung windows, with their old latticed blinds, seemed protective. Dense hardwood frames and mullions, generous in breadth, set off each pane as if it were a little painting. I imagined that whoever built these windows had a keen appreciation for durability, a sense of how to keep the bad spirits out and the good ones in.

My office was on the third floor. Outside my window a straggly tree grew every which way. Directly opposite were the modern windows of the other side of the horseshoe. That sleek, technocratic vision seemed out of keeping with what Windy Brae had been to so many people. The only other person I was likely to encounter on my floor was a researcher, not too sure of her project, who was testing patient blood samples for chemical and physiological periodicity in schizophrenia. She and I generally came on different days, and I rarely saw her. Thus, I had a whole wing of this old hospital, the Sheppard-Pratt of another time, era, set of conventions, to myself.

From time to time, I would try to conjure a sense of what the hospital had been like forty or fifty years ago. I imagined inhabitants for these rooms, perhaps a patient, raving or in tears, brought in by an old Chrysler ambulance, being soothed by the sheer intuitive empathy of the many talented mental health workers I met over the years. Or I tried to slip myself into the emotional space of a patient who had particularly moved me (or was it my own emotional space?), listening on soft spring afternoons to the sounds outside the window, to the breezes and the birdsong, or in January watching the snowflakes scatter themselves in indeterminate pattern, falling effortlessly and inevitably toward the unyielding surface of the earth.

On warm days I opened the window and sat breathing in the air of the place. I wondered what it had been like to live in this room that now was my office, to fight the internal demons, to suffer and weep, to listen to the banging of heads against the wall, to scream out in pain, to watch for death or the chance at it, to wait to cut open the screen and make a jump or fly head first to the ground below, to wonder if the voices would ever stop, to crave some sanity, lucidity, to wish for one day without the need to seek out razor blades, broken pieces of glass, tin, instruments to alleviate a pain so insistent that it registered itself, like a festering sore, on the surfaces of the body. That strangely comforting spring breeze, perfumed with the scents of roses, violets, pine, and heather, could also bring peace. And later the heat would grow by degrees. The humid heat of summer in this unairconditioned room seemed to surround the self in a cocoon of moist, sweaty oblivion.

Should I sleep here one night and try it out? Or would that be too presumptuous, nothing compared to the heartbreaking agony of whoever had lived here? What did the persons living in these rooms a half century ago, what did they think about, feel? Were they comforted, as I had been, by the lazy swaying of the trees? Did they perceive the curious closeness and serenity of strong limbs, thick leaves, a fellow being lending warmth and security? Did they see the imposing trees as friends, confidants, repositories of lost memories, secret communications? I am reminded of Mary, one of the first patients I interviewed at the hospital, who befriended the inhabitants of these trees, the sparrows, blue jays, woodpeckers who, as she said, carried messages to her "ears," giving her some relief from the unending parade of war, conflagration, and violence which impelled her internal world.

The silence was a luxury, of course, which thirty patients (or researchers) would have disrupted. It is difficult to pursue a reverie amid the screams, the curses, the end games required when emotions are stuffed tightly into the narrow cylinders of the self. On this empty hall I could recollect the long-forgotten occupants of these rooms, of my room. I could imagine the despair etched into every stone of the building and sense something of the healing potentiality of the grounds. In the building I could read the firm and stark commitment to provide constancy for those whose emotional lives were extraordinarily painful and turbulent. The building stood as a testimonial that Windy Brae, as a *place,* would be there, would not desert, that in the midst of the enduring anguish, there would be not only persons but an actual site, bounded and defined, a refuge from the abject horror of the internal world.

From this office I made my forays into the worlds of the patients, learning from their stories much about the nature of power. What is it about these narratives that comments on more abstract concerns of philosophy and political philosophy, and more specifically, what do the metaphors and messages of dislocated and torn selves reveal about the structure of power in groups? This book is about power; it elaborates the commentaries about power embedded in the experience and language of certain human beings society calls psychotic. Pain and abjection are not without meaning. These stories about pain—meditations, if you will—deal primarily, although not exclusively, with vicious forms of power appearing as assault, annihilation, and destruction. The delusional projection of power can be talked about, can be addressed at the microlevel of the self, can be interpreted in the context of more abstract theoretical formulations about political context. And its operation can be seen in group dynamics and behavior.

It may seem odd to draw inferences about the operation of power from the parables and stories of individuals who suffer from psychotic disintegration.[1] But that is precisely what I want to do in this book. I take these stories to be real experiences described by human beings who suffer, who know something about the structure and reality of power as it affects their lives, perceptions, and values. The feel of power, the reality of power for psychotic selves, suggests a firsthand knowledge of tyranny. In this sense, I believe, the raw, primitive, archaic quality of the schizophrenic experience demonstrates how power works.

What the schizophrenic self suffers is a microcosmic representation of the *political* form of power as tyranny and domination. Power is exercised on the self; it defines the world of knowledge and meaning in rigid terms of absolute good and evil. This power derives not from social or consensual bases but from narcissism and solipsism. It seeks omnipotence. It is destructive, parasitic, and violent. It pushes the self into masochism and physical mutilation. It attacks the surfaces of the body and inscribes itself in the hidden crevices of the psyche.

In the words of Julia Kristeva, tyrannical power situates the self between "suicide and barbarity" in "a world of psychical collapse, depression and anguish" (1993, 52, 88). This power holds no promise; it is deadly in its operation. Its origins lie in the dim, prehistorical reaches of the self, in unconscious phantasies, sometimes repressed, sometimes split off, which forge the self's experience of domination and its dependency on the images these phantasies project into consciousness.[2]

For Kristeva, psychosis suggests a self engulfed, fragmented by its own uncanniness, its otherness. "The boundaries between *imagination* and *reality* are erased," and there is "a crumbling of conscious defenses"

(1991, 188). Psychosis is bound up with how the self assimilates what is foreign to it or uncanny. It is like a "black angel clouding transparency"; it assaults the self with rage; it shatters any sense of place or home; it "wrecks . . . understanding and affinity" (1).

This foreignness may provoke a "violent, catastrophic" encounter; it may assail us with "ghosts and doubles . . . imaginary structures" (190, 191). If I am not aware of this side of who I am, if the uncanny inside of me becomes autonomous and powerful, it may engulf my perceptions, my consciousness. I then may become an "inner exile." "The other, stifled within myself, causes me to be a stranger to others and indifferent to everything" (26), eclipsing from my field of awareness any distinction between reality and delusion, between "phantasmal" projections and considered reciprocities. Bizarre projection, the "uncanny strangeness" (189) of sensations and percepts, "takes up again our infantile desires and fears of the other—the other of death, the other of woman, the other of uncontrollable drive. The foreigner is within us" (191). And that amalgam of anguish, dread, and fear, coming from the phantastical imagery of the foreigner, the outlaw or the uncanny *within*, may coalesce as delusion, psychosis—a lived reality whose truth lies in what delusion projects as knowledge. Places like Windy Brae testify to the power of delusion, its ability to assault consciousness and impose a regime of endless pain.

Yet, power as tyrannical domination of the self could be eclipsed by a developing experience of power as cooperation, mutuality, exchange—what might be called a democratic exercise of power. This was not a regular occurrence at Sheppard-Pratt, but it did happen, and these transformations were dramatic. There were some who relinquished omnipotent forms of identification and identity for consensual attachment, for connection with reality. Some moved away from what Jacques Lacan calls psychotic "foreclosure," to experience shared and reciprocal power, the world of law and history. These patients often expressed amazement that the experience of power need not be deadly, need not incorporate nihilistic images. It was astonishing that exchanges with other human beings might create a field between self and other in which power produced generative and creative promise. Invariably, the patients who told me such stories had become aware of unconscious projections in themselves, had examined the psychological origins of their own internal tyranny, including the effects of families, genes, chemistry, and physiology. With great struggle, they had attempted to unravel the terror of their own internal lives within the context of their relationships with the staff. Such persons had left Lacan's psychotic "real" and its projections and had entered the linguistically and historically defined "symbolic."

I have tried to make some sense of these stories of power on both an individual and a political level. I believe they demonstrate insights into larger political and group-dependent questions of power and estrangement. They provide a ground for understanding projective and dynamic processes in groups and political contexts. At the very least, the stories about psychosis or psychotic moments make us aware of how demanding tyrannical power can be, how vicious is its exercise, and on the other side, how reciprocal forms of power can produce experiences that restrain the narcissistic component of power.

My inquiry, then, takes as a starting point the estrangement of the schizophrenic as an almost pure type of victimization by tyrannical power and an example of how primitive phantasies dictate the form of delusional power demanding allegiance from the self. The difference between tyrannical and reciprocal power, the consensual power underpinning both the self and political states (a theme at the heart of this book), can be elaborated through modern psychoanalytic formulations that take seriously the effect of the unconscious on perceptions of reciprocity and mutuality.

I agree with Julia Kristeva that the self's projective capacities and actions play a significant role in dictating what forms of power govern group interactions. As she points out, "the complex relationships between cause and effect that govern social groups obviously do not coincide with the laws of the unconscious regarding a subject . . . Unconscious determinations remain a constituent part, an essential one, of social and therefore national [or group] dynamics" (1993, 50). An understanding of how these dynamics operate in ourselves (through a psychoanalytic investigation and demystification of the uncanny) may enable "people to give up hunting for the scapegoat outside their group, a search that allows them to withdraw into their own 'sanctum' " and to "worship" the "collective configuration" (51).

In Chapters 3 and 4 I look at this dialectic between self and group in the context of treatment on one of Sheppard's halls, specifically, the effect of one patient's perceptions on the treatment group's experience of its own power and on its strategy for treatment. In later chapters I examine regression in historical and political contexts and the effect of these processes on the configurations of power. At all times I am guided by the conviction that unconscious phantasies or structures motivate the employment of power; although these phantasies may not be accessible to consciousness, they exercise a decisive influence on how power is used and experienced by individuals and groups. In Chapters 10 and 11 I evaluate the psychodynamic underpinnings of democratic exchange: respect for otherness and difference, the capacity to sustain conflict, and trust in negotiation, ambivalence, and living with one another.

It is my belief that participatory power cannot be maintained without constant struggle against the tendency to fall back toward delusional or psychotic states in the self, particularly delusional *time,* or what I call psychotic time. This effort of the self to maintain a psychologically secure reciprocity and mutuality indicates a set of psychodevelopmental transitions from narcissism and omnipotence to consensual reality, or the world of society, law, and historical conceptions of time.

Similarly, on the political level, tyranny closes off dialogue. It projects hated scapegoats, mobilizes populations toward policies of domination, makes violent aggression into a desired national goal. It admires omnipotence and elevates to national interest those identifications that in an individual would be considered psychotic.

What, then, is essential to the health of the individual and the group is an experience of power which *defuses* or detoxifies the narcissistic or solipsistic impulses in the self, which allows us, in Kristeva's words, "to recognize ourselves as strange in order better to appreciate the foreigners outside us instead of striving to bend them to the norms of our own repression" (1993, 29). It may then be possible to build larger and more inclusive communities respecting difference.

This dynamic contributes to a sense of promise in the self that is attempting to assimilate and demystify terrifying introjects, frightening strangeness. A similar dynamic in the culture helps to create democratic processes and percepts and the respect for the rights of individuals and for difference which are critical to an experience of power as resistance to domination and tyranny. The ugliness in the human self, its conflicts and divisions, is not an insurmountable obstacle to democratic functioning, but we must oppose to it a determination to avoid locking human prejudice and particularism onto a religion, a nation, or an ideology.

Democracy requires belief in the human capacity to acknowledge and tolerate the other without positing some kind of "new self" based on utopian and utterly unreasonable expectations. To be human is indeed to feel impelled by division and negativity. "Individual particularistic tendencies, the desire to set oneself up as a private value, the attack against the other, identification with or rejection of the group," says Kristeva, "are inherent in human dignity" (1991, 154).

"Dignity," in Kristeva's reading, confronts and accepts the foreigner in the self, the capacity for strangeness, for being and doing in ways hardly noble or virtuous. Kristeva hopes that democratic institutions may hold or contain this strangeness, these split-off passions, which often reflect unpleasant, if not downright dangerous, aspects of the human self, the "conflict, hatred, violence, and distinctiveness that for two centuries since the *Declaration* [*of the Rights of Man*] has ceaselessly been unloaded upon the realities of wars and fratricidal closeness and that the Freudian discovery of the unconscious tells us is a surely modifiable but yet constituent portion of the human psyche" (1993, 27). It is up to the democratic process to modulate such forces in the self, to blanket them in an ethics relying, she says, on "education and psychoanalysis."

Perhaps Kristeva's faith in psychoanalysis is unrealistic; even so, her argument is important: to resist tyranny, democracy not only must acknowledge the "alienation, dramas and dead ends of our condition as speaking beings" (1991, 154); it must also set up institutions and perceptions dedicated to understanding and tolerating these forces in the self. This vision is neither utopian nor dystopian; rather, it reflects the psychoanalytic commitment to knowing *and* surviving, the belief that we do not want to destroy ourselves, that human ingenuity, moved by the life instinct, is capable of "achieving a polytopic and supple society, neither locked into the nation or its religion, nor anarchically exposed to all of its explosions" (154). It is critical that we take the "different" into account, that we allow for its expression, refuse to be pushed into cynicism by negative passions, learn not to hate difference, respect the "distinctive features" of what is other. We must understand a place like Windy Brae as a passage on a continuum of suffering and psychological torment and not a deviant manifestation of the human project.

This "adjustment," to use Kristeva's term, constructs a "cosmopolitanism interior to the 'nation-state,'" respecting the difference, the multiplicity, that lives and breathes within any national border. She argues for a "middle way" without nationalism, fanaticism, jingoism, or exclusion, a workable tolerance that repudiates "the utopia of a society without nations" (1991, 154). Tolerance and its practices drive Kristeva's reading of "cosmopolitanism," a respect for difference which accepts the infinite variability and multiplicity of human experience and belief and does not try to change them.

ONE

Psychotic Unhinging: The Terror of Delusion

FREUD viewed the frightening closed systems of belief embodied in delusion as dangerous to the self and as a serious threat to the stability of society and the organization of political life. He was particularly disturbed by the power of delusion to attack secondary process functions (the ego operations of reason, moderation, compromise, limitation, and negotiation) and to induce more violent primary process aggression that assaults the ego and, in the case of political life, those institutional artifacts capable of containing it. The Freudian approach to dreams provides a context for understanding the power of delusion, a kind of all-encompassing wide-awake dream that organizes reality and consciousness.

Dreams, in Freud's view, constitute the "royal road to the unconscious," a "regression to the dreamer's earliest condition, a revival of his childhood, of the instinctual impulses which dominated it and of the methods of expression which were then available to him" (1900, 587). The dream, full of clues like the delusion, is an "abbreviated recapitulation" of the repressed and denied. It leads directly to the self's psychological past. "We can guess," Freud remarks, "how much to the point is Nietzsche's assertion that in dreams 'some primeval relic of humanity is at work which we can now scarcely reach any longer by a direct path'; and we may expect that the analysis of dreams will lead us to a knowledge of man's archaic heritage, of what is psychically innate in him" (Freud 1900, 588). Like delusions, dreams represent "mental antiquities . . . reconstruction of the earliest and most obscure periods of the beginnings of the human race" (588); each contains its own structures; each writes its own logic; each symbolizes an aspect of the unconscious; each possesses its own characteristic time; and each asserts power over the self.

> These wishes in our unconscious, ever on the alert, and, so to say, immortal, remind one of the legendary Titans, weighed down since primeval ages by the massive bulk of the mountains which were once hurled upon them by the victorious gods and which are still shaken from time to time by the convulsion of their limbs. But these wishes, held under repression, are themselves of infantile origin, as we are taught by psychological research into the neurosis. . . . *a wish which is represented in a dream must be an infantile one*. (Freud 1900, 592)

Dreams, then, are "the true psychical reality," symbolic images that form elliptical commentaries on hidden currents of desire. Freud traces the recognition of dreams as knowledge, as forms of time, to the classical Greek poets, who paid "homage . . . to the uncontrolled and indestructible forces in the human mind, to the 'daemonic' power which produces the dream-wish and which we find at work in our unconscious" (1900, 652). Dreams derived from the past disguise the unconscious in highly complex symbols that make little sense on first reading. They comment on deep sources of desire and wish in the self; they hold clues to the self's suffering, to strange sensations and waking perceptions; they lend themselves to interpretation by the dreamer and the psychoanalyst. Yet, the dream is momentary, and the consciousness of the dreamer remains grounded in consensual reality. Dreams might be likened to texts, to be deciphered within the terms of the rational or social consensus.

Delusion, however, creates a different world, hermetically sealed, and rivets the self to separate knowledge forms. Delusion, says Kristeva, is "the disavowal of reality . . . a psychotic partition-wall" (1986a, 226, 229). Consciousness refuses interpretation of its inner constructs; no distance separates self from its symbolic productions. Unlike the dream, the delusion exists within consciousness as a set of tyrannical images. Tied to the messages of the inner world, delusion exceeds the governing reach of consensual reality; its images of power derive completely from internal perceptions. For example, when Chuck says, "I'm going into the woods to drink the blood of dogs and watch crippled children eat their carcasses," psychosis locks out any self-understanding or objectivity. It completely encloses reality in the specificity of its images, in the airtight chambers of psychotic time.

The dream provides the opportunity to confront resistance, to look at spontaneous associations and refract them through the analytic mirror. Through recollection, the dreamer can reflect on symbolizations that recreate the emotional lesions of the past. Psychosis, however, blocks the historical recovery of the self's truth. Psychotic time absorbs historical linearity and annihilates reciprocal understandings of consensual reality; it provides for no degree of communal attachment and refuses dialectical interpretation. The dream dissipates into historical time, permitting the self to remember it within a set of ongoing symbols. The delusion, however, encloses the self in psychotic time, seals it up in an epistemological cocoon.

Freud considered delusion a fundamental dimension of the self's infantile past. "Delusion," he wrote, "owes its convincing power to the element of historical truth which it inserts in the place of the rejected reality. . . . Those who are subject to [delusions] are suffering from their own reminiscences" (1937, 268). These recollections take the shape of bizarre imagery that thoroughly distorts the self's historical truth but nonetheless contains clues: "We have long understood that a portion of forgotten truth lies hidden in delusional ideas, that when this returns it has to put up with distortions and misunderstandings" (1939, 85). Delusion, then, in falsifying the self's historical logic (with "errors that wrap [delusion] round") functions as a mammoth defense (a "compulsive conviction") against looking at the real order of reasons buried in the unconscious.

Chuck observes: "I gave birth to myself yesterday; it was fun; I coughed and another Chuck grew out of my knee. I liked the new Chuck better, but I didn't know if it was a boy or a girl." Myths, as Claude Lévi-Strauss (1969) has convincingly argued, are full of such events. Physiological causality is distorted; human relations become secondary to fantasized wishes and omnipotent action; birth and death take on significantly different meaning; humans become animals; animals turn back into humans; monsters roam the world; human taboos are flouted.

Images possess a complex logic that defies Western concepts of reason and understanding. It is as if Chuck were caught up in a mythological time, a time outside of history; his observations consist of a symbolic projection of feelings stored up in an unconscious world, an indirect commentary that inverts causal and temporal associations.

Freud held that delusion, as the plan of psychotic time, extends throughout the culture; it is particularly noticeable in religion (1927), but it also underlies politically motivated ideological formulations that constitute closed belief systems. Echoing Plato in *The Republic,* Freud writes: "If we consider mankind as a whole and substitute it for the single human individual, we discover that it too has developed delusions which are inaccessible to logical criticism and which may contradict reality" (1937, 269). Like the individual, the collective may find itself overwhelmed by distortions in the form of ideology, war, intolerance, fanaticism, and murderous rage. The power of delusion may rearrange a culture's consciousness, its history and values, the structure of the state. Paranoia may find itself institutionalized as public policy; leaders may demand quick solutions; the populace may yearn for all-or-nothing resolutions; economic policy and fantasy may find themselves intertwined. Politically this kind of regression allows less patience for negotiation and tolerance; it induces a great reliance on violence, force, or Draconian law. History is replete with the results.

Power driven by delusion is vicious and sadistic, and delusion is no stranger to political actors and movements. On an individual level, the more differentiated and less regressed self tolerates ambivalence, resists all-or-nothing demands, is less likely to act impulsively. The more regressed self, however, may be prone to rigid positions, unable to sustain tolerance, and more susceptible to feelings of paranoia and threat. What happens on the individual level may be mirrored in the collective as well, and the regressed or split-off self may serve as an insight into the regressed and chaotic polity.

Regression: Threat to the Secondary Process

The concept of regression is particularly useful in understanding how the "time" characteristic of psychosis erodes the consensual process and disrupts the functioning of democratic exchange and tolerance. The conflict induced by regression breaks limits. Regression toward archaic or precivil spaces in the self, internal psychological operations pulling the self away from social or consensual points of reference, weakens what Freud calls secondary process thinking, the socially dependent cognitive structures of "reasonableness" or "rationality" which regulate the interaction of human beings, Lacan's symbolic. Secondary process thought is the "thought" of civilization or socialization; primary process—obsession, compulsion, hallucination, delusion, Lacan's "foreclosure," Kristeva's "true/real"—is the thinking of unconscious or psychotic time.

In political life, secondary process mental operations appear as the values of negotiation, tolerance, and limitation (democratic values); primary process operations take shape as intolerance, jingoism, racist and tyrannical appeals to action and repression. I want to emphasize the functional alliance in persons and polities between a regressive *psychodynamics* and delusional *projection*. The psychotic self, almost totally regressed toward infantile identifications and feelings, lives in delusional or psychotic time. Similarly, a political society that has lost contact with its historical and therefore consensual foundations may find itself overwhelmed by belief structures or actions that have devastating effects. Delusion and psychosis are as much a part of the political world as of the psychopathological self.

The ruptures in secondary process defenses in psychosis are far more devastating than those in neurosis. The failure to "repress" makes consciousness the victim of regression, or to put it another way, consciousness may regress to archaic psychological states that are largely constituted by delusion. For the schizophrenic, that regression moves the self away from the social or historical consensus; in the case of political life, regression forces the will of the collective toward more primitive or atavistic emotional currents. It may invoke what Heinz Kohut (1971) calls the "grandiose self," pathological variants of narcissistic fixations, or it may activate primitive reaction formations such as paranoid defensiveness, the search for enemies (Volkan, 1988) or scapegoats (Girard, 1986).

Freud understood regression to be politically dangerous; it threatened the social consensus, weakened the bonds of civilization, and diminished the capacity of reason to respond to aggression and destruction. This dark, split-off, potentially explosive unconscious, filled with terrifying and often violent wishes, Freud likens to the "legendary Titans, weighed down since primeval ages by the massive bulk of the mountains . . . hurled upon them by the victorious gods" (1900, 592). Imprisoned in the crater of Etna, the Titans, like the primitive wishes of the unconscious, have the power to shake the earth, to provoke great amounts of suffering. Immortal and in constant motion, these beings are appropriate symbols for transformation in delusion and psychotic time.

If the Titans have the power to shake the self's psychological reality, is it not reasonable to expect them to shake the political earth? Historical time is a measurement peculiar to mortals and their failings. The vicious and fantastic or delusional shifts and changes of the gods, on the other hand, happen in a timeless environment. When Chuck feels he is giving birth to himself through his knee or that different parts of his body are sprouting new "baby Chucks," he occupies a world psychically similar to that of these ancient mythical figures. Like the Titans, Chuck dwells and acts in an environment impervious to the corrosion of historical time. Chuck says he "operates on two calendars: yours, which is three hundred and sixty-five days, and mine, which moves much more slowly."

To say that the individual self bears no relation to what the collective represents and wishes is to ignore a central argument in the historical tradition of political theory: the connection between human nature, what today might be called the self or the subject, and the political life of the culture. I contend that the experience of the inner world, especially the language of psychosis, provides evidence for that connection. The relationship is significant if only in the sense that guilt, murder, violence, repression, and delusion are political phenomena. As agents of psychotic time, in Freud's view, the Titans produce the need for civilization; for example, the pantheon of Zeus may be understood as symbolic of the world of infantile entitlement and omnipotence. These forces or presences stand behind the creation of the *civitas,* and in their embodiment as gods, totems, religions, customs, and ideologies (instinct and desire as iconic representation), the Titans come to be enshrined in society as authority, power, law, and order. Civilization, acting as the guarantor of order, curbs instinct by taming these "Titans" and turning these mythic presences into moral and political injunction and prohibition. What stand behind "Thou shalt not," then, are anarchic impulses and wishes of the unconscious, the self caught up in its own narcissism, its rage against restraint, control, and limitation.

It is the Titan inside the self, as the imperious, angry unconscious, which society dominates, assimilates, and turns to its own interests. By binding desire and self, civilization not only assures its own posterity and survival and the domination of specific elites and interests; it also defends itself against entropic tendencies that threaten the fragile arrangements of history and community. What Freud recognized in *Civilization and Its Discontents* (1930) was the capacity of the wish, the imagination, the delusion, to pull the culture toward disintegration and violence. Jacques Lacan and Julia Kristeva forcefully resurrect this recognition in their psychoanalytic theory. Ideologically extreme politics frightened Freud, for he saw in political violence not a "new order" or a redeemed civilization but the Titans of the unconscious, the anarchic force in human nature and history, working to disorganize the collective and throw it into chaos. History, then, for Freud, Lacan, and Kristeva becomes the victim of the imagination, the hidden, split-off self; it replays the "dramas" of the primal crime and, according to Kristeva, maternal power. It is the stage on which the infantile or regressed wish takes concrete shape as political form and organization.

History, as the order of conventional or "normal" time, demonstrates the extent to which a culture's conscious politics binds its unconscious Titans. Laws, regulations, institutions, civil authority, mores—all become agents of a collective superego whose purpose it is to contain instinctual energy. Just as the social order moves to isolate the inner Titans of the schizophrenic self, the political order, as, for example, Hobbes argued in *Leviathan,* seeks to bend energy or desire to the interests of political sovereignty. Hobbes located the problem in "too much appearing passion" and the presence of that "passion" in disputes over the meaning of "political" names. Delusion, or what Hobbes called "phantasms," threatens order, because it strikes directly at the cohesiveness of political and social structure; it radically alters the interpretation of "names" and "signs."

No matter how benevolent political authority may be in its public appearances, in Freud's view it disguises a more fundamental psychological reality: the renunciation of desire and the anarchic self and the institutionalization of guilt and retaliation in a culture's public life. Reason in political life—institutions that mediate, judge, govern, that perform "secondary process" political operations—may obscure a deeper psychotic foundation, a realm of collective desire and rage having the power to erode or completely destroy the secondary process juristic and constitutional structures. Such a "core" persistently inscribes itself on the language, thought, and bodies of persons who in a psychological sense claim refuge from the governing consensus. Politics, like individuals, is subject to regressive dynamics that work on perception, action, and policy, and it may be naïve to think that the political process is some abstract series of events or calculations that bear no relation to the internal world of wish and desire so critical in other areas of human experience. Politically, delusion, the force Hobbes identifies with madness, finds itself embodied in the collective demand for war, retaliation, or vengeance; in the hatred of specific political, social, and racial groups; in the insistence on unlimited destruction; in the silencing of dissent and the imposition of terror; in fantasized wishes assuming the "persona" of public policy. The question for democratic theory is how to provide resilient institutional or public defenses against delusion.

Weakness in a culture's secondary process operations, its politics of law, its sense of limitation, restraint, prudence, and negotiation, may be a product of pathological distortion, the effect of unconscious structures on consciousness, changing the split-off self, with its currents of desire and wish, into public appeals for action. Some examples of this phenomenon might be political extremism as an attempt to recapture infantile omnipotence; hyperrationality in the form of behavioral engineering; nuclear planning with its omnipotent morbid fantasies; psychological conditioning as a defense against the fascination with the uncontrollable, the anarchic; the demand for punishment for "moral" transgressions as a defense against "unbearable" and therefore unacceptable desire within the self; political cruelty as a projection of uncontainable rage and vicious self-hatred.

The Titans in Freud's world never disappear. Moving through thought and action, their presence as power, particularly pronounced in regression, exercises tremendous influence. "Among those wishful impulses derived from infancy, which can neither be destroyed nor inhibited, there are some whose fulfillment would be a contradiction of the purposive ideas of secondary thinking" (Freud 1900, 643). And what emerges from the unconscious has the power to erode elaborate social defenses that protect the culture from the wishes of infantile entitlement, which all too often appear in the power claims and demands of political leaders. Delusion, nonhuman identification—both represent what Freud saw as primary process thinking, forcing its way into consciousness.

Knowledge of this psychological and political world of the Titans, psychotic time and its delusional projections, is hidden in politics. It is sometimes experienced as the "normal" or the "norm." Witness the acceptance of horrible acts in Nazi Germany as part of everyday life, the project of purification or cleansing which became the norm in the Nazis' biological vision of the world and the future (Lifton, 1986). The Titans, as part of the self, are seen and contained in persons the society classifies as mad, and the schizophrenic, the paradigmatic psychotic self, becomes the deviant, the abnormal, the other, Kristeva's "stranger," whom society denies and despises. Society feels safer this way; it is easier to repudiate an individual's insanity than a politics or policies that an entire culture may accept as "normal." In the Third Reich, it was not insane to kill Jews, but it was indeed abnormal and even criminal to refuse to participate in, if not the killing, then the entire administrative and legal apparatus that constructed and justified the killing machine.

The fragility of secondary process restraints perhaps implies that only a thin line separates a so-called democratic or participatory politics from equally powerful and dangerous tendencies within the culture to institute the infantile world of unlimited entitlement in the form of tyrannical power. What is repressed, as Freud discovered a century ago, refuses to disappear; it lingers; it affects action; it transforms life; it reappears.

Democracy and the Psychodynamics of Conflict

Regression destroys secondary process structures, pushes the self into a state of boundlessness, releases enormous amounts of aggression and intensifies feelings of psychotic anxiety and panic. Living without limits, possessed by a delusional epistemology, the self faces a loss of continuity and being. What emerges in both the self and the group are actions or forms of power that have nothing to do with tolerance, respect for rights, or what John Stuart Mill (1951) calls liberty.

Psychosis threatens democratic forms of conflict resolution by attacking a sense of limitation and those boundaries between groups which, while allowing each to pursue its own cultural ends, nonetheless protects the group's integrity. What psychosis releases—intense vulnerability, rage, and hatred, Kristeva's "unnameable space of need" (1986a, 235)—finds itself contained within democratic approaches to conflict resolution and negotiation, particularly acknowledgment of and respect for rights. A liberal democratic polity requires renunciation and sublimation and the willingness to endure restraint in the pursuit of self-interest. That willingness takes the form of constitutional protections and a common understanding that the protection of rights is critical in sustaining secondary process functions persistently threatened by regressive psychological forces. The acknowledgment of democratic *right,* the constitutional restraint on interests, and the commitment to protect those rights (see Galston 1991) become bulwarks against politically defined regressive impulses in the state. The willingness to sustain conflict without resort to tyranny requires, to use Peter Gay's words, "a capacity for tolerating delays, disappointments and ambiguities attendant upon any open society, an unimpaired capacity for reality testing, for curbing one's aggressiveness without turning against oneself, for reliance on defensive stratagems that remain moderate in scope and flexible in application" (1982, 524).

Democracy that respects rights and liberty is indeed fragile. But it may function in something of the style Wilfred Bion (1970) sees as critical to the mother-infant relationship. I treat this relationship in detail in Chapter 10; here, it is sufficient to mention that the psychoanalytic concept container-contained is helpful in thinking about how democratic processes tolerate or assimilate conflict and how they protect against tyrannical power. What allows for developing reciprocity between mother and infant, says Bion, is the mother's capacity to hold or contain the anxiety and rage of her infant. It is a vital relationship because it shows the infant that the expression of rage, anger, and hate not only will not destroy the mother but will also not destroy the self. Impulses of annihilation and self-destruction can be defused by the mother acting as container for this split-off side of the infantile self. The mother/container literally detoxifies the rage being projected into her; in that internalization, the infant comes to see that the mother accepts the whole range of being; the expression of rage, vulnerability, hate, therefore, need not be shattering for the emotional world of the infant. These feelings are bound back into the self through the mother's acceptance of the ugly, angry, spiteful side of her child. Because of her capacity to hold these passions and in the process of holding, not rejecting, her child's being, the child develops a sense of safety or place which forms the core of later elaborations of the self's security operations.

Bion believes that the infant's psychotic impulses or drives are protected by the mother's containing presence. The self comes to learn that the expression of rage, its existence in the self, need not create threatening anxiety or provoke intolerable rejection. The infant avoids self-annihilation and immobilizing despair because the mother contains the self's split-off emotional or affective pieces. In Bion's view, the dialectic established between containing and being contained prepares in the infant a ground for the later appearance of more sophisticated ego-dependent techniques of conflict resolution. It is possible to exist with others, to sustain their rage and hate without what Cynthia Burack (1994) calls "disagreeable passions," which threaten the self's relationship to itself and to others. The concept of container-contained offers a model for the creation of an ego resilient enough to function, its secondary process defenses protected from erosion or destruction by primary process psychotic impulses—hate and rage as limit-*breaking* passions.

Bion's theory is important because, like Kristeva, he accepts the notion that the self is composed of often quite ugly passions, which are natural to human experience and not necessarily destructive of the human projects of reciprocity and negotiation of conflict. Outcome depends on how these passions are contained and negotiated in the person or group serving as container, or other, or on the ability of the other to contain or hold a rage natural to the self's existence. Bion's concept provides a useful psychoanalytic model for approaching issues of conflict in democratic theory and action.

Democracy is, in its politics as well as its epistemology, a defense against more extreme (what I call psychotic) modes of being and power. It acts as a protection against regression, the tendency to embrace unyielding and totalizing ideological positions. And its method of conflict resolution functions in much the same way as the mother/container does for her infant's split-off, raging self. A resilient democratic culture (one embracing participatory modes of action) will hold or contain the rage of its constituent groups without allowing it to annihilate either the constitutional structures maintaining the community or the respect for rights which allows conflict to flourish without endangering individuality. Conflict is the lifeblood of democracy, but it consistently circulates around respect for the capacity of the other to contain and detoxify disruptive aspects of self or group emotion. Democratic institutions, from this perspective, do not eliminate conflict; rather, they detoxify anarchic or annihilating presence and consequence. Power becomes supportive and creative or, to use Erik Erikson's (1964) concept, "generative"; it fosters growth. Conflict is talked about and legislated rather than imposed and forced. Rage is held by institutional and *cultural* processes that work to bind the entropic tendency present in all expressions of political interest.

For Kristeva, this psychological dynamic is intertwined with democratic existence. As she notes in *Nations without Nationalism,* "To recognize the impetus of that hatred aroused by the other, within our own psychic dramas of psychosexual individuation—that is what psychoanalysis leads us to" (1993, 29–30). This kind of personal understanding or awareness can only help to maintain respect for otherness or difference and appreciation of the political consequences of tolerance—vital democratic processes. Psychoanalysis "thus links its own adventure with the meditations each one of us is called upon to engage in when confronted with the fascination and horror that a different being produces in us," Kristeva remarks (30). And later she asks, "Is there a way of thinking politically about the 'national' that does not degenerate into an exclusionary, murderous racism?" (51).

Obviously, there are real difficulties in taking Bion's argument as a model for conflict resolution in a democratic polity committed to rights and individuality. For example, what happens on the individual level to the mother if she fails to hold or detoxify her infant's rage, if she finds herself overwhelmed by the intolerability of destructive impulses, if her own boundaries begin to crumble, if she succumbs to her own internal "strangeness"? Similarly, on the political level what are the consequences for the polity of a virulent, toxic rage that escapes all containing mechanisms? What institutional or political mechanisms metabolize conflict so as to produce generative as opposed to destructive resolutions? Is it realistic to suppose hate can be metabolized democratically? And what happens if the politically defined projective mechanisms fail?

Bion and Kristeva offer useful insight, considering that the passions of individual life are quite often messy and destructive and hardly predictable or sanguine. There is no reason to suppose these passions do not seriously affect the political or public realm of human experience as well. The critical political question is how to resolve these passions without falling into a Hobbesian or Madisonian cynicism regarding the capacity of human beings to govern themselves and to create institutional forms capable of sustaining rights and conflict simultaneously. A democratic theory of rights and participation protects against the fragility of human defenses against regression (the psychotic substratum to all human experience, Kristeva's "hole" that threatens to engulf the "subject"), the unbinding of the self, the refuge in solipsism, a kind of political variant on what Otto Kernberg (1975) calls "pathological narcissism." Democracy respects conflict, works to contain its entropy; the dynamic is dialectical, and the relationship between container and contained is reciprocal. Hobbes and Madison fear conflict and its effects and desire to suppress or enchain its consequences; the push is to close off communication, to repress, hold down, crush.

Democracy as a political theory protects the values of liberty and autonomy, which at the level of individual psychology are parallel to the acceptance of boundary, proportion, limitation. Democracy opposes the affect or symptom of nonreciprocal power: unrestrained narcissism, unlimited entitlement, perceptions of omnipotence, delusions or images of grandeur and dominance. As Peter Gay puts it: "Cultures . . . regress just as individuals do. . . . Jingoism is a triumph of the primary process" (1982, 526, 541). It is one political equivalent of narcissistic rage.

Failures in Holding: A Political Analysis

Cultural regression signifies a failure of the holding functions of the container, the constitutional/rights mechanisms established through democratic institutions. Rage, in this situation, cannot be contained, and political impulses of annihilation are released. The culture or society moving toward primary process identifications falls into a condition mirroring psychotic collapse: boundaries are lost, huge quantities of rage are released, and violent or annihilatory resolution of conflict is urged. Nothing in the culture detoxifies this virulent and violently eruptive rage, for constitutional "containers" have been overrun. Groups wish to kill, not to negotiate. Difference itself is seen as a threat. Hate takes on limit-breaking properties that, as in the infant-mother prototype, threaten identity and its generative resilience.

Like the fall into psychotic boundlessness on the individual level, cultural regression brings with it disorder, chaos, a fascination with destruction and violence, the need to dominate and torture, and the assertion of ideological claims, which (much like delusion in the individual psychotic) show little respect for boundaries or civility. Anticivil totalizing or totalitarian impulses appear with increasing frequency both in the acts of leaders and in the demands of groups. Cultural regression of this type (for example, the policies leading to the Nazi final solution, the attack on Bosnian Muslims, or any scapegoating political policy) is not a political condition sympathetic to the ideals of the democratic polity; such regression, understood as the erosion of rights, the appearance of primary process passion, leads to a pathological distortion of the culture's values and its concepts of good and evil. The Manicheanism so characteristic of delusion often appears in cultural ideologies, shattering the capacity of institutions to contain raging, split-off affect in individuals and groups. Gay finds this kind of cultural primitivism in mystical, nationalistic, and militaristic ideologies.

A rights-based democratic theory acts as a restraint on this collective or communitarian sense of political entitlement—nationalism, for example, as a way of making demands on another's territory or a reason for annihilating that territory's inhabitants, or racism as a claim about one group's absolute entitlement to occupy or define a particular territory. And in the presence of ideologies that argue in exclusionary and frenetic statements for entitlement or for annihilation of the scapegoat, the values of forbearance, acceptance, and tolerance become extraordinarily weak. The capacity to sustain difference, so critical to what Bion sees as the *outcome* of the dialectic between container and projector of destructive passion, and the subsequent detoxification of these projections disappear.

Regression, then, in both the individual and the collective is activating identifications having about them a delusional and therefore psychotic quality, demands and ideologies that possess the power to disrupt the democratic commitment to conflict and its resolution, to mobilize hidden and split-off aspects of self (and agendas), and to embody unconscious structure and impulse in political calls to action. If democratic action is the outgrowth of a self that has not split off its rage, that holds projections of rage and detoxifies them through negotiation and acceptance, then antidemocratic politics externalizes and mobilizes rage through acts of tyranny and domination. The results appear in political or public manifestations of the group locked into preoedipal phantasies (Kristeva's argument), claims to entitlement, and ideologies that, very much like delusional systems, divide the world into good and bad. Overwhelmed by uncontained rage, by primitive aggression spilling out as calls for annihilation, the political world may come to mirror psychological or psychotic states in the self preceding the elaboration of what Lacan calls the law of the father. Or in Freudian drive-theory terms, the sophisticated secondary process ego defenses, providing boundaries between primitive aggression and nontoxic avenues of resolution, disintegrate.

Delusion, the frenzy of absolutist phantasies and unbridled hatred, appears historically in anti-Semitism, racist nationalisms, and the forms of mysticism which galvanize entire cultures and populations into instruments of annihilation. In its rage, disrespect for limits, and obsession with violence and the transvaluation of ethics, this kind of politics and its ideologies resemble the logic of psychosis and the phantasized actions of paranoid/delusional parables. Or to put it another way, the retreat into the preoedipal, psychotic world of unlimited entitlement, unrestrained narcissism, and the disappearance of boundaries may be thought of as the political assertion of what Kristeva calls abjection, a "violent, dark" revolt of being, filled with threat, a dissolution of outside and inside, acceptance of images that appear to be "beyond the scope of the possible, the tolerable, the thinkable" (1982, 1).[1] It is a horrifying state that places the self in a universe unrecognizable to consensual reality. Consciousness lives "on the edge of non-existence and hallucination, of a reality that, if I acknowledge it, annihilates me" (2). To be gripped by abjection is to perceive infinite threat: "I behold the breaking down of a world that has erased its borders. . . . It is death infecting life. Abject . . . imaginary uncanniness and real threat, it beckons to us and ends up engulfing us" (4).

Further, abjection signifies a real disturbance in "identity, system, order"; it does not "respect borders, positions, rules" (4). Abjection is living in horror; its politics is domination, annihilation; its public manifestations indicate a perversion of power; it is "immoral, sinister, scheming, and shady: a terror that dissembles, a hatred that smiles, a passion that uses the body for barter instead of inflaming it . . . a friend who stabs you." It is experience as the immanence of horror; Kristeva speaks of "the heap of children's shoes" at Auschwitz, "the abjection of Nazi crime." As a politics, abjection is terror; it "pulverizes the subject" (5). In the self it may appear as delusion, terrorizing and haunting consciousness with pain, domination, victimization, and crime.

In the midst of this descent toward psychosis, democratic politics as tolerance, acknowledging the boundary of the other, the integrity of rights, and respect for difference erodes; its perceptual universe, grounded in secondary process thinking, in the morality of liberty and proportion, disappears before the onslaught of psychotic fears, unconscious phantasies, and the annihilating power of rage. The culture, caught up in the abject, shows little patience with ambiguity, ambivalence, or individuality; it may embrace totalistic solutions, visions that posit others as all good or all bad. It may provoke bizarre ideological and cultural ideas and become scornful of deliberation. Primitive need overwhelms proportion. "Politicians and philosophers," in Peter Gay's words, proclaim "a world of saints in combat with devils" (1982, 537). The ideology of abjection defines nations, peoples, groups, values, beliefs, as inferior, noxious, corrupt, poisonous. Even the Hobbesian justification of economic appetite and the laws of the market—the nonempathic, frenetic, exclusionary, and often brutal properties of possessive individualism—might itself be an example of primitive entitlement, a historical representation of abjection working itself out in the marketplace, pathological narcissism as economic reality.

Abjection and its threat to a democratic politics may appear in a Hobbesian competition over power and will, power standing against liberty and tolerance; individual phantasies may feed into the group consciousness, stimulating shared anxiety through support for jingoistic policies, racist programs, antifeminist actions, the idealization of violence, national purpose, the brotherhood of war, the "hard" and "manly" virtues of domination and force. Mass insecurity, public frenzy, paranoid calls to action, rage involving economic strife, may emerge as a mystical call for the unity of the nation, the destiny of the community, the destruction of out-groups, the oppression of classes, the glory of the state, the "white man's burden," the legal enactment of murder and revenge, and the radical polarization of the culture into the good and the bad, victim and victimizer, god and devil. All-or-nothing solutions; primitive desire appearing in a political climate hostile to signs of weakness, vulnerability, and negotiation; boundless feelings of omnipotence, domination; unyielding concepts of good and bad; a sense of entitlement to all in the context of values and way of life—all these *precepts,* which in the individual would be considered psychotic, seriously threaten reciprocity (the outcome of a continuing dialectic between container and contained), and the respect for difference and mutuality at the center of democratic politics and the affirmation of individuality.

TWO

Psychotic Time: Withdrawal from Consensual Reality

IN regression to psychotic states the self experiences a form of time having absolutely nothing to do with linear historical time understood as part of public or consensual reality. Psychotic time, as I call it, exists beyond the self; psychotic consciousness dwells not in consensually or politically validated structures or in participatory relationships but in the realm of delusional power inaccessible to historical interpretation. The idea of being assumes that it exists in some recognizable and reciprocal embodied world, in an Aristotelian context of ends; nonbeing is immersion in psychotic time, in the totalizing imagery and frightening stories of delusional power and its capacity to define and direct action. It is the time experienced by that part of our selves which lives in unconscious phantasy, which precedes linguistic constructions and the development of social illusions. It is, in D. W. Winnicott's terms, "pre-transitional" time, where no boundaries exist between inner and outer, or what Julia Kristeva (1982) sees as a language-less eternal present.

Kristeva writes: "We confront two temporal dimensions: the time of linear history, or *cursive time* (as Nietzsche called it), and the time of another history, thus another time, *monumental time* (again, according to Nietzsche)" (1986b, 189). She posits a concept of duration neither linear nor historical in character. Monumental time subsumes or absorbs linear time; it is the time of the unconscious, specifically the maternal unconscious, archaic, preverbal, and therefore less dependent on causality and freer to construct and destroy according to dynamics having nothing to do with causal reasoning. She refers to this time in the context of "female subjectivity," identified as "the *chora,* matrix space, nourishing, unnameable, anterior to the One, to God and, consequently, defying metaphysics . . . extra-subjective time, cosmic time . . . vertiginous visions . . . all-encompassing and infinite like imaginary space" (191). This kind of time appears in myth, in images of gods celebrating the maternal, in the "maternal cult." It is also the horrifying time of abjection, without boundary and linear historical referent. "The fact that these types of temporality (cyclical and monumental) are traditionally linked to female subjectivity, insofar as the latter is thought of as necessarily maternal," says Kristeva, "should not make us forget that this repetition and this eternity are found to be the fundamental, if not the sole, conceptions of time in numerous civilizations and experiences, particularly mystical ones" (192). For Kristeva, female subjectivity runs counter to the "time of history"; it is a repudiation, a "rupture" of those continuities, rational and historical, that support the regime of paternal presence, Lacan's symbolic. "A psychoanalyst would call this 'obsessional time,' " (192) a less extreme version of psychotic time, which nonetheless inverts "normal" or rational causalities that give context to historical time. This time, Kristeva says, is "the unnameable repressed by the social [masculine] contract" (200).

Makiko Minow-Pinkney in her essay on Virginia Woolf (1990) addresses Kristeva's different levels or concepts of time. For example, in Woolf's novel *The Waves* (1978), "fragmentation of the self entails the disintegration of time." Rhoda finds herself "blown forever outside the loop of time." Time, instead of conforming "to the canons of constructive development," appears to be "discrete rather than continuous, cyclical rather than linear. . . . Woolfean time constantly confronts the 'whirling abysses of infinite space' " (1990, 170). In Kristeva's words, this is time "as *rhythmic* agency . . . spatialized, volume rather than line" (1980, 205).

Tina Chanter (1990) believes Kristeva's distinction between the time of the unconscious—semiotic, feminine, and maternal—and the time of "reason"—paternal, rational, legal, and progressive—has critical implications for the feminine concept of self: "The 'universal' structure of care characterizing women's activities, points . . . towards another time" (1990, 77).[1]

While Kristeva's approach to monumental time differs considerably from my concept of psychotic time, particularly in her association of this time exclusively with the feminine, there are significant similarities: both concepts refer to understandings and imagery that invert linear conceptions of time and are totally unconcerned with any notion of "progress"; both point to a different order of time which repudiates oedipal or paternal organizations of reality; both derive from perceptions generated in a preverbal emotional space literally outside any of the measurements specific to historical time; and both *experiences* of time derive, in large measure, from the power of maternal presence or absence.

Psychotic Time: The Imagery of Delusional Power

Psychotic time, in my reading, annihilates the possibility of any reciprocity or acknowledgment of otherness. It surrounds the self with the narcissistic projections of a totally closed system of belief and perception. It is the time of absolute power, tyranny, and unfreedom; it transforms otherness into torture, domination, and hate. To be within psychotic time is to be in the space of torture, a realm of nonbeing where power appears as torture, tyranny, and destruction of individuality.

Schizophrenics experience psychotic time as fragmented duration, so that normal temporal sequences have no meaning. Psychotic time can possess an oppressive power—the weight of centuries, for example, felt as an intolerable burden on the self or the sense of self-presence as a million years old or cracked and brittle with age. It is understood as "time" furiously invading the self's space through messages of pain and domination. Psychotic time compresses events and transforms physiological structure and situational relationships. For example, Chuck believes that ancestors grow from parts of his body: "I gave birth to my great grandfather yesterday; he came right out of my thigh." Or he believes that his head is considerably older than his body: "My brain must be a million years old, but they put new parts on me every hundred years, like new legs or fingers. My heart is old, though; they can never replace that; it's too hard, cold; how can you breathe life into death?"

Most important, psychotic time moves the self out of historical or consensual time, the time of the polis—Aristotelian administration, citizenship, responsibility—and places consciousness in a radically transformed level of nonbeing, delusion as power. It is, then, not what Winnicott called illusions or beliefs but the psychotic percept, a delusion, that defines the structures of this peculiar form of "inner" time.

Jenny believes that she turns into a camel or a monkey every day. She claims meal trays are made of dangerous plastic. "It's used to make explosives." She looks at the Coke machine on the hall and sees "rats in a cage." She feels she lives two thousand feet under the sea, in the body of a "wicked witch." She understands herself to be

> in a nightmare. . . . I don't know what I see. . . . I want to be outside, laugh, and come home and smell apple pie baking. But none of it's here; only planes, bombs, death, and massacres. Look outside that window, see those machines? I know you'll tell me the workmen are repairing pipes, but I know what's really going on. They're digging for old bones, robbing graves. Patients have been slaughtered here and buried under three hundred feet of concrete. . . . poisoned darts, all over me, in my body, piercing my flesh. . . . No one will have me; there's no place out there. It's empty outside. . . . I'm an empty shell . . . all alone, in here, in Sheppard-Pratt. This place is my home; no one else will have me. I'm tainted, full of poison.

Or Chuck comments he has been thrown "into shock," that his voice, which he calls Ed, "electrocuted me . . . but the voices shut down, sometime over the weekend. Last night, you know, they changed my face. . . . it makes them feel better; the uglier I am, the better, more powerful they feel." I ask him how the voices changed his face. "At night, with electrolytes, maybe even with radar. . . . Once I was beautiful . . . but they made me ugly. . . . I'll be ugly for fifty years. . . . I was young and beautiful . . . once."

Consciousness lives in a perceptual universe without any recognizable frame of reference, any grounding in history; the experience of time is dependent on inner connections established by psychotic symbols that assault the self with vicious tyrannical power. To be in the time of psychosis and its origins in unconscious phantasies is to be literally consumed by the presence of delusion; in a political sense, it is to stand outside the *civitas,* the walls of the polis.

In the dominion of psychotic time, the helpless become powerful; the lonely discover themselves surrounded by immense populations; the rejected become leaders revered by millions; the weak turn into strong heroes, rescuers of the victimized and tormented. Mary says, "Don't bother me; I'm leading my armies into victory." The small grow to great stature and dominate entire nations, worlds, galaxies. At one moment Louis says to me, "I'm so lonely I could roll up into a ball and be a hermit"; at another, he sees himself as a "great killer," a "ruler of the universe," who will pull my head off and "eat it for dinner." He claims he wants to shoot me because if I'm dead he will be able to live; he delights in living because of "extraordinary plans":

> I want to take your human blood into my animal veins. . . . I'm dead, I have no body, no feeling. What there is of me is filled with jelly; at least if I kill you, I can fill myself up and rule the world. Look around me, do you see my helpers, all those people there with their guns, my armies. I need them. We're going to take over the world and then crush you. I know what I'm going to do to you, inch by inch, cut up your body and throw it to the dogs.

Time circulates around these imperatives; distorted forms of power floating without anchor, *not* historical relationships, organize Louis's perceptual world. It is a universe sinking into the miasma of Kristeva's abject, where "the subject will always be marked by the uncertainty of his borders . . . opening the door to perversion or psychosis" (1982, 63).

Psychosis attacks the self's sense of its public being; it pulls consciousness away from an awareness of the public world and locates knowledge in an internal, hidden reality accessible only to the subject. It erodes attachments to community; it radically distorts normal duration. When I ask Chuck how he feels, he responds, "Well, pretty good, but kind of dead. . . . You know, I've been dead for a hundred trillion years; that makes you sort of tired." John Frosch reports a patient who persistently confused Friday with Saturday—a delusion that transformed the order of consensual time to conform with her inner sense of duration.

> Apparently, for many reasons, it has been necessary for it to be Friday. She made a particularly striking statement, however—the essence of which was that to admit the wrongness of her belief would, to her, have raised serious questions about her sanity. Whatever other reasons made it necessary to construct this belief, it had to be true since otherwise she was crazy. Craziness to her meant loss of control, disintegration, and complete negation of self. In a sense, it had to be Friday instead of Saturday to preserve her sanity, her identity, her self, from disintegration and dissolution. . . . Holding onto the delusional reality helps the psychotic combat the threat of dissolution and disintegration and facilitates psychic survival. (1983, 148–49)

Because of this fear, psychotic time, as it strikes consciousness in the form of delusion, takes on an immanence; it is always there, a consequence of an inner world defined by dread and the prospect of self-annihilation.

Internal Symbologies: The Language of the True/Real

Psychotic or unconscious time is not "time" in any historical or linear sense. It lacks a *civitas* or public space, for the identifications of unconscious phantasies are held inside. Time, for example, appears to Jenny and Chuck not as the historical progression of days, weeks, and years but in the action of symbological events, specifically in terms of enemies and threats. Jenny survives in an ozone layer in outer space, or she feels bombs exploding beneath her room. Time lies within that ozone layer, or it resides inside the exploding bomb or occurs as bodies are being dug out of the ground.

The psychotic self lives within the specificity of whatever event occupies consciousness, and time is represented in the action of a continuing parade of images related only by the logic of the unconscious. Chuck feels his face being sliced off under the surgeon's knife; he knows they operate on him with "acid-filled" scalpels. After each operation, he experiences himself as disfigured, convinced his face "grows back afterwards." What Lacan (1968) calls the imaginary and Kristeva "that ineradicable 'death drive' " (1982, 96) subsumes and defines time. I ask Chuck if he wishes to talk, and he responds, "I can't. I'm busy killing all those doctors, burning them, putting them into the electric chair. I'm with my armies in South Africa, we're putting them away where they belong; dead, ashes, in the ground." Duration and power merge in the psychotic construct, "the assignment of a *subject* to archaic, prelinguistic narcissism, . . . the hollowing out of anguish in the face of nothing" (Kristeva 1982, 43), the hermitage of delusion.

Psychosis provides the psychological space where self expresses its "nature," where it lives out an inner knowledge as parable, a narrative in which others, whether they are aware of it or not, participate. The self is "an 'I' overcome by the corpse," overwhelmed by "a choking sensation that does not separate inside from outside but draws them the one into the other, indefinitely" (Kristeva 1982, 25). Chuck may see me as a spy, a killer, an agent. He may or may not tell me what he sees, but his utterances are filled with his own inner references and a sense of who he believes I am. If I deny it, if I tell him I have no wish to kill him, he may smile, shake his head, or walk out of the room. If I suggest he lives in Towson and not South Africa, he will be silent or deny what I say. For Chuck, utterance, no matter what its source, is assimilated directly into his own delusional time. My telling him Sheppard-Pratt exists in Maryland might indicate that I'm an agent sent to South Africa to deceive him deliberately. An hour later, he might be somewhere else or "working with the boys in Baltimore making sausages from the carcasses of dead, cast-off winos." Chuck authors *and* conducts the action; he constructs time; he walls off (Frosch 1983, 343) the outside world; nothing cracks his system. Filled with "black sounds . . . forsaken bodies," it is "double, fuzzy, heterogeneous, animal, metamorphosed, altered, abject" (Kristeva 1982, 207).

Psychotic time fragments the ego; it refracts destruction in images circulating around the self like a spinning top; it pushes the self into "a face-to-face confrontation with the abject" (Kristeva 1982, 209). Each fall of the top represents the completion of a given duration within the psychotic set. At one moment, Jenny believes her shampoo seeps into her scalp and poisons her brain; after that "top" spins itself out, she may feel her body is riddled with worms. That delusion may persist for several hours, after which it loses its force and is replaced by yet another. A given delusion before it winds down or disappears or is repressed may last anywhere from a few seconds to weeks or even years. Jenny may complain of poison in her food, or she may think she flies and chirps with birds outside her bedroom window. Each of Jenny's delusions—brains disintegrating, worms eating her body, talking with birds, seeing poison in food—becomes a fixed reality absorbing all consensual definition. It is, in Kristeva's terms, "demoniacal—an inescapable, repulsive, and yet nurtured abomination . . . the fantasy of an archaic force . . . unconscious, tempting us to the point of losing our differences, our speech, our life; to the point of aphasia, decay, opprobrium, and death" (1982, 107). Each of Jenny's realities contains its own "conception" of time, generated by fragments of the unconscious which project specific conceptions of reality.

Psychotic time is global, absolute, and total; states of dread, fear, horror, fragmentation, destruction, imminent annihilation develop within psychological environments in which conventional notions of time have no significance. For example, dread lasts just as long as the feeling occupies awareness. It is understood through its momentary rhythms, part of an "elusive, fleeting, and baffling . . . instability" (Kristeva 1982, 46). If Chuck believes doctors are going to operate on his face, he lives in that fear for hours. While he may think a second or two has gone by, he may in fact have remained immobile in a chair or on his bed for an entire day. Or he may observe that "chirotechnics" has invaded his body; he means he has been frozen and his molecules stored up in "ice banks" for three trillion years. If I see him early in the morning, he might say that he has just been frozen and he feels stiff from a billion years in ice banks. A moment may be a lifetime or the self may experience itself as the victim of an annihilating power that has crumbled, exploded, split, fragmented consciousness into thousands of bits and pieces. Each of these pieces carries with it bizarre concepts of duration. Consciousness, in this blown-up internal world, loses the capacity to delineate the serial aspects of social and historical time; it falls away from civility and takes on delusional preoccupations.

Psychotic Percepts: Knowledge Systems in Psychotic Time

For the self living in psychotic time, the *civitas,* the Aristotelian ego of restraint, and secondary process operations become the enemy; psychotic time ruptures the link between consciousness and civilization, consensual reality and the self, historically continuous public space and personal responsibility. The power projections filling psychotic time destroy the self's attachment to the polity; what is being lived in delusional parable is a grim psychic prehistory filled with ruminations on violence, death, annihilation, despair.

Kristeva's evocative language captures this withdrawal, estrangement: "An ego, wounded to the point of annulment, barricaded and untouchable, cowers somewhere, nowhere, at no other place than the one that cannot be found" (1982, 47). Chuck, for example, closes himself off from others; he takes refuge, dramatically, in the solipsism of delusion. "Where objects are concerned he delegates phantoms, ghosts, 'false cards': a stream of spurious egos" (47) or delusional points of reference. Chuck does speak; he constructs extraordinary parables. "Separation exists and so does language, even brilliantly at times, with apparently remarkable intellectual realizations" (47).

The stories of those stuck in psychotic time are often quite complex and rich in symbol, but there is no connection between them, no thread of being that ties the self to an embodied sense of utterance or relationship, as Kristeva recognizes: "But no current flows—it is a pure and simple splitting, an abyss without any possible means of conveyance between its two edges" (1982, 47). Psychotic time keeps the self literally locked out of consensual reality; the meanings Chuck attaches to his utterances come from his very private, inaccessible, and disembodied emotional anguish, abjection, which delusion disguises with the tightness of an iron cage—"no subject, no object," no self, no other, no distinction between the identities projected in delusion and the identity of the self in a continuous flow of experience, "petrification on one side, falsehood on the other" (47). Chuck finds himself immobilized in the world of others, quite literally petrified, while his significant or signifying world, the one he pays attention to, evolves around the falsehoods of delusional reality, the space of psychotic time.

I believe the linguistic pictures of psychotic time may provide clues to the types of primitive drive structures motivating the more ominous sides of political life. Such images may mirror political systems that degenerate into nihilism and violence, into pathological obsession with private needs and distinctions between good and evil. Individuals who speak in delusion may provide a way of understanding the infinitely more destructive and pathological public delusions and their exercise of power.

Political theorists such as Plato, Machiavelli, and Hobbes have seen an intimate connection between destructive elements in human nature and the action of political life. And Freud observed that it might be instructive to reflect on "Plato's dictum that the virtuous man is content to *dream* what a wicked man really *does*" (1900, 658). Dreams contain a peculiar "commentary" on the truth; so, too, do the utterances of persons for whom the terror of the dream in the form of delusion has become the dominant element in waking life. It may well be that Plato's "virtuous man" disguises a more fundamental pathology that works itself out or through in the public space, the *civitas* of power and domination.

In 1924 Freud wrote: "Neurosis and psychosis are . . . the expression of a rebellion on the part of the id against the external world, of its unwillingness—or, if one prefers, its incapacity—to adapt itself to the exigencies of reality, to 'Avάykn [Necessity]" (185). Consciousness finds itself powerless to adapt; it is forced to reconstruct reality, to build a delusional habitat. "In neurosis a piece of reality is avoided by a sort of flight, whereas in psychosis, [reality] is remodelled" (185). Unconscious phantasies refuse accommodation with external reality, and the result is a painful and tortuous withdrawal from social exchange. To be in psychotic time, then, is to experience the social world as hostile and malevolent, as a negation. "Neurosis does not disavow the reality, it only ignores it; psychosis disavows it and tries to replace it," Freud remarked (1924, 185). What is substituted is delusion.

Let me illustrate Freud's argument by drawing on a clinical example. Dana, a twenty-seven-year-old woman diagnosed as schizophrenic, believes she lives inside the belly of a fish. Nothing is past; nothing is future. What "is" appears in the completely revealed existential present: the inside of the fish, the texture of its belly, feelings of darkness, suffocation, movement, fear the belly will fill up with water. It is like existing within a pure flow of experience, terrorized by a flood of perception. Knowledge of the world becomes profoundly delusional, deriving from projected images of domination, rather than from consensually validated sequences of past, present, and future in everyday life. Knowledge frames that guide action and interpretation lie embedded in the endless succession of fish images.

Dana knows her world through tactile sensations: slimy membranes, undigested food, stomach acids (her skin "burns"), a smothering darkness, drowning in fish intestines (she gasps for air), being tossed from side to side (complaints of a persistent nausea). She experiences pain when she sits in bright light or in front of a window (shielding her eyes), since she believes the presence of light means she has been "thrown up" out of the fish's belly. Dana may spend an entire day feeling herself caught in a storm, and the wriggling of the fish makes it impossible for her to remain still. She describes an overwhelming feeling of shut-up-ness. She senses herself tumbling around without any relief as the fish fights the surging currents. She may go days without sleep, understanding herself as swimming with the fish three hundred feet beneath the ocean's surface. She is convinced that whatever knowledge she has evolves around these kinds of experiences. Time, in its historical or conventional use, disappears; existence is "felt" only through what happens in the fish's belly.

Delusion encloses duration and experience. Chuck asks me to break down his feet and analyze them: "Will you please take a saw and remove the toes from my feet. Start with the little toe and pull the saw slowly so you won't crack any of the bone. . . . Be careful, my toes are poisoning my feet! These things happen in four-trillion-year-old men." It is not social rationality or conventional time that structures Chuck's perception; nor is Chuck's request sensible. It may be that even the "subject" requesting such action is not Chuck but a computer speaking through him which sends orders from an underground bunker in Ypsilanti, Michigan. Or the command to saw off his toes may come from an agent or a voice lurking in his mind. What is important here is that the knowledge of what duration *is* emerges not from the consensual world but from the beliefs of the delusional system which project specific "forms" for "interpreting" reality, time, and action.

Psychosis is autonomous, and for the subject it has enormous power to transform time and matter. Chuck's voice and the computer in Ypsilanti, provide the knowledge frames; both "speak" the truth; both create a special reality. When Chuck asks me to saw his toes off, he takes me into his universe of duration. I become an actor in his internal symbology; he believes that removal of his toes will assure his survival for another four trillion years. He designates me as the "agent" to make sure that happens. "I know I can live another four trillion years; but I have to be still to do it; I can't move; I have to be immobile to conserve my energy." It is a psychotic feeling state, but it is also filled with crucial knowledge that defines survival. The delusion, however, multiplies; it becomes even more bizarre; its logic literally grows on itself. It may be necessary, in addition to his toes, to slice off his feet.

> If you cut off my feet, you'll get to the root of my disease; it may take you three hundred years. I'm old, so to do these jobs takes lots of time. It was those shoes I stole in Honduras; they caused it. . . . they've become part of my feet and I know I'm here [Sheppard-Pratt] because of the poison Ed stuck in the soles. If I throw these shoes away, I'll be cured up, but you have to take my feet off too since the poison has seeped through the leather.

What I want to stress here is the degree to which the internal world encircles "external" reality; how the self assimilates "material" in the outer world to its delusional knowledge. The meaning of who I am for Chuck depends on what the voices tell him and the message the computer sends. Nothing else matters. External belief systems, consensual knowledge, historical patterns—all are secondary to what delusion defines as power, to what abjection constructs as a "fortified castle" in the self (Kristeva 1982, 47). For example, Chuck believes:

- He has died for three days, an event precipitated by computerized voices originating in Ypsilanti.
- He has been pickled in brine and sometimes been stuck in Sheppard-Pratt's main entrance hall for days.
- The hospital is a "museum" and Chuck is an ancient, long-dead "stuffed animal" put on display "for the doctors."
- Smoking cigarettes drives voices away; eating mustard and dirt creates a brain block the voices are unable to penetrate. The need for these defensive maneuvers may last until Chuck reaches his four trillionth birthday.
- He lives inside "killer mists that creep up on you in this part of Maryland," which may linger for thousands of years.
- A certain sound echoes through the hospital, the voice of the dead ancestor coming back from prehistoric times, and its rhythm has the power to keep Chuck awake for five consecutive centuries.
- He has an infection that seeps into his brain through holes in his skin; this infection began several centuries ago in an earlier animal incarnation.

- When he falls asleep, his skull is cracked open, and poison is fed into his brain, dissolving tissue, which oozes out through his sinuses. Three thousand years later Chuck wakes up, and the brain cells grow back.
- He is the target of a special ray (designed to kill him) that comes down through New York City. If it manages to find and touch him, Chuck will be dead for two million years; then he can be brought back to life through a special potion of tea and ground-up ants.

Each of these beliefs excludes the other, and Chuck's time frame depends on which delusion happens to be controlling his consciousness. He may move from one to another within a matter of seconds, but whatever delusion frames his world, his sense of duration depends on events central to the psychotic drama, to the presence of what Kristeva calls "abomination" (1982, 102).

Psychotic time may be enclosed in peculiar identifications. The nursing notes describe some of Jenny's behavior: "At lunch Jenny stood the entire time separating corn from lima beans, relating that she didn't want them to 'have to sit together.' Jenny asked this writer to give her a bath, but she refused after I had washed the coffee area, stating that I now had a virus on my hands and she didn't want my germs. . . . She is now writing notes while wearing socks as mittens on hands." On another occasion Jenny stated: "I've been in the dark for a hundred years. I'm blind. . . . they either want to kill me or eat me as trash. . . . I live in the garbage pail; I've eaten my heart, my liver, goats, horses, and cows. I've eaten everything that there is to eat . . . even cans of dead people."

She sees enemies all around her. Staff, patients, doctors, visitors—all want to kill her, hammer stakes through her heart, rip out her brain. Her sense of duration is bounded by the fear of death; and she expresses "some concern such as 'someone is stabbing me in the back because I have a pain there' " (nursing note). She thinks the staff is "going to give her film-developing solution . . . to poison her." She constructs her sense of "time" according to the dictates of her delusions, literally "reading" reality from the inside out. And no matter what staff members say or do, Jenny reacts according to how she believes she will be killed, mutilated, defiled, poisoned, or deceived. Psychotic time projects critical doubts, persistent fear she carries inside.

> Jenny attended a hall meeting and said she'd like to talk about "the violence that's going to occur on the Hall." She referred to this writer as a "nazi war criminal" and said that I was harassing people. . . . Jenny complained of pain in her ear and says there is "aluminum foil and bugs in her ear." . . . Jenny cried the early part of the evening and asked staff for a hug, questioning whether staff loved her and whether we would take care of her, and said, "I am dying of sorrow and loneliness." (Nursing note)

Psychotic time inverts both symbolic and real connections in consensual reality; it significantly distorts "truth." For example, in the disembodied voice of a computer Jenny drones at me:

> You're not Dr. Glass. How dare you come in here and impersonate him? I'm Dr. Glass, can't you see that? I don't know who you are, you imposter! Who are you? You stinking idiot, the computer is inside me, it's me. . . . it's stinking up my programs. I'm a stinking program . . . a shit stinking program. . . . why are you here? All you've done is kidnap me and take me to this place. . . . you're a killer . . . a monster! Get out of here, leave me alone. . . . if you're not out of here by three o'clock, I'm going to kill you.

Psychosis traverses vast reaches of developmental time; Jenny's identifications move from youth to old age within a few seconds. She may hate at one moment ("I'm five years old. . . . I hate you. Get out of here, you're not my Daddy."); the next she may speak with the wistfulness of a woman capable of caring for her vast brood of "grandchildren." "See the wrinkles on my face, the grey in my hair. I'm a hundred and fifty years old. I have to look after my grandchildren. . . . You can't imagine how much I love being a grandmother." Or she may feel fifteen, a teenager with irresistible infatuations and crushes; she builds a complex romantic fantasy about Jeffrey (a mental health worker). She writes to him: "Your eyes are the most lovely, your teeth are pearly white, you cause my heart palpitations in the middle of the night. . . . When I hear your beautiful voice singing so sweetly I melt into a pound of butter." Yet, her very real affection possesses a psychotic backdrop that has nothing to do with actual circumstances. It is a delusion that Jenny projects when she occupies the inner time frame of a love-struck teenager.

Conclusion: The Entrapment of Psychotic Time

Jenny, Chuck, Dana, Louis—all live as agents of their unconscious phantasies (structured as delusional action); each internal universe has its own compelling logic; normal or historical contexts of duration and consensuality have no meaning or purpose. Power is experienced not as consensual or shared, but as unyielding, tyrannical, and devouring. Not only are these patients capable of moving back and forth from infancy to old age, from teenager to adult to elderly, but each may actually experience the self as occupying the time frame specific to whatever life stage defines consciousness. It is not that Jenny plays at being a teenager or an old woman; she becomes that identification. She feels oldness in her bones; she moves bent over, complaining of "creaky joints"; or as a teenager, her infatuation and girlishness appear in her dress, her hairstyle. She may be coquettish or sit too close to Jeffrey; if he ignores her or asks her to sit "more appropriately," she follows him around and offers him money to make love to her. Depending on where she "is" in her inner self, Jenny changes, and the metamorphoses happen quickly and completely.

It is common for individuals trapped by psychotic time to identify, often grotesquely, with the nonhuman environment. Frosch describes a patient who "believed that as a child an observation machine had been implanted in her head. This machine could observe and even control her activities" (122). Another patient believed that if she "let the bad thoughts stay in her mind, she would die of dismemberment. This would begin with an incision of a lipoma on her forehead, and then different parts of her body would be dismembered and distributed to the other patients for the good of humanity" (127). Harold Searles relates a case of a twenty-five-year-old man who had been raised to think of himself as either a savage animal or a cute little doll, "but not in the form of a human being." His parents "chronically treated him as being a cute little doll, and shied away from real flesh-and-blood feeling of all sorts, giving the patient the unconscious conception that any such feelings within him were so unacceptable, among human beings, as to be in the nature of actual animal phenomena. His father's favorite mode of addressing him in conversation was 'Kewpie-boy' " (1960, 211). At Sheppard-Pratt Louis, on occasion, identifies with animals. He believes he occupies a dog's body, or he turns into a tiger, or he feels "wolves' teeth" growing in his mouth. "I feel my teeth growing bigger; and my hands, look at them, they're turning into claws."

Jenny living in a spaceship in the ozone layer, Chuck controlling a special freezing technique ("chirotechnics") that turns human beings into ice blocks, Louis becoming a wolf roaming Sheppard-Pratt's grounds—these nonhuman identifications permit the self to turn time to the imperatives of psychotic scripts. And since the self, through this kind of omnipotent image, changes the past, it need not act on the present or be frightened of the future. The self survives in a present surrounded by ahistorical images governed by what Searles calls the "pressure-towards-omnipotence" (1960, 236); this nonhuman identity drives the self away from the *civitas*, from any connection whatever with human community. It is a transformation that alters the structure of being. Searles quotes Marcel Heiman:

> The identification of the patient with the dog was so complete that almost imperceptibly she changed from talking about the dog to talking about herself. Her own libidinal wishes which she cannot master or accept are displaced on to the dog. She wonders, for instance, whether she should place the dog in an obedience class. In this session the patient herself howls and whines and is demanding, the same way that she describes her dog. (1960, 310–11)

Consciousness loses track of what is there, "not there," real, unreal, public and private. Searles describes a patient who "could only conclude that all of her surroundings were a giant movie set which was changed continuously. . . . she was certain that there were thousands of Chestnut Lodges, thousands of Rockvilles, thousands of Washingtons. Changes in these physical surroundings, as well as changes in the appearance of other persons, would occur right before her eyes" (1960, 315). Such identifications, removing the self from its temporal context, are projections "upon the nonhuman environment, of inner psychological change" (316), and the self regresses to a state of "becoming subjectively as one with the nonhuman environment" (324). Historical or temporal sequences (and their defining and orienting capacities) disappear.

Searles's patients identify with trees, rocks, cows, and wolves. One feels that a chain is attached to her heart; another, that a machine lives in his stomach; another, that flowers grow out of her legs. In the duration of psychotic time, peculiar and brutal events are experienced in the body, forces of immense power occupy the universe, the supernatural haunts action, cosmological transformations erupt spontaneously. Nothing makes sense in terms of historical time. It is as if history, for such patients, never existed. Perhaps this is what Jacques Lacan (1968) meant when he spoke of the "language" of the "unconscious," the eruption of the imaginary into speech.

Kristeva speaks of "our psychotic latencies and the fragility of our repression," seeing them as "an indication of the weakness of language as a symbolic barrier that, in the final analysis, structures the repressed . . . [the] threatening encounter with uncanny strangeness" (1991, 186, 187). Something of what Kristeva sees as central to the self's experience of its own foreignness, its own uncanniness, possesses an affinity with the indeterminacy of psychotic time: "I lose my boundaries, I no longer have a container, the memory of experiences when I had been abandoned overwhelm me, I lose my composure. I feel 'lost,' 'indistinct,' 'hazy' " (187). And perhaps the knowing of psychotic time is connected to what Kristeva describes as the "confrontation with *death* and . . . the feminine" and the "malevolent *powers*" of this "end" and "beginning that engross and compose us only to frighten us when they break through" (185), the feminine/maternal as abjection and the imminence of death annihilating the self's frames of reference in consensual reality.

THREE

Jenny: Power as Projection of the Inner

THE exercise of power through the projections of psychotic time is quite different from its operations within consensual reality. It is also the case, however, that forms of power with origins in unconscious phantasies exercise a considerable structuring influence over interactions within consensual reality. How, then, is it possible to demonstrate or trace the effects of psychotic time and its peculiar forms of delusional power on public or consensual power?

I would like to look at this question by examining a small interactive group on a hospital ward. The ostensible project was to create and implement treatment strategies for Jenny, a twenty-year-old schizophrenic patient; yet much of the discussion about her treatment involved figuring out how the projective power, distorted perceptions, and intensified conflict of Jenny's internal world skewed nursing attitudes and provoked distrust and tension between her therapist and the nurses. It proved necessary to disentangle the operations of power driven by her unconscious phantasies from those belonging to the consensual network of treatment. For successful therapy it was essential to distinguish the two and to observe their reciprocal effects. It was also critical for the sanity and participatory cooperation of the treatment team, particularly their ability to respect one another.

Unconscious Intentionality and Its Effect on Power

To find the being that was Jenny, to understand the contours of her self, those involved in her treatment had not only to listen to her utterance, to examine the content of her delusional imagery, but to observe how they themselves, as a group, embodied or acted out intentions not readily visible in the context of the action itself, how power was configured by the force of Jenny's unconscious phantasies.[1] The staff became the screen on which Jenny projected her internal maps; her unconscious exercised its power within the small group environment of the hospital ward. Jenny's unconscious intentions may be understood as inner images, *part-objects* that derive from the self's internalization of early infantile experiences of parental images. Part-objects are filled out and elaborated through the self's phantasizing, which represents a complex and often distorted blending of "inner" and "outer." Further, *pathological* object relations characteristically tend to *split* the object world between all-good and all-bad images. Therefore critical "others" in the self's existential field come to be perceived in absolute terms. Edith Jacobson, for example, speaks of the "child's need to keep the 'good' gratifying love object as part of himself, and to spit out and rid himself of the 'bad,' frustrating object" (1964, 62).[2]

The split in Jenny's internal world was absolute. She viewed her father and mother either as evil, consuming, murderous, rejecting, and poisonous or (rarely) as nurturing, protective, bountiful, loving, and pure, never as combinations of positive and negative qualities. This good/bad split in Jenny's inner world mapped itself onto the life of the unit and was "represented" or acted out in attitudes her treatment team had *toward one another*. Kernberg writes: "Both splitting and projective identification deal principally with the projection of bad inner objects and bad parts of the self—in short, with primitive aggression. Excessive aggression results in excessive splitting mechanisms in order to protect the good internal and external objects from contamination with badness. When aggression is particularly strong and bad objects predominate [the situation with Jenny], there may be secondary splitting of bad objects into fragments and these fragments may be projected into multiple external objects [staff], thus giving rise to multiple persecutors" (1975, 27).

This phenomenon persistently constructed Jenny's relationship with staff members, each of whom contained "fragments" of the bad object. When Jenny was feeling particularly close to her therapist, whom she might identify as "father protector," nurses J., L., and D. became extraordinarily bad. Closeness with any individual staff member was always accompanied by outbreaks of intensive hostility toward others.

Again, the argument: inner maps outer. Internal group or interactive dynamics, no matter how tortuous, affect external political relationships. Jenny's persecutors materialized in staff members whose actions and attitudes Jenny perceived as directed toward her. Staff members then actually became for Jenny "minute fragments of pathologically split and projected bad internal objects" (Kernberg 1980, 27). She brought this "reproduction" of past object relations with her to Hall A. Not only did she enact pathological self and object representations, but she induced in others *actions* that she had unconsciously projected onto them. Staff members performed for Jenny as carriers for shed part-objects ("multiple persecutors") she was unable to integrate into her self. Knowledge of oneself as whole, as a person, as coherent, depends on the integration of good and bad qualities, the position of "ambivalence." Jenny was not capable of this position. She lived in the midst of Kristeva's abject.

Jenny's Internal Divisions and Staff Perceptions

Enactment of Jenny's internal world in the treatment milieu occurred simultaneously on two levels: in Jenny's manifest behavior and in the staff's projectively defined behavior. Jenny's fragmented identity appeared not only in her actions but in the actions of those onto whom she projected all-good or all-bad properties. This dialectic structured the relations between Jenny's internal world and the staff's public actions.

Patients and staff participated in Jenny's dramatic reenactments; she unconsciously dictated the action and framed the movement. But the totality of the script, this in-dwelling in the horror of abjection, was hidden from both her and the staff. To pull the pieces together and construct coherent meaning out of unrelated bits of action, to decipher action as a comprehensible form of dramatic symbology, required considerable staff discussion, much of it hostile. Jenny "reproduced" her historical home on the unit, and her images of her "Sheppard home" were filled with part-object representations (good and bad) coming from her past and embodied symbolically within the actions of those with whom she was most connected. I cannot emphasize too strongly the extent to which Jenny recreated in her public treatment milieu the structure of her own internal object world. Jenny was not powerless in the context of the ward.

Staff members in relation to one another and to Jenny enacted "messages" that told stories about good and bad mothers and fathers. It was striking how deeply these messages lay buried and how strongly they were denied even in the "beings" of those carrying them. It was therefore extremely difficult to isolate these "messages" from the persons carrying them, to objectify them and locate them as part of *Jenny's* narrative. In consequence, staff countertransference was often stormy. Disentangling these messages from the feelings of staff members evolved into the major focus of Jenny's treatment. In the words of one staff member:

> I knew I was getting close to Jenny when I began to hate people around me, on the unit, other patients and staff. And in my hatred, I could see and come to terms with the connections between myself and Jenny. But I needed to talk about it, to express it to others, to have that hour a week when we focused on what we were doing to Jenny and what she was doing to us. For a long time I had trouble knowing what my hate meant. Why should I hate this person? I hardly know her. What was it in our relationship that provoked such feelings? And when we talked about it, when I began to see the kinds of messages flowing back, silently, between myself and Jenny, when I finally understood what she was doing with us, I could assimilate it and look at it in the context of treatment. When I could do that, I had a better sense not only of who Jenny was, but a much clearer understanding of the lack of boundaries between Jenny and myself. I don't know why I focused on Jenny; there were other patients as sick as she was. But when I went home, after the shift, it was her I thought about. And when I woke up in the morning, and if I had a nightmare, I knew she had been in it.

Jenny's Meeting: Making Public the Structure of the Private

The staff began to understand what stood in the way of Jenny's treatment, impeding its delineation, from three clues: Jenny's intractability and violence, her "impossible imagination" and its "race toward death" (Kristeva 1982, 24), and the difficulty in dealing with their own angry reactions toward her, their own unsettledness and anxiety. Early in Jenny's treatment, confusion and misunderstanding frequently pushed her and the staff into intolerable opposition. At last the service chief on Hall A set aside an hour a week to look at the effects of Jenny's treatment on the feelings and perceptions of the staff. "Jenny's meeting," as it came to be called, evolved into a systematic exploration of the patterns of psychotic power linking the public world of Jenny and staff. It was an effort to escape the pervasive hopelessness and fear that characterized Jenny's treatment, to evaluate the nurses' feeling that she ought to be transferred to another unit or discharged from the hospital, and to recognize and resolve the serious differences between her therapist and the nurses. Under the pressure of Jenny's unpredictability, violent outbursts, and sense of the world as imminent threat, relations among staff members had become highly fractious.

Jenny's meeting brought together the community of the unit: all sectors of treatment (psychiatry, social work, nursing, art, dance, activity) set out to explore Jenny's unconscious world in a completely open, intellectually free environment without an agenda, without preconceptions. The participants hoped to articulate the structure of hidden intentions and their power over states of mind and action, both Jenny's and the staff's. Over the months, staff members spoke about fears, anxieties, rage, anger, disgust, indifference, and hopelessness. They tried to see how Jenny's inner world encompassed and defined actions within the hall, how her experience framed conflict between nurses and psychotherapist, how her unconscious phantasies controlled the reactions to her.

Jenny's meeting became an opportunity to make visible what until that time had remained largely hidden and disguised. Gradually, specific scenarios (enactments) from Jenny's past, the "story" implicit in her split-off object representations, were identified, as were the modes of staff participation in these highly volatile affective structures. This focus on the nature and structure of reenactment distinguished Jenny's meeting and gave a significance to her treatment unique in the experience of the unit. The medical staff did not experience themselves as the "authority," making decisions and imposing them on the varied sectors of treatment; rather, they found themselves collaborating in the pursuit of candor. As Jenny's therapist put it,

> We tried to be as direct with each other as possible, to look at how Jenny made us feel, how we saw her, how we thought she saw us. We struggled with that, with the parts of Jenny wandering around in each of us, with her sense of disconnection (since we were all feeling so disconnected), with her confusion and despair that took root in each of us. Nothing was certain: all we knew was what we felt, and in treating Jenny we had to begin from that point; our own feelings and our interpretation of those feelings. We searched for common ground, an understanding about what Jenny was saying to us, how we acted out her inner world, fragments that had no coherence, no identifiable meaning. We needed to keep the circle open, and to maintain the framework of Jenny's treatment within the perspective of our own self criticism and our own willingness to see our reactions to Jenny in the context of Jenny's reenactments, her way of bringing the past into the present. [For insightful analysis of the psychotherapeutic treatment of schizophrenic patients see Searles, 1965; Schulz and Kilgalen, 1967.]

The major difficulty was that no single participant in Jenny's treatment could see the totality; no panoramic view made all elements of the dramatic action comprehensible. Staff members came into the play at random moments: one saw part of the first act; another arrived at intermission; another during the middle of the third act; another had to leave and came back the following night, only to find an understudy in the major role, and so on. Through collaboration, the participants hoped to reconstruct the dramatic narrative from the pieces of decipherable meaning each had discovered. Jenny's meeting made this reconstruction possible, and it also showed the staff members their place in the flow of often jumbled and incoherent experience. The meeting, then, provided a forum for bringing together the pieces, for collecting and analyzing the unconscious fragments, for locating common structures motivating public action, for working through the distorting impact of unconscious phantasies on the hall's patterns of communication.

Table 1. Phases in Jenny's treatment

	Observation	Hatred	Toleration	Love
Time frame	1–3 months	4–12 months	12–17 months	17–19 months
Staff feelings	curiosity guardedness superficial relatedness custodial care	anger frustration confusion fear hopelessness Jenny's meeting begins	limited tolerance effort at contact some (positive) emotional connection suspiciousness tempered by some humor staff protection by private-duty nurses	hope perception of likability considerable tolerance emotional care nurturance

Even though alliances, positions, and points of view developed over a period of months, the group survived its own hostility. Because the members of the treatment team were willing to involve themselves in a common project, however hostile their interactions, they were able to resist the very real temptation to push Jenny from the unit and the hospital as an untreatable case. The participants made a strong effort to provide a responsive holding environment (although intensely conflicted) as a way to maintain a process of reenactment that might at some point restore to Jenny her citizenship in the human world and ultimately give her some contact with consensual reality, thereby freeing her from the dominion of psychotic time. Jenny's treatment on Hall A, then, can be divided into four distinct phases: Jenny was observed, hated, tolerated, and finally, loved (Table 1).

It might be useful now to turn in somewhat more detail to the structure of Jenny's reenactments on Hall A.

Reenactment: Unconscious Splitting and Hidden Messages

Each image—or, better, part-image—Jenny held of her mother and father was defined as all-good or all-bad; no ambivalence entered into these pictures. The all-good mother and father appeared as perfect, loving, nurturing, almost godlike. The all-bad mother and father possessed only horrible, rejecting, vicious, cruel, tyrannical, and poisonous properties. Winnicott, for example, speaks of the infant's "two mothers," the "object-mother," who acts as the recipient of the infant's "id tensions," and the "environment-mother," who protects, cares, gives affection, and quietly satisfies (1965, 75). The object-mother embodies badness; she "becomes the target for excited experience backed by crude instinct-tension"; she acquires "the full force of fantasies of oral sadism . . . id-drives [of] attack and destruction" (76). The environment-mother, on the other hand, provides goodness; she forges a safe, secure relationship; as a "reliable presence," she offers "the opportunity for giving and for making reparation" (77). Jenny persistently acted on this split and promoted it on the unit.

Since Jenny's psychosis involved figures of persecution and torture, early in her treatment on Hall A the all-bad object world infused her conceptions of reality, her private Hobbesian "war of all against all." For example, one moment Jenny could see her therapist, Dr. M., as a jailer, a tyrant immersed in the "deepest blackness," wishing to defile her, "a source of evil . . . mingled with sin" (Kristeva 1982, 127); the next moment, she could weep in his presence, implore him to help her, ask him to take her home. In her view he could shift rapidly from good object to bad object, as if he were two different persons, rather than a single human being possessed of good and bad qualities. He remarked: "It was strange sitting there with Jenny, listening to her, watching her experience me. One moment I would feel myself come into her world as an all-giving mother, the next she would be looking at me as if I were a different person, even call me by a different name and yell at me what a horrible, disgusting person I was."

Projection of the negative aspect of the self onto (or into) the other determined much in Jenny's interaction with Dr. M. But the changeability of her view of him was also crucial. Her absolute identifications could shift almost instantaneously from the image of the ideal therapist who rescues her from "the crypt that encloses the dead," to the picture of a bearer of "phallic violence" (Kristeva 1989, 79). Dr. M. described this abrupt oscillation:

> Jenny could never see me as a complete person, as a human being with both good and bad qualities. I either became the tormenting father or the hostile, rejecting mother. Or I was idealized as a great, powerful protector, again as either her mother or father who had come to rescue her from torment. Jenny was incapable of seeing me as a whole person, separate and autonomous from her. I remember when my wife was pregnant, Jenny used to come to sessions with a pillow stuck into her abdomen, and stare at me with those adoring eyes. Then she could just as easily shift to telling me what a horrible person I was, how all I wanted to do was kill her, rape her, and so on; the next fifteen minutes she might sit silently weeping and looking at me as if she were going to climb right inside my skin.

Nurses, with one or two exceptions, took on primarily "bad" properties, seen as agents ripping flesh from Jenny's bones, poisoning her food, burning her scalp, imprisoning her body, consigning her to "a permanent vertigo," pushing her into a "black hole . . . invisible, crushing, cosmic anti-matter" (Kristeva 1989, 85, 87). One nurse recalled:

> Jenny made us feel as if we were jailers, and I often felt like a sadist with the power to inflict pain, a jailer whose only function lay in maintaining order and control. That's the way she made me feel; and I used to be mortified every time I took her on recesses [from seclusion]. She would look at me with those big blue eyes of hers, imploring, begging for relief, and my heart went out to her. It made me feel horrible, guilty. I would go home and weep my heart out and imagine myself to be some horrible person who could only bring pain. During that period, I had dreams I was a little girl constantly being spanked by her father and told how miserable I had been.

When Jenny cast her therapist as all-good and staff as all-bad, it was inevitable that the split would be mirrored in treatment, particularly in her therapist's view of the nursing care as "bad." Nurses "caused" problems, "poisoned" with treatment, "imposed" impossible conditions, "stifled" progress. Both Jenny's perception and her therapist's were at such times identical, as Dr. M. came to recognize:

> Sometimes I felt I had to save Jenny from nursing. I know it's irrational and doesn't make sense, but she provoked this splitting. I began to see the world as she saw it. But I believed I had reached this view of it on my own. It's almost as if in the patient there is an unconscious language that communicates messages, ideas, relationships which are acted on without anyone ever being aware of their presence. It took a long time for me to identify my own splitting of treatment in the context of Jenny's unconscious splitting of her object world. Jenny had real power in this respect; and whenever I found myself enraged at a nursing decision, I had to pull back and look at what I was doing. That's why Jenny's meeting was so useful; I could look at myself. I could see my actions in the context of nursing actions. I would listen to them. We could yell at each other, hate each other, and reach some kind of understanding.
>
> I have often wondered if Jenny's parents didn't in some way experience this kind of hostility and if we here at Sheppard were replaying Jenny's early family environment with the same psychological structures but a different cast with identical roles or part roles. Jenny placed pieces of herself, of her parents, in different staff members, never a whole self or a whole object but fragments that floated in and out of staff depending on the intensity of Jenny's projections.

Yet, Jenny could just as easily view her therapist's actions and feelings as all-bad, could just as easily see him as a torturer. Keeping her in seclusion, forcing intramuscular medications, complying with the nurses' need to keep Jenny restrained—all these could transform Dr. M. into an evil emissary from hell, the bearer of "violence, blood and death" (Kristeva 1982, 147). At such times he became a coconspirator with the nursing staff. He and the nurses, each acting out "bad" fragments of Jenny's inner script, felt as if treatment were proceeding with "direction" and "purpose" and "goals." Jenny, meanwhile, experienced a universe characterized by "dizziness, noises, buzzings, vomitings," "rotten and dead, full of discomfort and sickness," "the horror of hell without God" (Kristeva 1982, 146, 143, 147). She told me,

> Dr. M. that Nazi doctor wants to kill me, rip out my eyes and throw me into the incinerator. All he wants to do is eat my guts and grow fat on my blood. I hate him; he should be dead and buried, and I'll get him when he won't know it. I'll stick the knife into his heart and I'll watch him die. I remember how my father beat me, horribly, black and blue marks all over my body. He took the strap and lost control. But Dr. M. is worse; he's tougher than Dad because he cuts out pieces of my brain.

And Dr. M. found himself questioning his own actions: "Maybe I am her tormentor; maybe she's right; maybe I am a Hitler; what do you think, is she right?" He saw himself, to use Kristeva's words, as "an object of hatred and desire, of threat and aggressivity, of envy and abomination" (1982, 178).

The dramatic reenactment became quite dangerous when Jenny's projections were embodied in fruitless public argument and political territorial disputes between therapist and nurses. It was dangerous in the sense that treatment could be jeopardized because of frustration and the view that Jenny was the "enemy" and that the staff was engaged in heroic but unappreciated efforts to "save" her. For example, if Jenny believed herself to be in a Nazi concentration camp, if she felt herself being chopped up into bits and pieces or being burned by fires under the ground, her therapist might feel he was being "chopped up by nursing staff." Such unconscious connections unsettled boundaries and created intense friction in the public atmosphere of the hall.

Staff members found themselves enmeshed in images that Jenny could not possess as part of herself. It was as if inside of her were "nothing but bruises and paralysis . . . telescoped into a simultaneously killing and irretrievable burden that organize[d] her subjectivity" (Kristeva 1989, 87–88). She needed to "place" these images (or part-objects) in others because recognizing them in herself was intolerable. Images of aggression, murder, hate, hostility (the delusional substrate of psychotic time) or idealizations projecting love, devotion, and power appeared not only in Jenny's view of different staff members but also in their actions toward her. Jenny's unconscious phantasies wielded tremendous power.

Inner Mapping Outer: Some Scenarios

It is a mistake to think that the internal world of the patient has no effect on the perceptions and actions of the staff. Erving Goffman (1961) never considered projective identification as a dynamic in the small community of the mental ward. Certainly, the patient is powerless in terms of institutional politics. Nevertheless, in the context of treatment, power and its exercise *may* follow a dialectic established by the patient's projective enactments and the delusional contexts of psychotic time.

It is important, therefore, to distinguish relative levels and paths of power in any institution. Although the patient has nothing to do with administrative decisions and policies made by the hospital hierarchy (like the university professor or therapist in the context of higher-level bureaucratic decisions), it is *not* true that the patient is always powerless in the life situations of the treatment environment, the struggles or alignments of participants. The staff on Hall A was frequently beset by power struggles that originated in the subtlety of Jenny's projective processes. Splitting is just one instance of the manipulation of power relations which often threatened the authoritative relations on the unit.

Let me now turn in somewhat more detail to the actual operation of Jenny's "scenarios" in specific staff actions (Table 2). These scenarios were reconstructed from dialogues with Jenny, staff observations and records (nursing notes), periodic conversations with the social worker and the therapist and their report of conversations with Jenny's mother and father, previous hospital records, discussion in Jenny's meetings, observations of the art and activities therapists, interpretations of hall-based therapists familiar with Jenny, and the service chief's assessments. The scenarios should be understood as structures or ideal types of interactions. The evidence indicates, however, that these "types" and variations on their dynamics had an enormous impact on the unit's political relations and its distribution of power.

Take scenario A. The family dynamic operates as follows: mother becomes angry; Jenny identifies with mother's anger and becomes provocative, angry. Mother, now enraged, withdraws emotionally; Jenny develops rage-filled reactions, acting out her "bad" self-representations. Mother completely blocks off her feelings toward Jenny; Jenny becomes a nonperson within her mother's emotional world. Father screams at mother for ignoring their daughter.

Table 2. Jenny's dramatic enactments

Inner image	Action	Effect on staff
Scenario A. Mother as tormentor	Hostility toward staff (bad object)	Estrangement among staff (multiple persecutors)
Scenario B. Mother as protector	Jenny sitting quietly and having her hair combed (good object) Therapist paying close attention to nursing interventions; positive supports	Closeness and cooperation between Jenny and individual staff member Nursing and therapist in greater agreement
Scenario C. Father as protector from mother	Jenny physically striking head nurse (bad object) Quiet therapy sessions	Conflict among nursing staff Hostility between therapist and head nurse
Scenario D. Fear that sister will kill her	Refusing to come out of room because of belief that patient X will kill her (bad object) Withdrawal from other patients	Nursing taking sides with patient X against Jenny Therapist taking Jenny's side against intrusiveness and "hostile" gestures of patient X Conflict between therapist and nursing staff

On the hall this exchange of power reappears. The staff expresses anger toward Jenny. Jenny acts provocatively toward the staff. Jenny internalizes the staff's rage; she herself becomes enraged. The staff, angered by Jenny's actions, withdraws emotionally from Jenny's projected rage. Jenny develops rage-filled reactions toward the staff. The staff completely blocks any "good" feelings toward Jenny, views her as obnoxious, and withdraws caring or nurturing feelings. In day-to-day nursing interactions, Jenny becomes a nonperson in the staff's emotional constellation. She receives rudimentary nursing, but there is little willingness to engage her; other patients complain of not receiving enough time from the staff. The therapist expresses anger at the staff for neglecting Jenny's needs; he argues with the staff over Jenny's treatment, convinced she is not being given enough time, her needs are being ignored. Like Jenny's father, he takes on the role of advocate for her with the staff (mother).

Jenny's unconscious images of her mother as tormentor are thus enacted in staff hostility, even though the connection between staff conflict and Jenny's unconscious world is not readily apparent. Staff members feel estranged from Jenny; they experience her inner world as estrangement among themselves. They argue; nursing alliances work at cross-purposes; intense disagreement arises over vacation time; tension levels on the unit skyrocket. Nor is it a coincidence that Jenny's intractability takes an unusual amount of time in staff discussions. It is her family all over again, but this time Jenny's self, as it is being written by her unconscious phantasies, in large measure determines public discourse and action over her treatment. Jenny's internal world, with its "psychotic guise[s] . . . repugnance, disgust, abjection" (Kristeva 1982, 11), manipulates the distribution of power on the unit.

Similarly, in scenario B, Jenny places in a male mental health worker a beneficence and "goodness" that appears in her allowing him to comb her hair. She feels quiet in the presence of this older, somewhat fatherly man, whom she occasionally opposes to the rest of the nursing staff. She sits on the hall, drawing or playing with her toy monkeys, calm and peaceful. The therapist and the nurses work closely together during this quiet period; conflict diminishes; other patients seem to the nurses to be "doing well" or to "look good." Communication increases on the hall; the therapist and the nurses find themselves in agreement more often. Staff relations improve over matters having nothing to do with Jenny's treatment. It is vital to recognize that staff relations would become noticeably more cooperative when Jenny provoked feelings of care, protection, and closeness *toward her*. Conversely, when Jenny induced frustration, argument, and jealousy, staff relations deteriorated. Whatever mood was prominent or ascendant, it was Jenny's internal world, immersed in psychotic time, that moved the perception of power, the distribution of power, and the exercise of power on the hall.

The family structure in scenario C plays as follows: mother withholds from Jenny; father intervenes in mother's actions; mother distances from Jenny; father pushes for additional treatment, help; mother wants to commit Jenny, to free herself from responsibility; father seeks special care beyond what mother feels is necessary; mother rejects Jenny out of frustration; father offers to intervene and help, shoulders extra financial and emotional burdens.

And on the unit: the head nurse withholds from Jenny, misunderstands an action or a statement. Jenny then acts out; her therapist intervenes in the nurse's interpretation and reaction. He expresses hostility toward the head nurse. The head nurse distances herself from Jenny, pays less attention to her. The therapist schedules extra meetings for Jenny's treatment. The head nurse expresses a wish to have Jenny moved from the hall, to define her as medically untreatable; she raises the possibility of sending her to another hospital. The therapist makes a convincing case for extra discussion, more team meetings, special meetings, more money in terms of staff time for Jenny's treatment. The head nurse rejects all this extra effort, contending that the psychiatric staff is "overinvolved." The therapist/father intervenes and insists that Jenny stay on the unit, that her case is treatable but requires "time" and "attention"; the service chief (the head administrator of the unit) agrees with the therapist. Jenny is not "sacrificed" for the good of the group. She remains on the hall.

In scenario C, then, the father protects Jenny from the mother; the therapist acts as advocate for the patient in relation to the staff. The power split is good father/good therapist versus bad mother/bad staff. Power on the unit comes into play in decisions made about Jenny's treatment and when the therapist overrules nursing decisions or strenuously and often rancorously fights with nurses, especially the head nurse.

And finally, with scenario D, in the family, Jenny fears her sister's actions and feelings, and she is terrified of her own feelings toward her sister, the wish to murder her. Jenny comes to believe that her sister wants to murder her. Jenny withdraws from the family because of fear of her sister. Her parents tell Jenny that her sister has no interest in murdering her, that Jenny's belief is a figment of her imagination.

On the unit, Jenny fears certain female patients. She becomes terrified of her own feelings toward a specific female patient. Jenny comes to believe that the patient wants to murder her. Jenny hides in her room and refuses to come out. Staff members tell Jenny that the patient does not want to murder her and ask her to come out of her room. Staff members become exasperated with Jenny and take the side of other patients.

Dr. M. and the head nurse see each other as Jenny sees them; they act out "pieces" of Jenny's *internality* in their relationship with each other, and their interactions come to symbolize critical elements of Jenny's internal drama, the projection of split-off and denied fragments of herself. "Bad" mother torments Jenny; "good" father rescues her. Primitive part-object representations, therefore, find themselves mirrored in concrete differences in treatment approaches and in shifting power alliances and actions in the unit. From this perspective, it is a serious mistake to believe that the internal, the unconscious, the intrapsychic has no influence on public structures and power relations. At least in this instance, Jenny's tortures, the scenarios of her family constellation, the delusional projections of psychotic time were all played out in the very real power arrangements of the unit. Pieces of Jenny's inner world appeared, dissolved, recombined, and reappeared in the staff she hated, feared, loved, and denied.

FOUR

Tragedy: Power as Delusional Tyranny

THAT Jenny was obsessed with love, violence, confinement, and loneliness was understandable, given her situation and history. She organized the delusional percepts of her internal world with great sensitivity and even logic. She spoke with an inner playmate whom she tortured and who tortured her; she reflected on eating human flesh; she found herself in "places that sold rancid meat"; she kept diaries, recording events on the hall in minute details. Not all her entries were well organized or even comprehensible, but her discourse had a pattern, a set of themes or structures derived from the action of her unconscious phantasies.

Jenny's experience echoed Kristeva's abject: "I behold the breaking down of a world that has erased its borders: fainting away" (1982, 4). It was a universe provoked by phantasies of the absent and tormenting mother, in which a child, horrified by preoedipal images, "rejects and throws up everything that is given to him—all gifts, all objects. . . . Fear cements his compound, conjoined to another world, thrown up, driven out, forfeited" (6). Nothing can comfort the self; no innocence brackets the self's horrors. There is no refuge in the arms of a maternal *caritas*. "What [the abject] has swallowed up instead of maternal love is an emptiness, or rather a maternal hatred. . . . what solace does he come upon within such loathing? . . . a blank subject . . . at the dump for non-objects that are always forfeited . . . a deep well of memory" (6). Indeed, at a deep level Jenny felt as if she were a dump, a nonobject, a target for the world's hate and indifference. Her parents had rejected her, revealing in conversations with her therapist and social worker that they considered her a defective human being and would prefer to forget her, leaving her to the ministrations of the hospital and the state.

Jenny's projective dynamics turned consensual reality upside down. Yet, she could also be said to examine certain aspects of human experience and perception—the presence or absence of love; the destructiveness of others' actions and intentions; the impulse toward violence and torture; the dread of being confined; the fear and debilitation of loneliness; the lack of concern and regard from others; the misreading of others' intentions and wishes; the confusions of human sexuality and desire; the panic at being misunderstood and made invisible. Jenny's preoccupations were not so far removed from these concerns about humanity, care, closeness, freedom, and trust which extend throughout society. Her own fears, however, were so intense that it was impossible for her to experience love and intimacy. Jenny felt the social world had abandoned her (which was true); more often than not, she interpreted "closeness" as the opportunity for a staff member or a patient to stick a knife into her belly or poison her food.[1] She found collaboration intolerable and considered other persons' actions murderous, sadistic, and threatening. The closer she was to the distorting images of psychotic time, the more she removed herself from consensual reality.

Jenny's world *was* different. Her past was quite unlike that of a normal teenager growing up in a quiet American suburb. What could be expected from a twenty-year-old woman who since the age of fifteen had been in and out of mental hospitals. At sixteen, during an argument in the kitchen, she had accidentally stabbed her mother with a butcher knife. Several months later she had tried to kill herself with a twelve-gauge shotgun turned on her stomach. These experiences were compounded by her family's rejection. Her mother feared her daughter and refused to visit her. Her father was frustrated by her illness. Jenny's thoughts were encircled by abandonment and despair. Yet, the hatred, confusion, and violence of which she spoke may be typical of countless families plagued by intense unconscious and interpersonal conflict. Her feelings may simply represent the extremes of those feelings that characterize the so-called normal family. Her poems describe, at least symbolically, the extent to which communication within families is subverted and often destroyed by projective patterns of power that erode trust.

Certainly within her environment at Sheppard-Pratt, Jenny recreated aspects of her family situation; patients, staff, therapists elaborated her internal and split-off family dramas. She treated other patients like siblings; she provoked the staff in much the same way as a recalcitrant child might provoke her parents. She made good/bad mothers and fathers out of nurses and therapists. Even though she declared her hatred of the hospital, she made the world she was forced to occupy into a family. Here was the only place where others had ever expressed concern and respect for her as a person; for if their actions and feelings toward their daughter are any indication of how they felt in the years preceding hospitalization, it is unlikely Jenny ever experienced much care, affection, or trust from her parents.

That Jenny's immersion in psychotic time evolved around violence and power is unquestionable. Yet, her psychosis sealed off self-observation and self-reflection; it defended her against owning the external violence and rage, against internalizing it as part of her emotional constellation. Jenny knew, for example, that she had tried to kill herself with a shotgun. What she was incapable of understanding was that this desperate act was not the product of a voice telling her to die or a command from a computer but had something to do with her own feelings of utter despair and isolation. She was just as apt to see the hospital pulling the trigger as to recall pulling it herself.

Jenny could derive no comfort from the hospital, nor could it bring her any closer to consensual reality. In her mind's eye, she saw Sheppard-Pratt as a persecutor, existing to hurt her and other people, the agent of pain. The distortions of psychotic time and its projection of unconscious phantasies would not permit her to see the refuge the hospital provided. Where but in such a place, protected from the indifference and brutality of the consensual world, could Jenny be brought to realize the extent of her self-destructive impulses and the effects of her delusional projections on her physical and psychological self? The hospital was committed to keeping her alive. It allowed her to explore the horrifying intersections between her unconscious self and the conscious, functioning environment, to project her pain into the power relations of the unit. If Jenny were discharged, her paranoia, dread, and despair, compounded by the refusal or inability of family and friends to understand her, would rapidly push her toward suicide. Jenny interpreted confinement as torture, pain, insensitivity, and domination, but if she were released from this torment, she would undoubtedly listen to the voice telling her that death was preferable to life, or she would try to meet God by destroying her physical self.

From the perspective of the hospital, confinement makes it possible to contain Jenny's murderous impulses toward others and herself in an environment sensitive not only to her needs but also to her *language*. If an empathic staff found considerable difficulty in dealing with her often threatening language, imagine what it would be like outside the hospital. Jenny would soon find herself shunned, forced into a physical and emotional isolation that might ultimately degenerate into death. Power on the outside is not empathic; it is not always empathic on the unit, but it is more likely to be so, since the staff is constantly scrutinizing and criticizing the operations of power.

In many of her poems, Jenny's reality appears as an unfulfilled wish: her fantasy of love from a mental health worker; her desire for a place without nurses and staff or locked doors and keys; her need to fill up an inner emptiness; her despair over interminable loneliness and the invention of imaginary playmates. Yet Jenny's wishes had about them a no-exit desperation. She professed love, but her actions pushed the mental health worker away. She yearned to leave the hospital and yet found herself terrified at leaving the hall, convinced that people prowled in the corridors with darts and ray guns, ready to shoot her full of poisons. She hated the locked doors but became extremely agitated when strangers came onto the hall. She wondered if Nazis hid behind the Coke machines, if the nurses filled milk cartons with strychnine. She complained of loneliness but often rebuffed overtures with negativistic and hostile language.

Jenny feared entrapment and confinement, but without the bond of a place that acted toward her as a mother might toward an infant, she would kill herself. Jenny forcefully declared her hatred of staff, her sense of injustice; she experienced the hospital as a prison, a concentration camp, torture chamber, a place serving up dead meat. But whose perception is correct in the midst of this "gushing forth of the unconscious . . . neither jovial, nor trustful, nor sublime, nor enraptured" (Kristeva 1982, 206). Is the hospital a prison or a refuge from an outside world that would be deadly? Would Jenny be any freer if she were allowed to act on the commands of delusional voices that told her to cut off her legs, so she could turn into a stone; to build a fire, so she could die in hell; to let all the blood out of her veins, so she could disintegrate into particles and float up to the outer-space man; or to douse herself in acid, so she could become ether, able to meet God?

Jenny feared being poisoned, eaten, killed, and annihilated. She said she needed to destroy those she hated on the unit. Hers was a universe of absolute goods and absolute evils. The forces that tormented her were omnipotent. The only appeasement of her rages and hatreds was in torture and death. She felt overwhelmed by sexual confusion and violent intentions. Death squads and burning buildings, apes, baboons, monkeys, human and animal flesh, guns, knives, and bombs surrounded her. Frequently, what Jenny feared (being eaten, massacred, cut up into small pieces) was precisely what she threatened to inflict on others. Generally, she kept her world hidden in her notebooks, but occasionally, it appeared in her utterance. For example, she once told her therapist he had better "look out," for she would kill him, his wife, and his children. He responded that her thoughts frightened him, and Jenny replied, "I'm frightened too." Hers was a world of violent exchange, explosion, and transformation, and whatever love and tenderness she may have received in childhood was long ago obliterated by the horrifying effects of her disintegration.

It is not easy to treat a patient for whom the world is a continual state of nature, who believes life to be, in Hobbes's words, "nasty, brutish, and short," who may physically threaten the people around her. When Jenny was particularly agitated or lashed out physically, the staff found it necessary to place her in seclusion. But she was not confined capriciously. The staff, though they struggled with their own ambivalence and rage, made sincere efforts to care for Jenny with tolerance and understanding. Nevertheless, Jenny viewed them as sadists and tormentors. She hurled accusations, listed injustices, appealed for liberation from her jailers. She constructed the world in this way precisely because she was incapable of seeing the effects of her actions on others. Her psychosis destroyed any capacity for empathy. She therefore interpreted any restraint at all as persecution and domination, the illicit operation of power, even though she would unquestionably have killed herself if left to her own devices.

The trap cut both ways: Jenny felt victimized; the staff felt frustrated. Each began to hate the other. Yet, Jenny and the staff had a close relationship. During certain periods, indeed, the staff regarded her as the ideal or idealized patient. Psychotic time, however, manifests itself in language, and when this language confronts the language of treatment, misunderstanding is inevitable; reality differs depending on the language of the speaker.

Jenny never broke through her delusional world, but the hospital gave her some hope, some possibility for returning to the human world, for freeing herself from this delusional imprisonment. As she put it in one of her poems: "When will I stop seeing myself as an ape? When will Daddy Ape let me go?" Where else could she represent and therefore externalize this inner world and its power and not be punished for her thoughts? To demystify psychotic time, it would have been necessary for Jenny to make it public, consensually available, accessible to those she trusted, even though she never verbally acknowledged her trust. She was not capable of that accomplishment, but she did say to me regarding her diaries, "I hope what I've written here might help me in some way. It may seem weird to you, a little of my strangeness, but I'm tired of being lonely. And maybe others might learn from my experience. Besides, I'd like to give Daddy Ape a shot in the kisser."

After two and half years of treatment, the boundaries demarcating inside and outside remained hopelessly confused. When Jenny felt particularly anxious, it was not because of her own feelings or desires but because of the "electricity in the air that is killing all of us," or because the "electrocution chamber has been brought to Sheppard-Pratt, and I'm next on the list," or because of the "agents" on the hall secretly sent by her mother to kill her. When she felt depressed, it was not because of things that had actually happened to her but because the food was poisoned, or the staff was out to get her, or other patients secretly controlled dive bombers that were attacking her room. If the mental health worker refused to love her, it was not because he was married and had asked her on any number of occasions not to speak to him suggestively but because he was a vicious, horrible person who only wanted to treat her like an animal.

Jenny revealed the preoccupations and desires of a person considered clinically insane, but her language also suggested considerable intelligence, sensitivity, and feeling. Jenny divided the world between the free and the jailed, the masters and the slaves, humans and animals, but she was imprisoned as much by her own psychotic representations as by the institution. Both, for different reasons, kept her locked up.

The Stage of Tragedy

At the foundation of her schizophrenic psychosis, Jenny faced an undecidable psychic dilemma. She possessed an infantile conviction, expressed in delusion, that her rage had the power to kill. Yet that conviction, intolerable to sustain, had been projected outward, the power given to external agents: the hospital killed, it poisoned food, its water clogged her heart, gas burned her lungs, dive bombers roamed the skies, rays burned her brain, and so on. Unable to acknowledge anger or rage as part of her "self," as coming from inside her, she placed it outside as malevolent threat and presence. Machines, chemicals, poisons acted on Jenny the thing, the disembodied object; her otherness refracted itself in the persistence of a psychosis that reduced her to less than human, although she was occasionally capable of self-observation: "How can you like me? I'm so mean and nasty, full of prickles like a porcupine."

Jenny's statements could be terrifying to those who were caring for her. "If I get angry at Nurse J., will I kill her?" she might say, or "I hate Nurse J.; give me a knife and I'll stick it through her ribs," or "If I had a gun, I'd blow all your brains out." It was far safer for her to place her wishes in outside forces such as dive bombers, fires, and gases, since when she uttered threats she represented a part of herself caught in an uncontrollable panic. Further, if she were to realize her "wish" (the destruction of the head nurse, for example), she, like an infant, would be left emotionally alone, helpless, and abandoned. Better a bad mother—for that is the fragment the head nurse filled out—than no mother.

It was nevertheless quite difficult for staff to take such statements as *only* symbolic of inner states of mind. They were too real. Jenny's rage was ferocious, just as her delusions of being sliced apart by knives hanging from the sky portrayed an unrelenting viciousness. Further, she felt torn between the desire to express her rage and the knowledge that if she did express it and in her fantasy destroyed the bad objects, she might suffer the horrifying consequences of being left small and weak in a universe without comfort or hope. Jenny, therefore, surrounded herself with endless images of threat, counterthreat, and torture. Not only was it essential for her to split off this side of her being in the form of delusion, it was safer for her to place her own rage, her poison, the shed, unwanted parts of her self, in different staff members. If the staff could be brought to such rage as to isolate her in restraints or in seclusion, then she would be spared having to face the despair and hopelessness of an impotent internal wish to kill which could never hurt anyone but herself. Staff members, then, in particular the head nurse, were unconsciously chosen by Jenny to act out or embody different aspects of this enraged and uncontrollable self. It was in this way that Jenny wielded very real power on the unit.

Defenses against Annihilation

Jenny experienced the injection of intramuscular medication as the administration of a lethal poison, but it was far better for her to feel as if her caretakers were killing her than for her actually to annihilate both herself and the universe with her explosive feelings. With her power to place rage in the actions of the parent-staff toward her, Jenny successfully projected her frantic internal wishes into potent external impositions. She was able to make herself into the object of her own fury. She was able to place her phantasy of murdering her parents, or the part-object representation of either parent, outside herself (delusionally) in the staff, her therapist, and the hospital—all of whom, she believed, wanted to destroy her.

Jenny even denied her own attempted suicide. She claimed that the wound was made by an external agent, a sniper. Finally, in a soliloquy delivered to Hall B two days before her discharge, Jenny, for the first time, acknowledged she had tried to kill herself. More typical was denial:

J: Why am I here; why are they [staff] persecuting me?
JMG: They are here to care for you; they are afraid you may try to harm yourself.
J: Why should they think I would?
JMG: Because you once did try to take your own life.
J: That wasn't me, a sniper shot me.

On another occasion, she blamed her father: "He held the shotgun at me; and I couldn't let him go to jail; I love him so much; he's so good to me."

Psychiatrists, psychotherapists, nurses, and social workers in a mental hospital are not simply technicians ministering to a set of passive tissues, although psychiatrists and mental health care professionals find themselves increasingly drawn to this model. Treatment is not a matter of reconnecting organs or fighting bacteria or setting limbs. The wish to see the self in these terms, particularly noticeable in biological psychiatry, is traceable as much to the need for care givers to diminish frustration in treatment and the indeterminacy of psychotherapy as it is to have faith in so-called scientific objectivity and research. Psychiatric care, because of myriad factors including the complex psychodynamic structures and neurophysiological properties of the internal world, faces persistent disruption of any rigidly controlled scientific theory.

Psychically the mind extends outward and inward, and participants in treatment, just as in "life," find themselves caught up in invisible tentacles, the murky, confused, contradictory, and eminently nonquantifiable meanings that encircle the self. The unconscious phantasies of those doing the treating become entangled with the hidden and split-off phantasies of those being treated; private and public often become hopelessly intertwined. If these tentacles are not separated and examined, if their reciprocal effects are not looked at critically, then treatment, like politics, finds itself caught in a set of assumptions about a hypothetical, often even mythical objectivity that while it may bring certainty in an abstract, *scientific* sense, mystifies, disguises, and denies the complex intersubjectivity of patient and staff, self and other. When Jenny states, "Do you know my mother hired someone to kill me; I'm so lonely God needs to save me, but God hates me. I know because Jill [another patient] has a knife she wants to stick into my stomach," it is not only her biochemistry speaking but a terribly wounded psychological self trying to represent an inner world through symbolic projection. To ignore such imagery, to dismiss it, to conceptualize it solely as a management problem or a "chemical disorder" does a terrible disservice to the patient for whom language and actions represent hidden and denied aspects of self.

To speak with and treat seriously disturbed borderline and schizophrenic patients, is to find oneself, no matter how well defended by roles or status, in the midst of raging emotional currents that reach deep into the unconscious self. One mental health worker described it as "trying to keep afloat in an angry river of fifteen cross-cutting undertows." To be inside Jenny's orbit of projective identification, then, was to experience oneself, myself, beyond any specific role function or classification, since Jenny placed feelings in persons connected to her and those "feelings" intersected with unconscious phantasies being stirred up in the self. Jenny had the power to break through role definitions, to unsettle experience and expectation, and to induce reactions to her which were often an explosive amalgam of her part-objects and the inner conflicts of those who were treating her.

Let me give some examples to illustrate the connection between Jenny's internality and staff or public action:

1. The extra time her psychiatrist gave to Jenny's treatment created feelings of envy and anger in the nursing staff (good father versus bad mother); nurses were explicit in explaining how they felt and how they "resented" the focus on Jenny.

2. Nurses periodically became exasperated, particularly early in treatment, and emotionally withdrew from Jenny, playing out Jenny's relation to "bad" aspects of her self-representation. The wish expressed by many on the staff to abandon Jenny to another hall or to send her to a state hospital, reenacted earlier events in Jenny's life when her mother turned her care over to a reluctant aunt. "I wish we could get rid of her" describes staff feelings during the "hate Jenny" phase of treatment.

3. Private-duty nurses without any connection to the regular staff took over Jenny's nursing care; the staff felt with good reason that Jenny might try to commit suicide. She felt she had been "thrown out" of the hospital when private-duty nurses were interposed between her and the regular staff, another enactment of Jenny's extrusion from her mother and father's world. Staff members who participated in Jenny's meetings came primarily from the day and evening shifts; Jenny usually slept through the night shift. Since shifts were interchanged, however, most staff members did have the opportunity to participate in the case discussion.

4. Jenny's own feelings of isolation and worthlessness were mirrored through what she called her "imprisonment" in her room and the continual gaze of the private-duty nurses. Staff nurses felt that the private nurses gave Jenny intense one-to-one care, the sense of being cared for, watched over, and nurtured. Jenny's therapist agreed. A reevalua-

tion psychiatrist, however, suggested that the private-duty nurses might be acting as a buffer between the frustration and rage of nurses and therapists and Jenny's physical presence in the hospital.

5. Jenny periodically thought of herself as part of staff members' lives; for example, she called one mental health worker's wife and told her to "leave my husband alone." Jeffrey and his wife were unsettled by the call, but he began to focus considerably more time on Jenny because he was "concerned about her." Jenny said she had trouble figuring out if her body was Jeffrey's or hers. Or maybe Jeffrey was Jenny and she was he. Or maybe her brain was in his head and his brain in hers. Jeffrey became confused over Jenny's treatment and wondered why he was so "obsessed" with her. Jenny continued to write love letters to him.

6. Jenny's most volatile moments enabled staff members to focus their anger over other patients on her; she turned into the measure of the hall's (her family's) pathology. Nurses reenacted parental investment in their daughter's illness, the collusion among family members to "place" in Jenny their collective inadequacies, failings, anxieties, and rage. The therapist put the situation in psychotherapeutic terms: "Focusing all our anger, rage and frustration on one patient allows us to treat the other nineteen; we have the illusion of freedom; it gives us a sense of some control over who we treat. Or then again it may be that Jenny stirs up in us unwanted parts of ourselves that we are unwilling or unable to look at, parts that we have shed or metabolized years ago, but which come back to haunt us in the mirror of Jenny's world." It might be interesting to think about these observations in the context of Kristeva's notion of the unconscious as the "strange," "alien," or "foreign" presence in ourselves.

7. Jenny's mother and father became discouraged over her treatment and hinted they might be forced to have her transferred to a state hospital. The nursing staff during this time complained about psychiatry's overinvestment and overinvolvement with Jenny and nearly succeeded in having her transferred to another service. "Why do all the therapists focus so much time on Jenny? What is it about her that makes her so special?" the nurses wanted to know.

8. Jenny saw sickness in the staff and felt it was her "mission" to save them from "their own violence." She was reenacting her feelings as a child, that it was her responsibility to bring together her warring mother and father, that if she were sick, feeble, they might love each

other again. Similarly, on the hall Jenny unconsciously acted out the drama-phantasy: therapist and nurse battled over Jenny's situation, and as the battle intensified, Jenny became sicker and sicker.

9. Jenny's need to be at center stage appeared in the staff's growing view, after the initial disenchantment, that her case presented special difficulties and required considerable time and talent to treat. This significant shift from earlier sentiments occurred during the latter part of the "tolerate Jenny" phase. All came to believe they were involved in a "common enterprise" to treat a "classic" case with considerable potential for improvement which would demonstrate the effectiveness of collaborative treatment. Jenny's grandiose feelings came to be mirrored in the weight attached to her treatment. The general sentiment of the staff during this more hopeful phase was "If we can cure Jenny then we can do anything." The scrutiny of Jenny's case by the major departments in the hospital—psychiatry, nursing, social work, and activities—brought intense discussion outside the hall, on other units, during lunch. In the words of one nurse,

> At first that initial year we grew to hate Jenny. At least I hated her. She caused so many problems, was so unpredictable. She would strike out at us. I felt intense anger, even hatred towards her. We all talked about it; what she did to us, how she made us feel, what we took home with us when we left the hospital. If there weren't that opportunity for talking about what was being stirred up in me [Jenny's meeting], I couldn't have dealt with her. I would have been the first one on the bandwagon for transferring her to a state hospital. I have never met such a resistant patient.

For Jenny, treatment became a persistent struggle to make connections with those shed part-objects, inner images of her parents, which took root and grew in different staff members. "Imagine," she once commented, "what it feels like to know that in the eyes of the persons you most love you simply do not exist. When I was small no one wanted me, not even my favorite aunt. Sometimes I feel like that here; no one on staff really cares; and all I am is grist for their mill, shit for their toilets." Kristeva's words describe this sense of utter abandonment: "An ego, wounded to the point of annulment, barricaded and untouchable, cowers somewhere, nowhere, at no other place than the one that cannot be found" (1982, 47).

10. Therapist vacations reenacted parental abandonment, provoking expressions of intense hatred from Jenny: "I know I'll never see him again; I hope he dies; I hope a car falls on his head. I hate his guts." In leaving, her therapist, the all-good father, abandoned Jenny to evil, the bad mother. Jenny feigned indifference to his absence, but she listened to music about destruction, killing, and death. She slept a great deal, finding it necessary to "hibernate." She saw herself "bleeding over the floor"; the blood, she said, "streaks" her clothes, made a mess over the couch, flooded her eyes, and ran down her cheeks into the corners of her mouth. She screamed she wanted to pull "Dr. M.'s guts out of his stomach and strangle staff members with his intestines." She carefully scrutinized patient movements, believing that Dr. M. had hired someone to kill her while he was away, that her father kept a secret payroll to recruit patients as killers; that the cleaning lady conspired in a secret mission, initiated by Jenny's mother, to cart off her dead body in a plastic garbage bag. With her therapist gone, Jenny felt victimized, abandoned; staff hostility increased.

11. Earlier, in the "hate Jenny" phase, the staff had appeared to Jenny as concentration camp guards; staff members spoke of Jenny as the "elephant who wouldn't move." Treatment skidded between the twin poles of Jenny's unconscious phantasies and the staff's utter confusion over feelings Jenny induced in them. Jenny and the staff spent months locked in a power struggle. Treatment approaches were as dependent on the mobilization of unconscious phantasies in staff and patient as they were on medical interventions. Jenny saw herself as an outcast, a stranger, and the staff felt that she dwelled on the outermost fringes of whatever community existed on the hall. As staff countertransference diminished, however, and the meaning behind Jenny's dramatic symbologies became clearer in the context of the different action-texts, staff fears, hesitations, and reservations disappeared. They began to take a collective pride in what treatment had accomplished. As a mental health worker described it:

> When Jenny started kicking, it no longer bothered me because I knew exactly how we would stop it; every time we put our arms around her, she just curled up and went limp. It seemed that her kicking was an invitation to be held; I remember one time right after an unbelievably angry outburst (she was screaming all kinds of threats and names), I came towards her, put my arms around her and she started to weep.

All the tension went out of her body and she let herself fall into my arms. It was so abrupt, so sudden, the shift from raging, stormy infant to this totally helpless and pathetic human being.

Transitions toward Tragedy

Staff members during the "tolerate Jenny" phase found themselves more sensitized to what Jenny saw or placed in them. For example, for months, Jenny would periodically say a variation of the following to one of the nurses, usually the head nurse: "You bitch, slut, whore, get away from my face, or I'll bash your head in." Such comments were one reason for the initiation of Jenny's meeting. They distanced the staff and fed Jenny's profound fear that her rage could indeed kill. When those who were caring for her acted in fact as if her rage could kill, Jenny was terrified by what she saw in their eyes, by their *fright*. When staff members distanced themselves, Jenny felt rejected and in her desperation she lashed out physically. Once the staff was aware of how this dynamic worked, however, it became possible to defuse Jenny's anger not by withdrawing but by moving even closer and allowing her panic over abandonment to be expressed. The fear that her own rage might blow everyone, including herself, apart diminished. That kind of intimacy, "holding" in the face of intense hostility, enabled Jenny, perhaps for the first time in her life, to trust another human being, to experience her "Sheppard family" as responsive and caring. If her rage could be contained, even accepted, then she could feel safe.

This collaborative effort to understand Jenny from her own perspective—to look at negative countertransference, to read her actions and internality as commentary on a dialectic including the staff's unconscious reactions—had an extraordinary impact on treatment. Not only did Jenny's meeting clarify frustrating roadblocks and power conflicts, but it increased staff tolerance, allowing Jenny to feel safe enough to experience some measure of community, brief glimpses of a citizenship that had always been alien to her. For the first time on the hall, if not in her life, she seemed connected, excited about the human world and its *consensual* possibilities, although much in her actions and perceptions remained excluded from the social realm and its public understandings.

Yet, for a few months, the balance did lie on the side of inclusion and recognition, and Jenny's actions, recognitions, statements, and interactions were governed more by a sense of herself as a social participant in a larger group than as a solitary wanderer in an isolated inner universe. Her relations with the staff improved; the negative and hostile side of power relations among staff members diminished considerably; Jenny sustained contact with others for longer periods of time; her fear was not as omnipresent; she seemed less consumed by images of abjection, including delusions of destruction and death; she spoke with her therapist and the staff about actual events in her life, her recollections; she began to look more coherent; and she struggled to distinguish inner from outer. It was at this stage that she observed that "hope" was the "last pearl in Pandora's box."

Reappearance of Abjection: Jenny's Transfer

Almost twenty months after her admission to Hall A, Jenny was moved to Hall B. Since her therapist had been transferred to Hall B, both staff and therapist decided that Jenny should follow him. Unfortunately, removing Jenny from Hall A initiated what turned out to be a rapid psychological decline.

Even though the move was only one flight up, Jenny took it as a transfer to another world. "I have been taken to hell," she said to me. The disruption reinforced her conception of the world as enveloped in badness and defilement. Once again, she found herself grappling with images of death, disintegration, and destruction. Nevertheless, she left Hall A with good feelings. A few days before her transfer, Jenny wrote a letter and tacked it onto the patients' bulletin board:

> Dear Hall:
>
> I would like you to understand. Some days, I do not feel too well and other days I feel good. I would like to be your friend. All of you because I like you people. And I even like our staff.
>
> Please be patient with me.
>
> I have heart trouble and a lot of my problem is I cannot always keep up from not enough and too much hassling.
>
> Please be a little more considerate and do not be greedy over friendship because all of you hold a special thanks within me.
>
> With Love,
> Jenny

On the new unit Jenny's tie to the good object world was abruptly closed off; she felt ripped away from her family, kidnapped and deposited in an unfamiliar place. What good self-representations she had managed to take back into herself on Hall A dissolved, and the connections, the fragments of trust that had begun to emerge after months of work were shattered. In the new, unfamiliar environment, the subtle and intricate web between Jenny and the staff members who had learned to delineate unconscious intentions, came apart. New confusions and assumptions remobilized bad object representations. The move was a disaster.

On the old unit, the good object representations predominated in Jenny's relationship with the staff. Further, the images associated with the bad object world had decreased in intensity and frequency. On the new unit images (delusions) associated with the bad object world surged, and feelings representing the good object world in both Jenny and the staff were almost completely obliterated. Her imagery took on terrifying, apocalyptic proportions reminiscent of earlier phases on Hall A: gang rape, machine gunning, death by mutilation, the tearing out of innards, brain slicing, and so on. Jenny said she had lost her "Sheppard mothers" and had been put in "prison to die." She felt the new unit was a "blast furnace where they burned you at a million degrees Fahrenheit." She thought her move had been planned by her sister and asked, "What kind of thing is that for one sister to do to another?" She refused to acknowledge her real mother's identity; when she received a package of Easter gifts, she could not "figure out" who had sent them: "I don't know a Mrs. —— [Jenny's mother's name]." The nursing notes commented: "Pt. said she had no idea who that was. . . . Then I asked her what her mother's name is and pt. said she didn't remember."

Jenny spoke of "nerves popping all over" her face; she asked if I had seen a "wasp's nest" down her throat, and if I had, would I please pick it out. Did I see "killer knives" sticking out of the walls, and why had the "concentration camp guards," who had disappeared two or three months before her transfer, suddenly reappear on the new hall? It was not that the staff members on Hall B were any less caring or capable than those on Hall A. What had changed in Jenny's mind was her fragile sense of place. Further, the change in social environment, exacerbated by the Hall B staff's lack of familiarity with the subtlety of her case, so disrupted Jenny's inner frames of meaning, boundary, and identity that the transfer pushed her into an acute panic, eroding whatever trust she had discovered inside herself and in those around her.

Superficially, Jenny adapted, but in my conversations with her, she revealed that her adaptation involved defending herself from what she saw as a monstrous battlefield. "Everyone around here has knives and guns; I have to hide from them." Her sense of safety disintegrated, and it became even more precarious when her therapist told her that her insurance would run out within the next eight to twelve months and she might have to leave Sheppard-Pratt. A day or two later she remarked that she had difficulty sleeping because murderers lurked underneath the floor, waiting for darkness before they emerged and killed her. Jenny's hostility toward the staff increased. "If I had a bazooka right now, I'd blow all their heads off." She felt if she were discharged from the hospital, her father might try to kill her; yet, she could show moments of remarkable lucidity: "Half my life is a delusion, I don't know truth from reality; sometimes I think I may pass out from fear."

The fear of discharge contributed to her rising panic; images of dismemberment preoccupied her. At the same time, staff members felt they were being "torn apart" by Jenny's unpredictability, distance, and outbursts. Her delusions reflected her sense of self as shreds, parts, fragments, broken or ripped pieces. The nursing notes contain this entry:

> Pt. said she is missing part of her pelvis. She put powder all over her head. She took a shower and asked for the razor to shave her legs, but [instead] shaved off about an inch of her hair in the front "so it will grow back thicker." She believes that the blood technician killed her "baby." [Jenny believed that every time she moved her bowels she produced a baby.] Jenny reported to staff that she smelled her skin and it smelled as though she had been "bombarded with a virus"; and [even though it was late spring and sometimes quite warm] she wore a fur coat to protect her from "viruses."

Jenny perceived all movement as a form of assault. A patient walking down the hallway turned into a crazed killer; a stranger in the hall became a vicious sadist with orders to pull her skin off her back. She felt compelled to "fight back." When a nurse told her that she was being given a new room, Jenny told her, "You slut, I'd like to poke your eyes out" (nursing note). Images of annihilation permeated her relationship with her therapist: "I hate Dr. M.; he only wants to kill me; I wish I could stick a shotgun in his mouth and pull the trigger. . . . The world is going to explode; I have a bomb inside me; it's about ready to go off . . . blood is squirting through my head!"

Kristeva speaks of this "horror within . . . the collapse of the border between inside and outside. It is as if the skin, a fragile container, no longer guaranteed the integrity of one's 'own and clean self' but, scraped or transparent, invisible or taut, gave way before the dejection of its contents. Urine, blood, sperm, excrement, then show up in order to reassure a subject that is lacking its 'own and clean self' " (1982, 53). Jenny experienced her isolation, her disintegration, as absolute, irrevocable: "I have no friends here; I don't want to make friends; please take me home, bury me somewhere, put a stake through my heart."

Two months before her discharge, Jenny's delusional universe and its unrelenting horror completely consumed her, effectively cutting her off from any contact with consensual reality. For example, after striking a nurse and being put in locked-door seclusion, Jenny spoke of "being trapped." The nursing notes reported:

> She denied that this was a hall in the hospital, instead saying it was a "power plant." Pt. spoke of having five bullets in her. She insisted that she was "full of pus" and "rotting away." She was also threatening towards a male staff member, saying she "felt like sticking a pen in his head." She later called a female staff [member] a "murderess." Jenny announced suddenly in the living room that she was doing worse than ever, that she was a "mess." When asked how we could help her, she responded, "kill me, you'll all be better off without me."

The journey into acceptance and understanding which Jenny and the staff had taken on Hall A was never repeated in the new unit. Further, if the drive toward tolerance and rights can be described as political (the creation of a public space among persons involving negotiation, decision, the administration of power, and the exercise of authority), then what Jenny's treatment lacked in her new unit was political, the dimension of reciprocity. In the new place, she could not escape her private world and establish any connection with public modes of being, mutuality as the foundation for recognition.

The Annihilation of Reciprocity

For Jenny, community on Hall A had worked itself out as the embodiment of her own internal, split-off feelings in various staff persons, and the collective acknowledgment and intensive analysis of these projections. Further, the continuing scrutiny of her unconscious intentions in scenarios acted out on the hall, the public discourse over their effects, had enabled Jenny to feel safe enough to take tentative steps back into the social world and accept the hall's reality as her own. When the transfer broke that process, her attachment to the public world, the intersubjective space between her and the staff, disintegrated together with whatever was left of her fragile core self.

Her previous treatment team had won its knowledge of Jenny by dint of hard psychotherapeutic work, long experience, and deep self-reflection, not through instruments of technology or science. In Jenny's case medications never helped; what did help was the willingness of all concerned to throw themselves into the "flows" of her experience, refracting it through self-criticism and rigorous public analysis. This political process, the public representation of feeling, characterized by conflict, struggle, resolution, and tolerance, was unavailable on the new unit. I would like to stress that Jenny received highly empathic nursing care and responsive long-term psychotherapy on the new hall. It was not that the staff was unaware of psychodynamic issues or insensitive to the relation between inner and outer "realities." Nevertheless, the new place radically disoriented Jenny, and the staff could not afford to devote as much time and resources to her as the treatment team on Hall A had given.

Without attachment to the shared experience of consensual reality, Jenny's inner life was again dominated by the torture of psychotic identification. "Badness" returned to devour her body, to threaten her physical integrity; "evil" stood ready to tear her into shreds; the "badness" of the universe possessed "teeth and knives." She had the feeling that there "was something inside her that needs to get cut out," according to the nursing notes. She "requested staff to cut off her head so she would die. . . . [After placing] her hands around [a] nurse's neck and attempting to choke her, Jenny asked the staff to put her to death. She stated she wanted to form a therapy group called 'kill the staff group.' " Such utterances increased the emotional distance between Jenny and her treatment environment. Her therapist wrote: "The patient's clinical condition still evidences floridly paranoid ideation with several instances of assaultive behaviors towards staff. The plan is to provide a highly organized and protected environment for the patient with the use of LDS [locked-door seclusion] as required until the patient is less afraid and able to tolerate greater autonomy on the Hall." In seclusion Jenny screamed about gasoline being poured over her body; she called nurses "ugly sluts"; she urinated and defecated on the floor and smeared feces over the walls. She believed that a "rat lives in her vagina" and that a "coral snake" crawled around her bathroom. She associated the production of feces with giving birth and saw her excrement as a baby. The nursing notes reported: "Jenny examined her excrement this morning because she thought she may have excreted parts of a baby; Jenny thinks she's pregnant."

Life as Delusional Imprisonment

In seclusion Jenny became the actual prisoner, tied down to a hospital bed, leather restraints on ankles and wrists for several days. Her removal from the human community attained a certain finality. It was a victimization that recreated the structure of her inner world. She induced the action of power *on* her to dominate and torture her being; she reproduced in her hospital environment the very imprisoning tortures she experiences in her delusional world. During her time in restraints, Jenny was given periodic recesses and rubdowns; considerable attention was paid to her physical "comfort." Nevertheless, she spent her last five weeks at Sheppard with at least one wrist bound at all times.

Internally dominated by psychotic time, removed from human interaction by her physical bonds, Jenny suffered the reenactment of the most tragic and painful moments of her emotional past: becoming invisible to those on whom she was most dependent. For the staff she became a recalcitrant bundle of energy without identity or meaning, a mass of physical motion to be restrained as efficiently as possible. Her delusions reflected the radical alienation of a being no longer considered human. Her body, she believed, existed as an object to be acted upon, a thing to be defiled and rearranged through violent assault; she felt "dangerous objects [had been] put up her rectum that might cause her to have a heart attack," according to the nursing notes. She remarked, "I would rather be cut into little pieces instead of being embalmed." She believed that the leather restraints were being used to make it easier for technicians to draw blood from her body and refill her veins with formaldehyde. "I think they're going to try to graft my leg onto my head; what kind of experiments are they running here? Why are they going to cut off all my limbs and put them where they shouldn't be?" The nursing notes reported:

> Pt. was combative (scratching and kicking) when put in five-point restraints. And very verbally abusive; speaking of wanting to murder staff members; quite graphic and gruesome descriptions. Also mentioned fear of splitting open or having "heart attack." Pt. has been testing restraints . . . hostile, delusional. . . . "you're all liars, killers, this is going to make me deaf, dumb and blind. . . . you're an old whore, she's a retarded mongoloid. . . . bitch I'm going to murder you. . . . I need major bone surgery. There's my stupid butt-faced Doctor. . . . You look like my dead guinea pig. . . . my bladder was taken out. . . . are you executing me. . . ." Pt. screaming that we removed her kidney and pee-hole . . . wants to be catheterized, trying to tear off her panties. . . . Pt. tried to bite male staff . . . said that she is burning up. . . . Pt. removed sheepskin wrist protector from right wrist restraints with her teeth. [She asked one of the nurses] "Are you frightened? 'Cause I'm frightened and I want you to be frightened." . . . stated in quiet tone: "You sado-masochist, you machete artists. . . . they're trying to kill me, I have Novocaine in my brain. . . ." Pt. talking of wanting her head bit off by writer.

Jenny no longer thought of herself as a person but as a collection of decaying or fragmented body parts. "My heart has turned into gangrene; I wish I could pull it out." She felt that the "dentist screwed me up; I think I have a tooth coming in or that's what he thinks, but it's really a blood clot in my brain that came out of my mouth" (nursing notes). The hospital intercom system, wired to her tooth, sent messages directly to her brain; staff put "cement" into her milkshake, blocking off the entrance to her stomach. She saw herself as an "animal roaming in the woods" feeding off infected, rotting carcasses. She said that "the brain in her head was not her own, but came from a dead person smashed up in a jetliner crash." She would "like to see a million people die and then cut her throat." She wished she had a "machete" so she could "cut everyone down just to stay out of restraints." She asked staff members to "cut off her head and kill her. . . . Pt. began screaming loudly about hating the hospital, all the patients and all the staff, yelling that she could bash our heads in; demanded seclusion and stripped herself naked in the hallway." She repeatedly threatened violence: "I'm at a point where I could kill someone." She saw "army men in camouflage shooting bullets through the walls at her." She asked if "someone will remove the bullets from out of her head"; she discovered "bat eggs on the ceiling" and wondered if "we are in Germany" (nursing notes).

By the end of her hospitalization Jenny was surrounded by destructive power. It lay everywhere in her perceptual field. It lived with her, filled her consciousness, defined her relationships. It was as if she had descended, with no possibility of exit, into a universe of imminent annihilation.[2]

Completely trapped by her own delusional introjects, unable to contain her fear, with staff equally estranged, Jenny finally left the hospital prostrate, tied hand and foot to an "emergency" stretcher. The world of human citizenship was closed to her. She found herself banished not only from Sheppard-Pratt but from the state of Maryland, since the state hospitals had refused to admit her. Her therapist had explored the possibility of keeping Jenny in Maryland, but in the words of one staff member, the state hospitals "got wind of what she was like and refused to have anything to do with her." The ostensible excuse was that since Jenny was not a legal resident of Maryland, the state system was under no obligation to accept her, although a case certainly could have been made that living at Sheppard-Pratt for thirty months was sufficient reason to consider her a resident.

Literally a self without a "place," her juristic citizenship questioned, her psychological state regarded as untreatable, Jenny returned to the same hospital and ward that had originally attempted to treat—or, better, "manage"—her psychosis. Jenny was discharged from Sheppard-Pratt in July, although her insurance would have continued to pay until October. The staff on Hall B felt that her treatment was at an impasse, that she was untreatable. Early discharge would leave at least a few months on her insurance in case she later needed crisis care in a private psychiatric facility. It is tempting to see Jenny's plight as analogous to that of a political refugee, turned back from a country that holds out the possibility of a less-persecuted existence, forced to return to the scene of unbearable pain. Jenny did regard Sheppard-Pratt as her home, and her therapist felt that sending her to a local state hospital would have kept her closer to "home."

I want to reproduce what might be read as a soliloquy, the major substance of Jenny's farewell speech to Hall B, composed from nurses' accounts.

> I guess I'm going to be leaving here; this place is dangerous; I don't feel safe because of all the gas leaks. I have called BG and E [Baltimore Gas and Electric] several times and I even tried to call my father. I have done all I can do and it still remains unsafe.[3] During this time I really need your emotional support. I know my mind is messed up right now, but when I first came here the hospital didn't understand that I was being reborn. When I shot myself, I wanted to die, but when I saw the blood running out, flowing down my sides, and felt the pain, I didn't want to die anymore. I felt like I was being reborn; after so much blood ran out of me, I was like a new-hatched egg; and I could feel the blood was cleaning me up, and I was ready to begin anew. But they brought me here and no one understood. They locked me up and didn't understand that I did not want to die. After a time I tried to hang myself.[4] It was out of desperation since they never saw what I was going through and how I felt about things.[5] But now I'm finally going home; and I'm glad, because I think it will be a nice home in the countryside, with flowers and a little garden and peapods and baked bread in the morning, and the birds singing me little songs. And I'll be able to wake up in the morning and look through my lace curtains and watch the dew fall from the trees.

Of course, Jenny's destination had nothing to do with the countryside or a nice home with baked bread and birds singing little songs. She was to be taken by air ambulance to a chronic ward in a state mental hospital located in the downtown section of a large midwestern industrial city. In a ward of fifty or sixty patients, Jenny's presence would fade into the dull, green walls and the long corridors. There, she would languish probably for the rest of her life. The final entry in the nursing notes reads: "Jenny left the Hospital at 8:30 a.m. to transfer to [——]. . . . Pt. left Hall on a stretcher to be taken to airport in ambulance to [home state]. Pt. was accompanied by head nurse and nursing supervisor and was alert, cooperative and in fair spirits upon leaving Hall. Pt. was hugged by several peers and staff members before leaving Hall."

Conclusion: Disintegration and the Failure of Community

Jenny's case received attention throughout the various levels of the hospital hierarchy. Her treatment had taken on considerable significance; it had been studied in some detail not only by me but by staff members in every department. She had been the subject of several Grand Rounds presentations. Yet even though staff members on Hall B and those who had worked with her on Hall A expressed regret that she had to leave, there was also relief. A weight had been taken off the hospital's and the unit's back. A source of tragic misunderstanding was no longer visible to remind people of the failure of tolerance. For Jenny, her experience on Hall A had indeed been the last pearl in Pandora's box, and she had lost that pearl of hope. Existence in a consensual world could not be retrieved.

What remained of the contents of Pandora's box, scattered over the earth after the pearl had been smashed by Jenny's despair, were terrifying presences distinguished by their power to torment. It was a madness, in Yeats's words, "let loose upon the world," from which Jenny could not pull back. With hope gone, nothing was left for Jenny except the pain of the universe.

It would be wrong to see Jenny's treatment on Hall B as lacking in sensitivity or care. Her disintegration could not have been predicted; nor were the causes apparent in her troubled relations with the Hall B staff. Both staff and Jenny were confused, uncertain, and disoriented by each other's "strangeness." Both were caught up in ever-widening circles of misunderstanding. It was reasonable to assume that the advances on Hall A could be carried over into the new unit, that even though Jenny might feel unsettled for a brief period, she could establish new connections with the persons around her, for treatment on Hall A had forged a tenuous sense of trust and an attachment to consensual understandings. Yet, on Hall B treatment could not overcome Jenny's mistrust, hostility, and intense fear of the new environment, her dread of reality and "otherness." Staff members withdrew to their familiar language, and Jenny, surrounded by the dybbuks let out of Pandora's box, succumbed to the language of psychosis.

Even though the staff on Hall A had made a profound alteration in the structure of Jenny's inner scenarios and unconscious phantasies, the transfer disrupted that tentative change and forced Jenny to reoccupy a delusional space that removed her from a common humanity. In her overwhelming panic, she took the only pathway open to her: withdrawal into the delusional symbologies of psychosis. Jenny had defined Hall A as home, and she found it unbearable to leave home once again, to be ejected as she had been from her childhood home. The transfer took her beyond hope, to a place where otherness could be refracted only in the deadly images of perpetual torment. The fate of Sisyphus, condemned to an eternity of repetition, came into play. Hopelessness overcame her, and delusion displaced reality, revealing to her the only knowledge she could understand.

Jenny, when she finally understood she had to leave, could not hold an image of Sheppard within herself. She could not take with her what she had worked so hard to attain on Hall A; trust simply had not taken root. It had not settled down inside her, and when she left Hall A, the image of the good object, her experience of Sheppard-Pratt as home, disappeared. Nothing remained; delusional power became the defining element of her life. The intensity of the bad object world invaded Jenny like a fever, like an infection that triumphs over all the antibodies and wreaks havoc on the body.

Indeed, much of what happened to Jenny on Hall B was physical. It was necessary to place her in restraints, to seclude her from other patients, to respond on a basic physical level to the disastrous fear that possessed her from morning to night. Nurses had to live with her, listen to her threats, and deal with her rage. Faced with a patient as totally out of control as Jenny was on Hall B, to have unraveled the complex fractures in her internal world would have required superhuman efforts.

On Hall B, Jenny returned to her private universe of terror, became the "old Jenny" who had created so much frustration and despair among the staff on Hall A. For a moment, the Hall A team members had felt they could do something for her, had nurtured the good object fragments and constructed links between themselves and Jenny and between

Jenny and the external world. But transfer lost the thread; Jenny lost the thread. It was nobody's fault; no single factor accounted for the regression and ultimate collapse of such a difficult and confounding patient. Her therapist explained:

> If we had to do all over again, perhaps she shouldn't have been transferred; but she was, and as you saw, the outcome was tragic. She went too far away from us; and we couldn't afford here to devote the staff time and dialogue that had sustained us and pointed the direction on Hall A. When I told Jenny her insurance would run out and that at some point she might have to leave the hospital, she lost faith, her hope, what she used to talk about as the last pearl in Pandora's box. She came to see us all as enemies; her trust was destroyed and her despair so great that treatment could do nothing; it had no effect. I have no doubt that if we had released her into the streets, that she would have committed suicide within twenty-four hours; and we had no choice but to send her back to [the state hospital in the Midwest].

Jenny's desperate efforts to establish relationships and friendships on Hall A were, in the context of her illness, heroic, monumental. They required great courage and faith. The idea of beginning again, of refinding her sense of place, must have seemed terrifying. Her anguish at being abandoned to another hall so alienated her from the human project that she felt impelled to close off those fragile channels of connection, her rudimentary basic trust, in order to protect herself from a final emotional death. Psychosis, then, defended her against her own grief, and she took refuge in inner symbologies that had served her well in the past. It became far easier to live with the fear, rage, and violence of psychotic time than with the horrifying and life-threatening consequences of trusting other human beings.

Moving from what she had known as her home, her place of safety, seemed yet another rejection in a whole lifetime of being put "somewhere else," of psychically and physically wandering around a society that brought her no safety, no asylum, no firm sense of boundary or settledness. Jenny, therefore, in the last months of her stay at Sheppard-Pratt, returned to her internal world, her own personal state of war, whose familiar forms of power seemed to grant an understanding and self-definition that external forms of reality did not. If she had to guard against death at every moment, there would be neither time nor energy to feel grief and despair. As she defended against her profound sense of loss, the last pearl in Pandora's box was exchanged for the gaze of the Medusa. Jenny, lost in the unreachable spaces of psychotic time, became as impenetrable as stone.

FIVE

Maureen: Power as Assault on the Flesh

A TRAGIC element of the psychotic employment and experience of power is its fundamentally destructive and alienating effect on the self. Power attacks not only consciousness but also the *embodied* self: the body becomes the object of attack; the movement of power is literally written into the flesh. The body suffers. Psychotic obsessions or preoccupations set up an extraordinary tyranny whose objective is physical mutilation. For Jenny, psychosis constituted these preoccupations symbolically, as delusional projection—spaceships attacking, fires burning, poisonous gases spilling through air vents. She experienced actions on a symbolic plane, as well. The fires from beneath the hospital burned her; spaceships turned their guns on her and shredded her flesh; poisonous gases eroded her lung tissue. The schizophrenic may experience even suicide as an assault from someone else. Jenny, for example, believed it was a sniper, not herself, who had shot her in the belly.

For Maureen, a thirty-four-year-old mother of two daughters, the exercise of power against the self derived from split-off unconscious phantasies, but the assaults to her body were not symbolic; they came not from outside herself (the schizophrenic resolution) but from conscious actions that derived from deeply held feelings of worthlessness and rage which could be resolved only by literally using her body as a surface on which to register anxiety and dread.

Maureen felt the persistent and uncontrollable need to cut herself. Unlike Jenny or Chuck, she did not live in psychotic time; nor was delusion her epistemological frame of reference. Technically her diagnosis was "borderline personality disorder." A piece of her being remained riveted in unconscious phantasies that dictated to her, through the explosive eruption of affect, that told her her being was worthless, life was futile, and her abiding worthlessness had to be shown to the world through assaults on her body such as cutting or through physical actions (bingeing and purging with laxatives) that had the effect of literally altering the form or container of her self.

On the level of affect, not epistemology (she did not explain reality through delusion), Maureen found herself radically alienated from attachment and intimacy; in this respect, she could not be touched by the needs of others. For the schizophrenic, the images of delusion encircle the self and define experience for the body; for Maureen, and borderline patients generally, self-destruction (such as mutilating the body) was a day-to-day project involving ingenious and often hideous efforts to lacerate, defile, rip or tear the flesh and to hide these mutilations from the nursing staff.

Maureen had been in and out of mental hospitals for a period of six years. She found herself fascinated by razor blades, thin knives, pieces of glass, the tabs of soda cans. She spent most of her conscious hours contemplating ways to mutilate herself. She imagined razor blade cuts moving up her breasts, slicing into her vagina, making tiny lines of blood down her arms, stomach, thighs. She locked herself in closets; she carved messages into her body. Her life consisted of one series of obsessional, abject, mutilating acts after another. She neglected her children; she ignored her husband. He himself was often away for days at the time because of the travel demanded by his job. There was little if any communication between them; she hid and disguised all traces of physical self-abuse.

All that concerned Maureen was disfiguring her body. From time to time, her obsessional preoccupations appeared to possess psychotic features, and the historical pattern of her existence became secondary to the impulses and operations of a set of unconscious phantasies striving to define themselves through acts of self-mutilation. Yet, Maureen never lost linguistic or cognitive attachment to consensual reality, though she did lose affective attachment. Whether she was in a hotel room cutting herself or at a fast-food restaurant wolfing down burger after burger or in a closet staring at the blank walls, she always knew where she was. It was not the outer-space man taking her to the hotel room; Maureen knew it was she who acted, not a force outside of herself. She experienced her body as a war zone, a place where power appeared in the mutilation or distortion of her embodied self, her flesh. She desired this war, had Kristeva's "passion for death" (1989, 221). She told me it gave her pleasure to hurt herself. She drew pictures in her art therapy depicting bleeding genitals. The impulse to mutilate gave contour and direction to her life; for her, to torture one's flesh and to cut and distort its shape and form confirmed the reality of power and its exercise.

Maureen suffered an extraordinary imprisonment; she found herself tyrannized by the power her obsessions exercised over her body. It was a state of mind and being that resembled, in some respects, Plato's description in book 9 of *The Republic* of how the "tyrannical man" develops, although in Maureen's case, the only one she sought to enslave was herself. Plato speaks of the language of inner destructiveness spoken by the irrational part of the self: impulses lose boundedness; desire gives up limitation. What rules the self is excess, lack of proportion: "The beastly and savage part, replete with food and wine, gambols and, repelling sleep, endeavors to sally forth and satisfy its own instincts" (1964, 571c). Reason, civility, virtue—all disappear under the onslaught of the inner tyrant. The unrestrained, anticivil self breaks all limits: "[It] does not shrink from attempting to lie with a mother in fancy or with anyone else, man, god or brute. It is ready for any foul deed of blood; it abstains from no food, and, in a word, falls short of no extreme of folly and shamelessness." (571cd).

This is obviously not a happy or hopeful picture of human nature; it has a close affinity with the thinking of Freud and a similar fatalism regarding desire. Freud would agree with the Platonic observation that "there exists in every one of us, even in some reputed most respectable, a terrible, fierce, and lawless brood of desires" (572b). In Maureen, that "lawless brood of desires" was turned against both the physical and the psychological self. She became the central victim of a power she authored, enacted, and prosecuted. It was as if Maureen, at the root of her being, portrayed in microcosm the tragedy of the collective caught up in that which is uncontrollable, dreadful, and in Kristeva's terms, unnamable. Plato takes the uncontained self seriously, for he fears madness, understands its power, its capacity to destroy. Madness, whether in the individual or the state, provokes disintegration by destroying reason, limitation, and virtue. Both constitutions, the state and the self, have a great deal to fear from psychosis: unleashed tyrannies.

I do not contend that clinical narratives or situations actually represent the state one-to-one. The links are more complex, subtle, indirect, and symbolic. I do, however, want to suggest that clinical conditions may mirror, in their linguistic form, larger cultural and social processes of disintegration. And madness or psychosis on the individual level may demonstrate (in something of a "pure culture") what Freud (1920) addressed in *Beyond the Pleasure Principle* as the power of destructive impulses or drives to break up human identity and relationship.

Jacques Lacan and Julia Kristeva are right to attach much importance to this dynamic in studying the individual self. Most psychoanalytic observations on Freud's formulation of the "death instinct" take a critical attitude. By contrast, Lacan's concept of primordial masochism (1968, 80–81) and Kristeva's reflections on abjection locate Freud's drive for destruction in a psychoanalytic narrative, a psychic prehistory and an effort to recover it linguistically. Each interrogates the presence of death in the frame of the imaginary, what the unconscious produces, as strange, uncanny, and dreadful. Maureen's narrative, in this context, becomes instructive and frightening; it was an excursion into abjection as a form of masochistic assault.[1]

Lacan comments on the symbolism of death: "When we wish to attain in the subject what was before the serial articulations of the Word, and what is primordial to the birth of symbols, we find it in death, from which his existence takes on all the meaning it has" (1968, 85). Images of death, the grave or "sepulture" (1968, 84) as a symbol, are constant reminders of our mortality, our vulnerability, death as an "intermediary" facing the self, with the power to define action and identity. Although it is doubtful if a death "instinct" can be proved, or grounded as an epistemological proposition, Lacan nevertheless sees the facts and experience of death (the interplay of symbols of death in the imaginary and the real) as an overpowering *presence:* desire, objects, persons die, reappear, and suffer pain and annihilation at the hands of power. To name or signify death in language becomes a central object of the psychoanalytic inquiry.

Life as the Continuing Project of Death

Maureen had been admitted to Sheppard-Pratt because of several recent suicide attempts involving pills and knives. She expressed disappointment that she had failed. On one occasion she had been rescued by paramedics who traced a phone call from a hotel room near her home. She told me she felt completely cut off from her family and wished her younger daughter (who at twelve was beginning to show disturbances remarkably similar to those of her mother) were dead or had never been born. After the birth of her second child, Maureen told the nurse to take her back, that the child was not hers; why did she have to keep her? She believed that both her husband and daughters would be better off if she (Maureen) were dead.

Maureen was fascinated with death and annihilation. She spoke about it endlessly, drew pictures describing it, some of them in horrifying graphic detail. Her world had nothing of what Freud calls Eros, no "life instinct" or love of community. Rather, her existence was defined by what Freud in *Civilization and Its Discontents* (1930) called the "instinct to aggression and destruction," except that the object of aggression became her own flesh, her own body. Punishment, masochism, was written in her body; the language of her unconscious (abjection) appeared in the marks and notes inscribed in her flesh.

Maureen's body was a literal battleground; when she gave up her cache of razor blades to a departing therapist, she turned to laxatives. She consumed over fifty laxative pills a day; she said eating made her feel "dirty," and she felt compelled to get rid of the "filth" (Kristeva's abject as defilement). When the nurses took away her laxatives, she turned to "purging," vomiting after every meal in a very private "ritual of purification" (Kristeva 1982, 82). When her behavior was monitored so she could not go into the bathroom after eating, she vomited into the wastebasket in her room.

Periodically her husband would visit, and on their outings, Maureen invariably found an excuse to stop somewhere. What she wanted was to find a drugstore so she could replenish her supply of razor blades, laxatives, and sleeping pills—all of which, whether she used them or not, gave her comfort. She was careful to designate one package of razor blades for cutting. The others, including packages of pills and laxatives, she carried around with her as a kind of "protection." She felt unsafe unless she had a purseful of objects that could kill her. Death seemed comforting; its finality imposed a limit that gave her, as she put it, "enormous security." When, at the hospital, she finally gave up her hoard of blades, she said it was one of the most difficult things she had ever done: "It left me feeling terribly unsafe, unprotected. I had nothing, no one; my favorite objects were no longer there to keep me company. I felt alone and unprotected."

Maureen was not clinically schizophrenic; she did not live inside a delusional system that unsettled her linguistic connection to life. Yet, she was subject to moments of psychotic disintegration. She often appeared to be normal or collected, but her unconscious phantasies severed her *affective* (not cognitive) connection to consensual reality. Maureen was somewhat overweight—the opposite of her purging was bingeing—but it would be difficult to detect anything pathological in her ordinary conversation. She was able to hide, sometimes for weeks, her cutting and self-laceration. When the nursing staff discovered the deception, perhaps because the cuts had become severely infected, these mutilations became vivid reminders of her essential alienation. Maureen felt she had nowhere to go except into the bathroom, to lie in warm water, watching herself slice her flesh. Scarring herself and then living with the pain from the festering wound as long as she could without being detected became the fundamental project of her life. Cutting, she said, kept her from committing suicide; it relieved the pressure. When razor blades were no longer available, laxatives served their purpose, and when laxatives were discovered, daily purging and head banging replaced them.

Maureen was trapped by impulses she could not contain. They were driving forces, like Plato's drones, incessantly impelling her to action, powerful currents of desire out of control, assaulting her self, with the consequence of long periods of confusion, disorientation, and self-destructive behavior. During these psychotic regressions (when, for example, she hid in closets, left home for days, wandered the streets), her identity literally fell apart. She had no idea who she was; every other presence in her life became secondary. Her husband, family, job—nothing mattered in the face of drives that left Maureen feeling helpless, terrorized, as if she might explode into a thousand fragments. Power was turned on the self as relentless and unforgiving torture.

Yet, Maureen also felt an overwhelming guilt at having failed her family. She wanted to go back home, but she believed that if she did, the entire cycle of self-destruction and the obsession with annihilation might start again. She felt ill equipped to deal with the anger of her daughters and with her hatred for the younger, who was having terrible difficulties with weight, school, and just "living." Maureen's husband, emotionally isolated and guarded, away on the road for several days a week, contributed to her sense of emptiness and isolation.

The Death Instinct: Mutilating and Distorting Self

Nothing mattered except this wish to carve messages into the flesh and to recover her "clean and proper" body (Kristeva 1982, 78) by taking laxatives and purging herself of the "poisons" and uncleanliness of food. Yet, Maureen's eating and the physical distortions induced by eating were also symbolic languages, mirrors of her abjection, ways to tell the world about the self. To become fat, grotesquely overweight, was to convey through the medium of her own "embodiedness" the extent and pain of her alienation, her inner sense of disgust and ugliness. She once described to me what it was like to find oneself obsessed by food:

> You go from fast-food place to fast-food place; you buy several hamburgers and sit in the parking lot, wolfing 'em down, so fast you almost gag. You don't even taste them; they are like substance, but you know you must eat them, as fast as possible. Then you go somewhere else, an empty lot or a bathroom in a gas station, or another fast-food place, and vomit it all back up. Then you buy another batch, and you keep on and on. You do this hour after hour; and if it's not cheeseburgers, it's donuts; and if it's not donuts, it's cookies; and if it's not cookies, it's soft, white, mushy bread. And if it's not a McDonald's, it's a Seven-Eleven, whatever. You seek out these places, and eating, stuffing down the emptiness, becomes your life, your whole day.

Maureen's words describe intense aggression turned against the self, languages of her unconscious phantasies inscribed in the body as acts of physical self-mutilation, distortion, and ego disintegration. In the hospital, Maureen ranted and raved; she was capable of an intense, devastating anger. But more often than not, her domination by an unconscious that composed itself as action appeared in frantic moments of laceration, as a life built around the obsession with razor blades, laxatives, sleeping pills, and soft foods that could be swallowed quickly. Maureen's existence defined itself from the inside out; her inner compulsions, her regressed, primitive behavior, her need to fill up the pervasive emptiness, her hatred of "being," to use D. W. Winnicott's (1952) term, made up the contours of her life. Nothing, not language or therapeutic mirroring, could resurrect her shattered sense of self, its absorption into loneliness and loathing, the power of her abjection.

But Maureen is not unusual in this regard; consider a clinical vignette recounted to me by a staff psychiatrist. A patient brings a teddy bear to her therapy sessions. She puts the teddy bear down and then cuts herself with a razor blade. She bleeds all over the therapist's office before he succeeds in suturing the wound. Shortly thereafter she admits herself to the hospital. In another incident, the same patient attends her evening college class. Later, at home thinking about the class, she comes to believe she spoke too much. She needs to do something about her uncontrollable talking. So, before going to bed, she takes a needle and thread and sews her lips together. She saves the tissues that soaked up her blood, but several days later, throws the sutures away. She tells her therapist that she regrets dumping her sutures in the garbage. Whenever she cuts herself, she offers to give her therapist her bloodstained tissues. He politely refuses them. She is an intelligent woman, obsessed with punishing herself. She hates her body; feels she is not female but a "blob," without sexual identity, without any gendered connection to the world around her. She hates the idea of being a woman and hates the idea and drives of sexuality.[2]

In a sense Maureen was preoccupied with the "desire of nothing nameable," as Lacan called it (1985, 1038), a desire for nothingness so overwhelming that she could name it only by carving lines into her flesh, by annihilating her body through willed acts of self-destruction. Louis, similarly, observed to his therapist that he was fighting the "dictator within"; he saw himself as a "government" and then corrected himself: a "self-government; maybe I'm a dictatorship." He understood all "will" in his life to be determined by a power outside of himself which "dictated" to him. Something external, in the sense of Victor Tausk's (1948) idea of an "influencing machine," controlled his actions, filled his identity, defined his boundary. Louis's world was composed of endless rituals and terrors; each required elaborate defensive maneuvers so bizarre they appeared to be the movements of a mime. Louis responded to inaudible voices and unseen spirits that built monuments of meaning around such mundane objects or places as ashtrays, carpets, hallways, blankets, and so on.

Louis's "unnamable" but ritualized inner world was subject to sheer terror, power run amok. It was structured as a schizophrenic discourse in both language and movement. Maureen, however, composed her world cognitively in acceptable social names; she adapted to the appearances of normality. Yet, as for Louis, the real for her (as opposed to the symbolic, which she tolerates) lay in that hidden, unconscious universe of inner compulsions, drives, and obsessions that relentlessly pushed her away from the human community and toward death.

Louis spoke of himself as Gumpy and Pokey: Gumpy, completely pliable, a rubberlike moldable figure, and Pokey, who refused to move or moved very slowly without much purpose. Maureen framed her existence with cuts and with closed, dark spaces, cramped and uncomfortable, which became the receptacles for her experience of emptiness. Neither Louis nor Maureen advanced historically; with the linear movement of time and growth denied to them, each lived in a prison of endlessly repeating obsessions; both found themselves trapped by the projections of a psychotic unraveling.

Notice how this sense of an unnamable inside, a corrosive internal world that pulls at "being," appears in the language of another suicidal borderline patient, Paula.

> When I leave the hospital, I don't feel I'll miss anyone because there's nothing inside of me, so there is nothing to lose. I haven't gained anything. If you are nothing, you don't gain anything, so there's nothing to lose. . . . It's like an acceptance. Sometimes I feel like I exist in an eternity, like my body is somewhere else and then lives inside me. I can be terrified in my soul and no one knows. The real action of who I am lies not in my body, but in this place where my soul is, that no one can see; . . . death and terror, it's around you; . . . that's who I am; it's what my body feels. . . . If you're already dead, why feel anything? How can a dead, numb person feel anything? That's the acceptance, the part of me that knows I'm dead and wants to accept it. . . . Also, if you're dead, there is never anything to lose, nothing to take with you; dead people can't take anything with them.

Psychotic Objects: Subversion of Consensual Reality

Maureen waged a war against herself with razor blades, food, and laxatives; Louis with delusions and fantasized rituals and terrors. Each suffered under the productions of an unconscious filled with aggression and desire which intersected the social world in forms accompanied by disintegration and death. Although much of that imaginary world is translated into symbolic frames, it remains a powerful but often unstated dynamic exercising a dominating influence on behavior and action. The unconscious and Lacan's drive-based unnamable are enmeshed in an ongoing confrontation with the outer world and with the experience produced by the intersection of outer with inner. What is self and what is other become secondary to what unconscious phantasies project as reality, meaning, form, *and* power. In this respect, Louis and, on occasion, Maureen suffered from the identifications of psychotic time, a sense of duration specifically induced by a delusion or obsessional ritual that severs the self's psychic connection to consensual reality. Intersubjective experience or reality is subverted by a disintegration induced through psychotic images and symbols. That disintegration draws the self away from life, from Eros, toward the images of death and torture that constitute the driving force of a tyrannical power.

Maureen lived on the border between a civil world and the grim projections of her unconscious compulsions. She refused to direct aggression outward, toward others, although she might dispute this assessment with regard to her somewhat sadistic relationship with her younger daughter. Nor did she organize violence or find herself, like Jenny, at the center of complex delusions of power. But what she experienced as anger turned on her body, the intensity of her rage, the violence of her impulses, represented not only her being but also the tragedy of a self lost to her emotions, enslaved by masochistic impulses that literally wrote messages on her flesh, a massive disintegration, or what Lacan sees as a falling away from the symbolic, the world of law and historical continuity. Maureen confronted her self at the intersection of the imaginary, as psychotic preoccupation, and desire, as the impulse to turn power, as mutilation and distortion, onto the physical boundaries of her being.

For example, she believed there were "two" Maureens, two selves: one she presented to her husband, and the ugly destructive self she carried inside, hidden, away from public view. This was the self that cut into her body, carving the messages of the self-hating phantasies that possessed her. Maureen saw her own body as a psychotic object, on the border between the civil world and the finality of death. If she could mutilate her body, she might not submit to the suicidal impulses, might not deny her body altogether. By hurting parts of her physical self, she believed she could preserve existence. It was the only release.

The self-defilement of abjection persistently motivated Maureen's masochism. On a number of occasions, she cut around or in her genitalia, as if she were saying through her actions that the "feminine" is a "radical evil that is to be suppressed" (Kristeva 1982, 70). Kristeva observes that the borderline patient "will always be marked by the uncertainty of his borders and of his affective valency as well." Such selves are tormented by the "horror" of an internal "war" with all its "terror, and the ensuing fear [or knowledge] of being rotten, drained, or blocked" (63).

Maureen described to me how she enjoyed watching her blood flow. Making the cuts excited her. She spent hours deciding which veins to lacerate and how extensively to injure them. The feel of the blood, its color, had a reality separate from her, and it gave her a "strange pleasure" to see her arms smeared with her own blood. Cutting only intensified her sense of detachment from whatever signified or symbolized life. And she found peace—"a balance of power" inside herself, a truce in the endless war of self-defilement—only when contemplating death, cutting, and the mutilation of her genitals.

Indeed, Maureen's conception of sexuality had, in the view of her therapist, a psychotic self-destructiveness. He noted:

> Maureen had fantasies of abuse when making love; she hated it and him [her husband]. She felt she should be hurt, mutilated, that she deserved it; . . . she experienced sex as detached, a disconnected experience that she only understood in the context of her phantasy of annihilation. There is no pleasure here, just a source of intense pain and self-degradation. It had a sado-masochistic quality and it sounded almost as if her descriptions of sexuality were the descriptions of a self being torn up, exploded, ripped into fragments and pieces of herself. It was quite horrible listening to all of this. I had the feeling I was inside the mind of an infant.

Any interpersonal encounter that might involve some intimacy terrified Maureen. She imagined blood dripping down on her, her car going off a cliff, and her body torn to shreds by its fall down a steep, rocky ravine. Before intercourse, she saw her arms and legs and body parts being torn off her trunk, leaving her husband to make love to an indistinguishable bloody mass without form, shape, or sexual identity.

There were concrete, historical reasons why Maureen experienced sexuality as a fragmented form of violence. When she was eight or nine, she and her fifteen-year-old half brother began an incestuous relationship that lasted for a number of years until it was discovered by *her* father. The half brother joined the army and was away for some time. When he returned, Maureen, by then in her midteens, wanted to resume the sexual relationship. Her brother rejected her offer but expressed an interest in remaining "friends" with Maureen. Maureen said she was "crushed" by his rejection and hated him when, a year or two later, he married another woman.

Maureen's incestuous relationship; its discovery by her father, for whom she had little or no respect; the obvious damage to sexual and psychological development—all these factors still powerfully influenced the grown woman. Her therapist, however, maintained that the incest with her brother, which Maureen had encouraged, was not sufficient grounds to explain the psychotic terror that accompanied her later sexual encounters. Incest, he believed, had aggravated early, preoedipal defenses against annihilation and implosion (mutilation) whose origins may very well have had something to do with Maureen's relationship or lack of it with maternal presence. Some of the clinical clues to such early deprivation, the failure of maternal provision and its effect on the "body's territory" (Kristeva 1982, 74), included extreme dependency; oral rage; images of biting, tearing, devouring, incorporation; her pathological fear of being left alone; *extreme* demandingness; her sense of fragmentation, body flying apart, when themes of intimacy or sexual contact were broached in therapy; her urge to sexual masochism; her fear of her own identity whenever she found herself feeling "close" to another person; and finally, her rejection of her second daughter at birth, her dread of holding and protecting her, which may have replayed an archaic script in Maureen's own dim psychic prehistory.

The Functions of Masochism

Maureen's phantasies performed a function: they released her from inner torment and fear and, at least momentarily, provided masochistic enjoyment, a form of self-comforting, a seeking after pleasure in the dim underworld of psychic and physical pain. Maureen's pleasure/pain calculus found itself radically inverted. Instead of the Benthamite calculus, a recognizable catalog of pleasures and pains, it conveyed a much grimmer sense of pleasure and the meaning of life. It was an often stark commentary on her "basic incompleteness" (Kristeva 1982, 89), determined by her unconscious phantasies, and the realization of their intent through the power she turned against her body.

> I don't know why such acts [cutting] give me pleasure but they do. I like to rub my wrists to irritate the scars; I like that they're there. . . . They give me a great deal of comfort and it makes me feel good to know I can touch them when I want to. . . . Of course I'm concerned that I hurt myself, who wouldn't be? But it's something I have to do; it's something I like to do. Oh, I control it; I'm not suicidal; I'm not going to cut so deep I'll sever an artery or do something crazy like that; . . . it's just that I like the pleasure of cutting. . . . I've often asked myself, why don't I follow through with it; why don't I finally kill myself, buy a gun, jump off a bridge? I like the idea of contemplating death. . . . I know the cutting, the pills, razor blades, the fantasies, make me feel good when I think about them. . . . As a kid I used to cut crosses into my breasts and think about guns and ropes and different ways to hang myself. It's a temptation that grows and grows.

At home, Maureen stayed away from the kitchen because the knives tempted her; she took down the belts in her closet because she saw them as instruments for hanging. She was afraid to drive her car for fear she might mangle herself in an auto accident. Objects took on ominous properties: a dining room table might be hurled at her; drinking glasses could be broken and used to scar her flesh. Objects had the power to destroy; she had to flee the dining room, run from the knives, hide the glasses. It was almost as if she and objects were engaged in a kind of mutual dialectic of destruction in which things became actors in intricate phantasies of mutilation. Maureen herself imagined the consequences of any given object in her house; she refused to move, since the object might assault her at any moment. Only her terror mattered; nothing else. Life had become an exercise in the sustaining and experiencing of terror.

Completely conscious of her own borderline and psychotic tendencies, capable of articulating the terms of her psychiatric condition, Maureen nonetheless remained trapped by an internal emotional world that ruthlessly dominated her. She was a prisoner in the dim half light of Plato's shadows, the rough shapes of anomic desire. Unable to experience erotic pleasure, caught in an endless series of masochistic identifications, seeking out abusive power, Maureen lived in that madness Plato called "tyranny," a state of nonbeing in which the rational self found "itself" absorbed by impulses and drives whose origins lay in an obscure, unsettled reach of her unconscious. Therapy became an often fruitless effort to disentangle these chaotic part-objects of a wounded self.

Maureen's horrifying fears, the domination of the unnamable in her actions, her confusion about self and other, body and psyche—all testified to a psychotic boundlessness, a limitless world where inner and outer, self and other, real and unreal, often merged in frightening aggregations of images, thoughts, and sensations. Never sure of who she was, her identity, Maureen could never be sure of what the world was. The consequence was a terrifying inability to "be" in the world either according to the pleasures of Eros or in relationships that brought gratification and joy instead of torture, fear, and domination. Maureen's aggression, her disappointment, her hatred and fear found their way not to the world but to the self, specifically the embodied self. Maureen communicated, but it was an often nonverbal communication bearing messages of annihilation and death. If any credence at all is to be given to Freud's notion of the death instinct, Maureen carried within herself its pure culture.

SIX

Power and Its Construction: An Argument between Alice Miller and Michel Foucault

TO what extent are societies subject to the same kind of regressive or splitting forces as individuals? Might clinical reality be suggestive in examining configurations of power which do not derive from consensually shared perceptions and reality but objectify and enslave the self? If death or the wish to die (the wish to kill the self)—a critical dynamic of the ends of power in a patient such as Maureen—can become the motivating drive of a person, a self, is it not possible that a similar dynamic might appear in collective forms of behavior? States and communities find themselves subject to very real psychotic conditions, such as the loss of boundary, the presence of uncontrollable rage, and the failure to distinguish between self and other.

The kind of rage Maureen directed toward her body, the self-destructive impulses pulling her toward the horror of Lacan's imaginary, may in fact appear in the actions of groups and states. I am reminded here of Kurtz's last observations as Marlowe reports them in Joseph Conrad's *Heart of Darkness:* "The horror . . . the horror." Kurtz's utterance, certainly about himself and his own drives, also foreshadows the succeeding decades of a European culture that turned into a charnel house. In this respect, what Maureen represents as a self living in a life-world that includes others and possesses a history can be seen to have a certain political significance. Her borderline, periodically psychotic impulses have about them a constitution or structure that, in terms of what they mean as a regression from civil or consensual norms, may be thought of as appearing in the behaviors of communities.

Plato's argument in book 9 of *The Republic* and Lacan's fascination with the death instinct as a psychotic unhinging or foreclosure are compelling; it may be worthwhile to explore these views of self in the context of a psychoanalytic perspective on power understood as the wish to torture or destroy other human beings or groups of human beings designated as scapegoats. In a clinical sense, power may take on sadistic and destructive properties; it is hardly a benign presence in psychotic or borderline frames of being.

I would like to turn to an analysis of power which takes seriously the phantasies of the unconscious and the horror they produce in political or public contexts. I frame this theory of power as an argument between Alice Miller and Michel Foucault, although neither ever addresses the other directly. To posit their theories of power as a disagreement over the importance of psychological explanation not only demonstrates different approaches to the understanding of power but shows how distant psychoanalytic theory is from Foucault's social/historical analysis of power *dispersion*.

Two caveats: First, I find Miller's argument interesting and important but not entirely convincing; I present her interpretation as faithfully as possible because I think her position deserves to be understood and because I think it offers unusual insights to help clarify how power functions and what it is capable of. But her fundamental argument, that the origins of power are to be found in the effects of repeated physical and psychological abuse in childhood, though right to an extent, overlooks other major factors. I address some of these factors in the next chapter.

Second, I recognize the danger that even though I use Miller to critique Foucault, both may in fact share a similar aversion to what Freud calls psychical reality. A sharp distinction should be drawn between Foucault and Miller, on one side, and Freud and Lacan (the unconscious as the source of negation), on the other.[1]

The Parental View of Childhood Freedom

Miller, unlike Foucault, takes the individual leader quite seriously as an exemplar and practitioner of power. In this respect her theory might be considered more "political" than his, in the sense that while she refuses to downplay the historical and social context (epistemes) central to the Foucaultian analysis, she focuses on the psychodynamic symbolism of power in ideological and political acts. For Miller, the parent-child relationship constitutes the fundamental source for understanding the distribution and practice of power, and power cannot be dissociated from its origins in childhood percepts, particularly in considering the relations between leader and led and what the leader appeals to in specific historical environments.

Miller writes: "One is not normally aware of something that is a continuation of one's own childhood" (1984, 75). If childhood has involved the constant harassment of the self by a brutalizing authority, she maintains, the experience of power will reflect similar properties. The self loses sight of what it has experienced, but what it does in its relationship with others is to replay early parental relationships or scenarios as dramas involving the exercise of power. If the child experiences authority as frustrating and debilitating, then the self and perhaps the culture may perceive power as punitive and retaliatory.

What Miller looks for in delineating the sources of the experience of power, at least in a clinical sense, is a parental context dominated by patterns of harassment and abuse. For example, when parental authority establishes the relationship through beating (psychological or physical), the parent compulsively repeats the past; it is a phenomenon that psychoanalytic theory calls the "return of the repressed." Miller writes: "In beating their children, [parents] are struggling to regain the power they once lost to their own parents" (1984, 16). Power is a very real phenomenon in family environments, but its definitions and context come entirely from parental *authority* and the value parents attach to obedience to authority. "It is perfectly normal to speak of the necessity of striking and humiliating children and robbing them of their autonomy, at the same time using such high-sounding words as *chastising, upbringing,* and *guiding onto the right path*" (16).

Parental attribution creates the qualities attached to power. Thus, if parental authority is experienced as punitive, the child will come to believe that "normal" power is repressive, negative, and punitive. In addition, the belief will be established that the exercise of repressive power is just. The child internalizes the parental percept; the succeeding generation repeats the pattern. It is a depressing vicious cycle; the compulsion to repeat plagues family relationships and weighs heavily on political concepts such as justice and fairness. The exercise of power, then, comes to be seen in primarily *negative* terms.

Miller (1990b) argues quite strenuously that negative or punitive ways of exercising power breed an enormous quantity of hatred in the self; therefore, in many children the exercise of power and the gratification of hatred become psychologically bound up with each other. It is a trap in which hate and evil come to be identified. What is hated is evil, poisonous, and bad, Kristeva's abject. The trap is set quite early in life by positing the unconscious conviction that love and cruelty are synonymous. The equation of cruelty and love breeds a sadism in the self easily translated into vicious acts of aggression against an other defined as evil.

In Miller's view, most parental education is "poisonous pedagogy," misguided and repressive. She traces this educational philosophy that supports repression of spontaneity and humiliation of self to the child-rearing texts of the nineteenth century. In these texts, the child appears as an impulse-driven monster who must be tamed and civilized. Modern methods, Miller believes, differ only in degree. The abuse of the child in the service of obedience to parental will has grown into a major social problem in contemporary society, and the practices of child abuse should be a factor in understanding what power is and where it originates. Obedience to authority remains a major pedagogical assumption of most families and social contexts. Stanley Milgrim's experiments in following orders, conducted in 1974, suggest an even more extensive acquiescence to and idealization of authority. And even though children may flout authority and rebel against it, parental authority asserts itself as domination, command, disrespect of the child's will, and in many instances, physical abuse.

The Assault on Exuberance: Spontaneity as Enemy

Power as a creative, fluid, reciprocal expression of self finds itself under siege from a very early age (possibly one of the ancestors of the paranoid component of political power). Miller quotes from an 1896 text on child rearing which in her view conveys much about how children were expected to present themselves.

> As in the case of all illnesses that are difficult to cure, so too, in the case of the psychic fault of exuberance, the greatest care must be devoted to prophylaxis, to prevention of the disorder. The best way for an education to reach this goal is by adhering unswervingly to the principle of shielding the child as much as possible from all influences that might stimulate feelings, be they pleasant or painful. (1984, 30)

Miller reads a vicious cycle in these injunctions against exuberance. "Once 'wickedness' has been produced in a child by suppressing vitality, any measure taken to stamp it out is justified" (31). Inevitably, this attitude influences actions in the public realm: if the norm in families involves discipline, repression, and the containment of exuberance; if this style of upbringing is generally accepted in the culture; if power within the family takes on abusive properties, then, Miller says, it follows that both political leadership *and* the individual's relation to the presence and feel of power will be affected. Whatever the distribution of power in the society, its *form* cannot escape the projective dynamics of unconscious phantasies generated during early childhood.

One of Miller's central critiques of Freud is his abandonment of the seduction theory. In building his psychoanalytic theory on the notion that sexual wishes directed toward the parents incite desire, Freud ignored what Miller, Jeffrey Masson (1984), and others consider a far more important relationship: the *actual* or attempted seduction or abuse of the child by the parent. Miller's attack on the primacy of the oedipal phantasy in Freudian theory reflects her conviction that neurosis *and* psychosis are rooted in the *facts* of childhood abuse and the repression of these very *real* memories. In my view, she draws too sharp a distinction between abuse as etiology and Freud's theory of sexual wishes or fantasies. The two positions are not necessarily exclusive. Interpretation depends on the clinical evidence, the skillful listening of the therapist, and the therapist's capacity to distinguish reality from fantasy. A therapist can accept evidence of child abuse and treat accordingly without overturning the entire oedipal theory of self and experience.

Many of Miller's examples of the *political* consequences of child abuse come from extreme contexts: terrorism, mass murder, state-sanctioned violence. Extremely repressive familial environments, where power is experienced as hate and pain, reproduce themselves in the public space. The "enemy" stands in for the parent; the wish to murder the hated other is a return of the repressed, but in a public context, where the absent but punitive parental authority finds itself transformed into a scapegoat. Projective processes work themselves out in the context of the leader-populace dialectic; long-repressed memories and hatreds take conscious shape in calls for destruction of the enemy.

Leader and populace feed off each other, and the underlying affect—hate—comes to be manifested as ideological representations of state policy. Miller suggests that in Nazi Germany the effects of abusive parental authority on the self found expression in mass murder and revenge against Jews and others defined as "poisonous."

Miller not only argues the obvious proposition that Hitler was psychopathic; she sees broader, more ominous implications in the sense that the Nazi use of power embodied or represented retribution against an other the entire culture defined as evil. This other, those named as inferior, biologically tainted, allowed the political agents of Nazi Germany to fulfil *unconscious* phantasies of retribution against abusive and hated parental authority. The Jew, as a distinct cultural type, took on the status of a projection and allowed an entire society to enact in conscious form these violent unconscious phantasies of hate. Seemingly ordinary citizens took great pleasure in contributing to this effort.[2]

The Jews became a scapegoat for what was in fact a cultural pathology taking political form as National Socialist ideology and as the political practice of murder. The murderousness of the Third Reich, Miller maintains, was a cultural phenomenon rooted in a widely shared belief that punishing children, abusing them, was necessary to curb impulsiveness. Miller insists that Hitler's obsessional perceptions and their unconscious patterns fed into and kindled similarly hostile feelings in his audience. Both experienced the reparation of childhood humiliation as an assault on a hated other; and the Jew served that purpose. To exterminate Jewish badness and evil was to purge the self of its own historical experience of self-loathing, and the symbol of the Jew further enabled the cultural *German* self to deflect power from its own hated self—the consequence of abusive parental authority—to the hated other. Purification of self, then, and purification of nation became synonymous in the enactment of the unconscious wish for revenge. The projected wish against the father was transformed into the politically defined other-as-enemy.

> Where does anti-Semitism's perpetual ability to renew itself come from? The answer is not difficult to find. A Jew is not hated for doing or being something specific. Everything Jews do or the way they are

> applies to other groups as well. Jews are hated because people harbor a forbidden hatred and are eager to legitimate it. The Jewish people are particularly well suited objects of this need. . . . A child who has been required to don the armor of "virtue" [obedience to authority] at too early an age will seize upon the only permissible discharge; he will seize upon anti-Semitism (i.e., his right to hate), retaining it for the rest of his life. (166)

Evil here takes on a very ugly face; it is hardly banal: it is born in abuse and then works itself out in history through a political ideology that uses power to annihilate.

Is this psychoanalytic reading of destructive complicity between leader and audience plausible? Plausible, yes; convincing, no. But what sorts of "explanations" for the destruction of the Holocaust can possibly be convincing? Even with its interpretive faults, however, Miller's argument attempts to answer some fairly vexing questions. How *does* one explain the general enthusiasm for Hitler and his anti-Semitic ideology?

Is every battered child a potential follower of Hitler? Of course not. Is the destruction of European Jewry to be explained only as the projection of Hitler's unconscious phantasies, the consequences of the beatings and physical abuse Hitler received from his father? ("What didn't the son do to forget the trauma of the beatings his father gave him?" [173]). Of course not. Yet, the facts of child abuse are undeniable, particularly in Germany and the Europe of the late nineteenth and early twentieth centuries. Racism and hate lay behind much of the willing participation of many European sympathizers with the Germans; and it is unreasonable, Miller suggests, to *exclude* the effects of physical abuse in childhood from political questions regarding the origins and deployment of repressive power:

> The Jews were characterized by a special mixture of Lucifer-like grandeur and superiority (world Jewry and its readiness to destroy the entire world) on the one hand and ugliness and ludicrous weakness and infirmity on the other. This view reflects the omnipotence even the weakest father exercises over his child seen in Hitler's case in the wild rages of the insecure customs official who succeeded in destroying his son's world. (178)

For the audience, the German people and the pan-European audience for anti-Semitism, "forbidden, long avoided feelings [were] given free rein. The more they had filled and pressed in upon one, the happier one feels at having finally found an ersatz object" (179). Hate found its fulfillment in an out-group defined as other/evil. Both leader and followers sought gratification, fulfillment, and reparation in the prosecution of that hate.

To beat the child is literally to beat back that part of one's "self" which is hateful, frightening, and most important, vengeful; to beat one's child is to avoid beating oneself. Therefore, beating, whether psychological beating or actual physical abuse, "is a never ending task—behind it hovers fear of the emergence of one's own repressed weakness, humiliation, and helplessness, which one has tried to escape all one's life by means of grandiose behavior" (188). These mechanisms of defense were embedded in child-rearing patterns that became part of the culture's collective unconscious. Miller is not, however, arguing a Jungian position: her concept of a cultural unconscious is created through the shared *experience* of abuse and brutality; Jung posits a collective unconscious with mystical qualities that give to the group or nation or state a moral or religious unity. Not so Miller. Extensive patterns of abuse, aided by brutal forms of child rearing, made an entire culture sympathetic to political messages that generalized the experience and situated it within an out-group—the Jews.

The Plausibility of a Theory of Power

It is not unreasonable to assume that psychological factors influence extraordinary acts. Cultures do not, without motivation, enshrine genocide as national policy. The complicity of millions of people throughout Europe in the destruction of European Jews, Gypsies, and others defined as biologically inferior suggests a deep level of hate. It is hard to interpret it as the banal actions of mindless bureaucrats or to attribute it to the complacency of officials "just obeying orders." What is banal about Auschwitz or the caricatures of Jews throughout the thirties in German newspapers, gymnasiums, public institutions, as poisonous, corrupting, impure, dirty, and so on? To stage the mass murder of millions of people requires the criminal complicity not only of the technocrats responsible for building the camps and supplying them but of millions who tacitly, if not actively, supported the concentration and transportation of Jewish populations. To suggest that such massive operations of death were possible because of banal indifference to suffering or the sheer joy of doing one's job well (Hannah Arendt's [1976] thesis in *Eichmann in Jerusalem*) stretches the imagination.

When evil takes such forms, it is hardly banal; nor can such widespread insensitivity to horror be explained by mere willingness to follow orders, as Christopher Browning (1993) demonstrates, or "authoritarian" hierarchical patterns in the culture. After all, millions of men, women, and children were murdered within a relatively short period of time; the room filled with infants' and children's shoes at the Auschwitz memorial in Poland symbolizes more than the consequence of efficient bureaucrats trying to do a good job.

It is my sense that Miller's theory is certainly as plausible as Hannah Arendt's; both theories explain aspects of the mass destruction of human life. It is a mistake to dismiss Miller's approach as nonexplanatory; she names Auschwitz for what it was—evil. And if evil has a face, its gruesome look underscores what it accomplished: the hideous deaths of uncomprehending innocents. Miller's analysis of the projection of hateful phantasies within a culture and the culture's unconscious identification with the aggressive and vengeful side of these phantasies offers a human and moral context for the politics that made a certain group of human beings into a scapegoat whose blood sacrifice would assure the purity of the nation. Is it so implausible to suggest that such "sacrifice" disguises a collectively shared wish that by ridding the culture of its "badness," somehow magically one's self, family, and nation might be saved or redeemed or purified or granted eternal happiness? "Every delusion has its own meaning," Miller writes, "which is very easy to understand once the childhood situation is known. . . . the persecution of the Jews permitted [Hitler] to *persecute* the weak child in his own self that was not projected onto the victims. . . . In this, as well as in his unconscious revenge on his early childhood persecutor, Hitler resembled a great number of Germans who had grown up in a similar situation" (1984, 190–91).

The Foucaultian Lapse: Power Disembodied

Even discounting aspects of Miller's argument which suggest psychological and cultural determinism, even for a moment dismissing her argument about the relationship between Hitler's childhood past and what he mobilized in his German audience—even holding all this in abeyance, her argument strongly suggests that the relationship between power and its practice involves critical psychological and projective components.

Just as the charge of reductionism might be leveled against Miller's psychological theory, so a similar charge might be justified for historical theories that dismiss the importance of psychology. It seems to me this is a problem in Foucault's and poststructuralism's analysis of disciplinary power: the theorizing about power dismisses the projective intensity of *affect* and the structuring properties of unconscious phantasies in the exercise of power.

Miller asks: What are the origins of these concepts of disciplinary power; what sorts of unconscious memories motivate their realization and their practice? It is not enough to say that this kind of educational practice is the product of historically dependent forms of knowledge influencing social practice. It is not disembodied knowledge, disconnected from affect, which produces power; rather, it is that knowledge which directly springs from sexuality, spontaneity, and fear which motivates the construction of bulwarks against "willfulness."

Miller's point is that it makes just as much sense to turn to the psychological for explanations regarding power as to the historical and social. Indeed, she suggests the convergence of knowledge and power in practices may have a great deal to do with the projection of unconscious phantasies into specific cultural areas of action and control. The content of these phantasies depends on the arena in which they are operating, for example, the school, the family, the political regime. Whatever the territory, however, the hatred of willfulness emerges from complex patterns of projective identification which appear as cultural practice, each generation repeating the abuse of the previous one. Hate, fear, and terror find themselves enshrined as desirable educational tools. Brutal social and political forms arise precisely because of the fluid dialectic linking actions in the family, educational practice, and political ideology.

Part of what I am posing as a disagreement between Michel Foucault and Alice Miller lies in the general theoretical category of leadership, or what Foucault (1980) in one of his interviews called sovereignty and its effects. He distinguishes sovereignty from disciplinary power and rightly demonstrates how social practices develop their own autonomy, literally their own will. In *Discipline and Punish* (1979), he shows how concepts of punishment emerged from disciplinary practices, without any specific leadership intervention. It was not the sovereign who produced the prison but generally accepted beliefs about surveillance dispersed throughout the culture. This kind of knowledge was demonstrated, for example, by the symbolism of Jeremy Bentham's panoptical prison. Power is dispersed; it flows throughout the culture; it is not concentrated but manifest in extensive surveillance in environments such as schools, prisons, mental institutions, and so on. Power is exercised throughout the social order; it is not a sovereign imposition or fiat from the top down.

Panoptical power in the nineteenth century monitored and contained deviance, and the unruly impulses in a culture, whether in schools, prisons, or madhouses, found themselves restrained not only by bars and chains but through moral injunctions that were internalized. In mental hospitals, for example, chains were superseded by shame; the wrongdoer was controlled by being made to think of the self as tainted, impure, or evil. This "shaming" constituted a repressive form of moral surveillance, used to train madmen, criminals, deviants, and children in normalizing standards and codes. In fact, moral surveillance assured the domination of normalizing values *and* institutions.

Bentham's panoptical vision served as an icon for a type of punishment society accepted as essential for its well-being. Panoptical power, however, is only one form of power, and the weakness in Foucault's argument is that it overlooks political concepts of power which depend in large measure on leaders' ideological and public pronouncements and on the willingness of followers to embrace the messages, intents, and weaknesses of their leaders.

Miller's inquiry has different but not necessarily antagonistic objectives from Foucault's. She is no less interested in power, but she means to consider motive as well and she focuses power within a frame of leadership. Yet, paradoxically, both Miller and Foucault diminish, if not banish outright, any consideration of the effect of psychic reality (not traceable, for example, to the practices of child abuse) on power. Both emphasize the effects of external reality—for Miller, the parents, for Foucault, disciplinary practices—on the self; both ignore the internal life of the self, the whole range of fantasies, wishes, and displacements that may have nothing at all to do with specific external actions and their behavioral consequences. And both privilege social over psychic reality in such a way as to take from the operation of the unconscious any laws, processes, or mechanisms specifically its own and, more important, independent of behavioral forces in external reality.

Miller insists on understanding the unconscious as an internalization of the *social* acts of parents, which come to reside in a repressed psychological substratum of memory. Foucault insists that the subject is constituted through the effects of a fully externalized range of disciplinary power. In each case, what constructs identity and a sense of self is a totalizing power that consumes the subject because of its origins in actions *external to the self.* Miller, like Foucault, allows for little meaningful resistance to the presence of such power; it is a weakness in her argument as it is in Foucault's. Miller in this respect veers sharply from psychoanalytic formulations that posit the unconscious as a repository of phantasies having nothing at all to do with external reality and from psychoanalytic theorists (for example, Wilhelm Reich, Herbert Marcuse, and Luce Irigaray) who see the unconscious as a possible site of resistance to tyrannizing forms of power.

Foucault says that power must be understood in what he calls its "external visage," its dispersed manifestations throughout society, appearing as micromechanisms of control or domination. One example is the moral power of the tea parties the inmates of the York asylum were required to attend. Power, for Foucault, looks, peers, judges, and scrutinizes (1965).

It is not that Foucault is wrong about the micropolitics of power and its foundations in practice and knowledge. It is, rather, that he has an incomplete notion of what power *is*. For example, he declares that the analysis of power "should not concern itself with power at the level of conscious intention or decision; that it should not attempt to consider power from its internal point of view and that it should refrain from posing the labyrinthine and unanswerable question: 'Who then has power and what has he in mind? What is the aim of someone who possesses power?' " (1980, 97).

Foucault's judgment in this matter can be disputed. From a psychoanalytic perspective, it certainly does not seem impossible to consider the psycho-structures of power and their origins in projected phantasies of aggression and hate. Foucault believes that any question of intention, much less unconscious intentionality or phantasy, distorts analysis.

Nothing that lies below the surface is to be considered; the only intentionality worth analyzing is that which appears in visible social practice: "It is a case of studying power at a point where its intention, if it has one, is completely invested in its real and effective practices. What is needed is a study of power in its external visage, at the point where it is in direct and immediate relationship with that which we can provisionally call its object, its target, its field of application, there—that is to say—where it installs itself and produces its real effects" (97).

Alice Miller takes a very close look at the real effects of power, effects understood as bodies and psyches being hurt by an almost innate hostility in the operations of power. Like Foucault, she draws a close connection between practice and effects: stored up memories of abuse are projected into concrete political situations. Are not parents who demonstrate sexuality to their children by forcing them to witness the dissection of corpses, a recommendation of an eighteenth-century educator, engaging in real forms of psychologically coercive power? Are not complex machines for strapping down four- and five-year-olds to keep them from masturbating, a common practice in the mid-nineteenth century, real impositions of power?

Willfulness in children was regarded in the eighteenth and nineteenth centuries as an illness to be wiped out. Miller argues these practices are indicative, still, of attitudes toward childrearing; force, repression, and brutality are used even today to contain childhood impulses and energy. She wonders if we are very far removed from those times when respected educators argued that corpses be used to instruct children in sexuality (consider, for example, the eighteenth-century educator J. Oest's claim that "the sight of a corpse evokes solemnity and reflection" [46]),[3] and that anatomical lectures, dissections, and demonstrations utilizing dead bodies should be part of standard educational practice. Miller cites a 1887 reference entitled *Comprehensive Encyclodia of Education and Instruction,* which advises: "The will of the adult must be a fortress, inaccessible to duplicity or defiance and granting admittance only when obedience knocks at the gate" (42). Such disciplinary practices were meant, at the time, to enhance the health of the individual body and the body politic. Even though we have become more sophisticated in our techniques of control, Miller suggests, similar value assumptions still hold: childhood impulses and actions that are regarded as threatening to adult authority must be repressed, brutalized, and discouraged.

Is, then, what happens to one's body and psyche as a child at all explanatory of psychological alienation, of, for example, the anguish of women with multiple personalities? Is it idle speculation to ask psychological questions about intentions and reasons behind psychological environments filled with hallucination and delusion? Is the psychological ground of coercive power to be completely ignored in considering the origins of affective structures that motivate cultural norms and power practices?

Foucault dismisses psychology: "Let us not, therefore, ask why certain people want to dominate, what they seek, what is their overall strategy. Let us ask, instead, how things work at the level of on-going subjugation, at the level of those continuous and uninterrupted processes which subject our bodies, govern our gestures, dictate our behaviors, etc." But this is precisely the point: how does one understand events, actions, or persons at the level of "ongoing subjugation" without inquiring into the emotional origins, the *place* of affect behind subjugation?[4] Foucault declares: "We should try to discover how it is that subjects are gradually, progressively, really and materially constituted through a multiplicity of organisms, forces, energies, materials, desires, thoughts, etc." (97). Yet, it is precisely this question Alice Miller explores, tracing cultural attitudes to the vigorous suppression of childhood spontaneity. Is not, as Miller puts it, the "murder of the child's soul," a consequence of the psychological practice of power?[5]

Conclusion: Practices and the Context of Power

Alice Miller and those psychoanalysts who look at the functions of groups do not regard the historical or social lightly. They contend, however, that an understanding of these realms of experience is incomplete without a consideration of the relation between internal psychological structures, collective forms of projection, and political and social action. Foucault says that "the individual is an effect of power, and at the same time, or precisely to the extent to which it is that effect, it is the element of its articulation" (98). Yet, what "is" the individual or, perhaps better, the individual "self"? What constitutes the individual self's psychological "articulation"? And is such knowledge important in uncovering the archeology of power?

Miller would agree that the individual is "object of the prime effects of power," but she would also analyze historical influence and examine the psychological past, the self's history in its own childhood and familial context. She would engage in precisely the kind of inquiry, in addition to more classical psychoanalytic approaches, Foucault found suspicious. It is a fact that individuals, leaders, have enormous impact on the distribution and exercise of power; to remove power from its close alliance to leaders and leadership is to diminish the political context and environment of power. It is to narrow the field of analysis to what is visible. From a psychoanalytic perspective—including Freud, Lacan, and Kristeva—this strategy unnecessarily restricts the evidence available to the historian and social theorist for understanding the workings of power.

"Power," Foucault says, "is employed and exercised through a net-like organisation. And not only do individuals circulate between its threads; they are always in the position of simultaneously undergoing and exercising this power" (98). This is an accurate description of such professions as psychiatry, law, penology, and education. Certainly, Foucault delineates the genealogy of these forms of control. Yet, power also exercises itself in ideological constructions that extract violence from their participants. Leaders do lead; leadership is a central ingredient of power, particularly the kind of power that scapegoats a designated historical other.

Whereas history produces institutional arrangements and knowledge imposes itself as power, however, political leadership often descends from a more uncertain and unpredictable genealogy. What the leader speaks may articulate phantasies, both conscious and unconscious, which have not been historically defined, which cannot be uncovered and identified as governing epistemes. It is not that Foucault is wrong, but that his approach cannot be sensitive to the psychoanalytic notion of projection and the political contingencies springing from unconscious phantasies that leaders articulate as ideology. Foucault believes that in any study of power "one must rather conduct an *ascending* analysis of power, starting, that is, from its infinitesimal mechanisms, which each have their own history, their own trajectory, their own techniques and tactics, and then see how these mechanisms of power have been—and continue to be—invested, colonised, utilised, involuted, transformed, displaced, extended, etc., by ever more general mechanisms and by forms of global domination" (99). Yet, the psychoanalyst finds the "infinitesimal" in those psychological dispositions that give rise to phantasy and uncertainty—precisely the phenomena Foucault excludes.

For Foucault the infinitesimal mechanisms are the microoperations of power, for example, what happens in the prison cell, the classroom, the asylum ward, the clinic. For Miller the infinitesimal mechanisms are found in such evidence as dreams, reports of childhood abuse, educational techniques, cultural patterns of action and reaction which may coalesce as ideologies a leader uses to appeal to specific populations and audiences. "Technologies of power" are not the same social phenomena as the identification of scapegoats. Technologies of power, control, and surveillance *do* exist; indeed, Foucault has demonstrated their omnipresence. Nevertheless, locating the genealogy of power exclusively in historic epistemes minimizes the place of historical leaders, their policies, and the contingent effects of their actions *and* pasts on given historical audiences. Foucault wants to examine and deconstruct the "mechanisms of . . . exclusion that are necessary, the apparatuses of surveillance, the medicalisation of sexuality, of madness, of delinquency, all the micromechanisms of power." (101) Yet, from a psychoanalytic viewpoint, the phantasies motivating these micromechanisms contain significant affective "reasons" for the establishment and exercise of power, particularly power that hurts and represses. They should not be ignored.

Further, as Joan Copjec (1990) notes, Foucault seriously underestimates the importance of negation in the construction of identity. "Foucault is not analyzing the positive operation of negation, he is instead *eliminating* negation and replacing it with the purely positive force of 'construction.' " Copjec sees negation as the stance of the divided subject, its internal position, the effect of desire in alienating the self from alignment with society. Foucault, however, endorses a determinism that leaves the subject not only without this potential for detachment from convention but as an empty shell at the mercy of normalizing power. Although Copjec agrees with Foucault's analysis of practices, she believes his theory lacks a place for individual action and resistance. "Foucault jettisons one of his own basic principles and commits himself to the concept of construction as a process that has no internal constraints and that must then always result in its own realization, in the production of determinate properties and positions" (14). He dismisses the unconscious (notably, repression) and in so doing discards the creativity with which a conflicted or divided subject might negate what is perceived as a hostile, cold, indifferent social world.

For Foucault, the individual is only what social practices construct; desire in his terms emerges from social practices that govern and constitute the "proper" and "appropriate" forms of desire. In Copjec's view, however, and in Freudian drive theory, the unconscious, acting as a negation of normalization, affirms or at least participates in the construction of an autonomous, divided, and often alienated subject whose relation to desire might be radically "other" than society's. What this means is that the divided subject may in fact not be a complete and absolute pawn of social practices. What is "inside," the unconscious, what Kristeva calls the "stranger within," may resist or negate what social practices impose on self and consciousness. The Freudian subject owes its affective being and existence (in addition to existent social practices), to drives, imagoes, and negations deriving from internal struggles with desire, recognition (and misrecognition), dimensions of self-experience not necessarily governed by normalizing power. This is particularly the case with Freud's notion of drives, the Kleinian theory of infantile phantasy, Kristeva's concept of the maternal *chora* (and the psychodynamics of abjection), and to a limited extent, Alice Miller's analysis of parental authority.

What Foucault has accomplished in delineating the power of "disciplinary normalizations" is extraordinary, but what he excludes is equally important. The effect of Foucaultian analysis is to diminish the place of psychodynamic etiology in respect of power. At least in Alice Miller's view of the effects of child abuse on an understanding of power, this minimization of psychological factors sidesteps serious interpretive and historical issues.

SEVEN

Psychosis in the Collective: The Group as Agent of Unconscious Phantasy

ALICE MILLER offers a theory that links repressed memories of the self to forms of collective political action. She uncovers forces that may help to account for the psychotic exercise of power in political contexts. For Miller the facts of child abuse are critical in structuring unconscious phantasies. But—and this I believe is a real limitation in her theory—she ignores or downplays several object-relational factors that figure into preoedipal pathology, notably the role and function of maternal identification and its consequences for group behavior.

Both Otto Kernberg and Janine Chasseguet-Smirgel see in the operations of certain kinds of groups a preoedipal pathology, psychological distortions suggesting a collective projection of wishes or phantasies involving *maternal* reunion or fusing. They supply the psychodevelopmental component that is missing in Miller's psychoanalytic "revisions" and which aligns their work more closely with the functions Melanie Klein (1935, 1946) assigns to phantasy in mental operations and the power Kristeva attaches to the maternal *chora*.

In the psychoanalytic theory that derives from Freud and Klein, it is not essential that child abuse exist as a historical fact for the unconscious to forge destructive group-dependent phantasies and to determine the configurations of power. Further, both Chasseguet-Smirgel and Kernberg move beyond the classic Freudian view of group behavior as a replay of the oedipal situation or as solely circulating around paternal presence and authority. The group's presence in what the leader is and what the leader formulates is much more dramatic in these theories than in Miller's. Leader and followers exist in a dialectical relationship with each other. It is not so much that the leader frames the political project and then imposes a harsh paternal will on the group, but that the group selects the leader who most clearly acts out and formulates the group's unconscious, preoedipal aims.

For Chasseguet-Smirgel, significant components of *maternal* identification account for group action that takes as its objective the violent imposition of power on others. Groups whose identity derives from collective acts of violence may be "auto-engendered," she believes, evolving "not around a central admonitory figure [for example, Freud's primal father] but around the group itself." The group makes frenzied efforts to forge an identity by destroying difference and fusing with an omnipotent maternal ego ideal. In its regression toward oneness, the group may push its individual members toward less-differentiated and therefore more totalizing and absolute forms of psychological organization; identification of self with group in these instances suggests the "hope of a fusion between the ego and the ego ideal by the most regressive means" (xv), that is, by the annihilation of difference and glorification of an omnipotent unity that duplicates, on a political level, the infant's primal narcissistic fusion with the maternal object or part-object. Otto Kernberg, Wilfred Bion, and Julia Kristeva (notably her work on the "foreigner" and nationalism) also see evidence in group behavior of these preoedipal dynamics, irresistible regressive strivings for merger and fusion, primitive defenses, like Maureen's, that imply critical deficiencies in preoedipal psychological development. It is an argument quite at odds with Alice Miller's.

Chasseguet-Smirgel uses the theory of regression to describe aspects of the collective behavior of Nazis, who, in her view, insisted on the glorification of the Aryan mother and the "veritable eradication of the father and the paternal universe as well as everything that derives from the Oedipus complex" (xv), namely, rebellion, individuation, the attainment of autonomy, and the respect for otherness. The idealization of nature, the appeal to biological purity, the fantasies of union with an idealized racial history and the untainted unity of race and self in early Germanic mythology revealed "an aspiration to merge with the all-powerful mother" (xv). Nazi ideology embodied these idealizations. (This kind of phantasy receives little attention in Miller's psychoanalytic interpretation.) In the midst of this highly charged imagery, delusions masquerading as knowledge, group identity and its consuming visions overwhelm individual autonomy. The group encourages a pathological dependency and belief that inhibits participatory deliberation and destroys tolerance. Oedipal detachment, individual resistance to the group dynamic, becomes impossible and undesirable. From Chasseguet-Smirgel's perspective, it is not child abuse that creates the unconscious phantasy but strong preoedipal wishes for merging with an omnipresent maternal oneness; this wish for fusion obliterates any respect for otherness and opens the possibility for targets of annihilation.

Wilfred Bion and the Basic Assumptions

It is Wilfred Bion (1961) who initially formulated the theory which holds that the group produces a leader to fit its own destructive psychopathological formations. Bion sees a relentless dialectic at work, considerably more complex than Alice Miller's linkage of child abuse and historically destructive ideologies. In Bion's view not only does the leader influence the group, but unconscious processes indigenous to the group and hidden from its members' conscious awareness continually affect the relation between what the leader does and says and what the group experiences. Unlike Alice Miller, Bion does not trace the origins of group behavior to specific abusive events in the pasts of individual group members, including that person "chosen" as leader. In this respect, Bion amplifies the Platonic argument that the individual self and the group, or collective self, exist in a reciprocally infusing relationship. In particular, he shows how collective action frames experience for the individual, how tendencies toward psychotic resolutions in groups induce similar feelings of fragmentation and disintegration in the individual. Bion writes: "The individual is a group animal at war, both with the group and with those aspects of his personality that constitute his groupishness" (168). In Plato's terms, groups harbor "fevers," "deceit," and "violence."

Plato equates madness, or at least one "type" of madness, with tyranny. Book 9 of *The Republic* demonstrates that the character of the tyrannical self and the character of the tyrannical state exist in a kind of reciprocal prison, a psychotic condition. Further, the corrupt state as a group affects the "nature" or character of the corrupt leader. Bion's theory (1961) grounds the collective side of this dialectic in a psychoanalytic inquiry.

Bion in addition has a distinctly Platonic view of "emotion." He thinks of emotions as universal states that contain a "form" or "essence" that may not be seen or known through the sensation of the emotion itself. It is an argument reminiscent of Plato's distinction between appearance and reality. For example, Bion suggests:

> Envy is typical of other elements of the personality in that everyone would be prepared to admit its existence. Yet it does not smell; it is invisible, inaudible, intangible. It has no shape. It must have invariance, or it could not be so widely and surely recognized; and if it has invariants it must be invariant with regard to some kind of operation and therefore there must be an underlying group of such operations. (1970, 54)

His description of the effective analyst involves a degree of rationality and distance immune to the effects of "memory and desire." Bion's analyst possesses or should possess a kind of pure, translucent "reason," a Platonic detachment from passion. "Reciprocally his freedom from being 'blinded' by the qualities (or his perception of them) that belong to the domain of the senses should enable the analyst to 'see' those evolved aspects of [experience, the 'things' in themselves] that are invariant in the analysand" (58–59). Again, consider another very Platonic sounding idea: "Nobody need think the true thought: it awaits the advent of the thinker who achieves significance through the true thought" (103).

Bion (1961) describes three different unconscious impulses (what he calls basic assumptions) which he says determine the affective identity of the group and its relation to the uses of power. Each "assumption"—fight/flight, dependency, and pairing—affects the kind of leader chosen by that group to carry out its unconscious aims. Bion understands the basic assumptions as essentially regressive, potentially psychotic. Even so-called "stable" groups harbor "psychotic anxiety . . . phantasies and mechanisms" (163–66) that may realize, on a public level, the horror of psychotic power.

Each basic assumption defines the group's will, and each appears with striking clarity when specific task functions break down, when the group's work-related identity fails to produce effective results. Each basic assumption exists almost as an independent hidden or unconscious relation within the group; each carries with it the dangers of a fall into psychotic time; and each conditions the kind of leader a group in turmoil will seek. For example, the dependency group, in Kernberg's view, "perceives the leader as omnipotent and omniscient and themselves inadequate, immature and incompetent" (1980, 213). This collective state of mind maps the external world with inner percepts that radically skew "consensual" reality. Kernberg continues: "Primitive idealization, projected omnipotence, denial, envy, and greed, together with defenses against these, characterize the dependency group. Its members feel united by a common sense of needfulness, helplessness, and a fear of an outside world vaguely experienced as empty or frustrating" (213).

Bion contrasts conscious processes of group interaction, used by what he calls the work or task group, to the unconscious structures that appear in the processes of the basic assumption group and seem to drive it relentlessly, frequently with disastrous results. Often the basic assumptions take the group to the psychotic border, erode its historic and social identity. As work functions or tasks break down or become obscure or confused, the group finds itself overwhelmed by the basic assumptions. The consequence is a group defined by feelings that are motivated by primitive unconscious phantasies. Power, in these instances, becomes perverse. Projection, idealization, projective identification, omnipotence, crippling anxiety, and fear (the omnipresence of psychotic time) dominate the group's thinking. Dependency, pairing, fight/flight derive from a psychotic core, which, like psychosis in individuals, erodes rational judgment, historical structure, and consensual reality and intensifies the self's sense of fragmentation, helplessness, and depersonalization. Fear, aggression, rage, anxiety, panic—all these "Hobbesian" qualities of experience, which Bion sees as the product of preoedipal object relations, characterize the dominion of the basic assumptions. The group may turn power to self-destruction, or it may perceive that its survival requires turning power on others outside the immediate boundary of the group.

One major consequence of this dynamic, he contends, is that groups often choose their sickest members as leaders. The paranoid schizophrenic, the pathological narcissist, and other antisocial types often find themselves selected by the group to carry out its basic assumption. Countering Freud's argument in *Group Psychology and the Analysis of the Ego* (1921), Bion gives much more power to the group in defining the structure of leadership and the nature of its task. Kernberg, Chasseguet-Smirgel, and (interestingly) Kristeva follow Bion in this respect. The leader, in Bion's interpretation, does not impose his or her will on the group; rather, the leader is an extension of the group will. It is not that the character of the self determines the character of the group but the other way around: the group's affective identity determines the nature of the individual "self." Each exists in a reciprocal relationship with the other.[1]

Bion maintains that these reactions or feelings are not based on a neurotic structure (Freud's argument in *Group Psychology*) but involve more diffuse and primitive dynamics (for example, abjection) that suggest the group is reacting not to a father figure but to deep-seated fears of its own fragmentation and helplessness. Maureen's preoedipal pathology, the consequence of maternal absence or abandonment, is a microcosm of this collective event. "Groups would, in Freud's view, approximate to neurotic patterns of behaviour," Bion writes, "whereas in my view, they would approximate to the patterns of psychotic behaviour" (1961, 181). Kristeva and Chasseguet-Smirgel seem inclined to follow Bion in this respect.

The Group as Psychotic Agent

Bion's basic assumption groups possess frightening properties; he describes a parable of descent into a psychotic time where nothing is familiar, where the world appears in the ominous gray of panic, anxiety, fear, compulsion, and fragmentation. Attacking Aristotelian values of cooperation, participation, reason, the basic assumptions push aggregations and individuals into anticivil Hobbesian "natural conditions" where life *and* power indeed appear to be "nasty, brutish, and short." The wish to murder and annihilate, the wish to be murdered and to be annihilated, the sense of the world as full of hostility, foreboding, imminent death—all these states of mind (power as domination, aggression, and ultimately fragmentation), what Bion calls the group mentality, serve to erode whatever connection the self and the group self had to "rational," calm, deliberative procedure or law.

The basic assumptions cut through law, history, and time; they propel the individual into a psychological place that obliterates historical identity. Nothing remains but impulse and power; the secondary process defenses—work, task, purpose, agreement, volunteerism, cooperation—are washed away in the omnipotent identities of the basic assumptions. This is a presymbolic understanding, an assertion of unconscious phantasy as both will and desire, prelinguistic recognitions. In a strangely Lacanian observation, Bion suggests that "the 'language' of the basic-assumption group lacks the precision and scope that is conferred by a capacity for the formation and use of symbols" (186). Periodically, a mystical (almost Jungian) tone intrudes in Bion's conception of the valency or unity of group life: "Every human group instantaneously understands every other human group, no matter how diverse its culture, language, and tradition, on the level of the basic assumptions" (186).

Take, for example, pairing. Bion sees it as a universal wish that something yet unborn will spring from the group and deliver it from its hopelessness and despair. That function may be imputed to a "couple" or an idea or an activity indigenous to the group's immediate experience. But in Bion's terms, the basic assumption of pairing is a profound unconscious *wish* that represents itself in the group as a whole. Pairing is not culture dependent; it is a universal aspiration, to be found in all groups, in all times and places. This is what I mean when I suggest that Bion's theory possesses a peculiar Jungian "tone." At times the basic assumptions resemble the Jungian archetypes. Like archetypes, the basic assumptions are timeless, not dependent on linear time frames. They exist independently of the group's conscious collective will.

Again I want to emphasize that the basic assumption leader may be a person who embodies the group's own anxieties and articulates them in the context of group action. Therefore, the person *nominally* "in charge" or "leading" or administering in any given group may not be the person chosen by the group to represent its *irrationality:* "The basic-assumption phenomena appear far more to have the characteristic of defensive reactions to psychotic anxiety" (189). The real, effective leader will arise spontaneously, the product of an unconscious group will. As in Plato's tyranny, it is not reason or administrative rationality that guides the deliberations of such groups but the driving force of psychotic time and its embodiment in power. Impatient with intellectualism, with restraint, the basic assumption group seeks action; impulse motivates the phantasy; and the individual within the group may not be considered to be "master of his fate" (91).[2]

A curious paradox runs through Bion's analysis. On the one hand, he contends that all individuals begin and end in groups; the self is a group or, as he puts it, an "Aristotelian" creature. All human beings have some valency for groups. Yet, on the other hand, the dimmer side of his argument is equally compelling. Groups may become highly fluid and regress to "structure-less" conditions that permit their transformation into frightening engines of annihilation employing power in the service of tyranny or breakup. It is a state of being Bion likens to psychosis. In a particularly chilling passage, he speaks of the basic assumption, dependency: "The belief in the holiness of idiots, the belief that genius is akin to madness all indicate this same tendency of the group to choose, when left unstructured, its most ill member as its leader. Perhaps it is an unconscious recognition that the baby, if only we had not become accustomed to associating its behavior with its physical development, is really insane" (122). Imagine the destructiveness, Bion seems to be saying, of the infant's rage. Look at what it signifies in the context of collective power, the actions of groups, and by implication, the policies of nations.

Bion acknowledges the need for rationality and cooperation; yet, he reminds us of the forces that threaten these essential social goods. Cooperation and reason, the dynamics of consensual reality which are basic to the human project, become fragile under the influence of the basic assumption group and its totalizing forms of power. Intellectual understanding, scientific investigation, limits and constraints are vital to a democratic society, but the basic assumptions, propelled only by a dangerous, absorbing phantasy derive from a more absolutist and archaic preverbal "knowledge." Bion, like Kristeva, criticizes the proposition that "individuals are rational people and that the governing consideration is the limitation imposed by reality" (129), *but* he firmly believes that goodwill and reason clarify all disputes. With proper education in the basic assumptions, the group process, which requires cooperation, enhances human life and sensibility. The pessimism in Bion's argument derives from his conviction that it is impossible to escape the force of the basic assumptions' *presence:* the work group, devoted to a consensual function or task, "is constantly perturbed by influences which come from other group mental phenomena" (129), the basic assumptions as identity.

Bion sees certain social groups as paradigms for the basic assumption processes: for dependency, the church; for fight/flight, the army; for pairing, the aristocracy (because of the importance it attaches to breeding). Yet, he refuses to limit his analysis of the basic assumptions to any sociological definition or nomenclature. It is a psychological concept that appears in all human group formations. Bion accepts as ideals the constitutionalism and liberty posited by Mill, but he retains a Hobbesian pessimism regarding human cooperation.

Psychotic Process and the Erosion of Limitation

Whether it be Jenny's psychosis, Maureen's need to cut herself, or what Kernberg sees as primitive defenses in organizations and Bion as basic assumption groups—the movement toward psychotic forms of identification in all these situations determines power configurations. In none of these cases are psychological structures of restraint and differentiation capable of impeding the appearance of more violent forms of restitution. Further, each of these events suggests that psychotic forces lie closer to the surface than is usually accepted or realized.

That may very well be the historical fact. Societies, like individuals, can find themselves overwhelmed by psychotic power. Psychosis unleashes violence; whether directed toward the embodied self, as with Maureen, or toward nations and groups defined in Kristeva's terms as "other," psychotic phantasies induce violent, chaotic events. States that lose their sense of boundedness, restraint, and tolerance and find themselves pursuing destruction as an unlimited assertion of will demonstrate a radical psychotic inversion. Reading Robert Jay Lifton's *The Nazi Doctors* (1986), for example, one receives the impression that behind the scientific vision of a purified Germany lay a madness, a limitlessness, of incomprehensible proportions. "To move in a genocidal direction, that cure [the purge of biological impurity] must be *total*. It becomes an all-or-none matter, equally absolute in its claim to truth and in its rejection of alternative claims" (471). Genocide is an utter annihilation of meaning and value driven by an insatiable appetite for destruction. To live, to endure that world of absolute power, to be its victim, the object on which the racial vision masquerading as scientific fact *acts,* is to exist within a psychotic universe. It is to be completely trapped, surrounded by grotesque representations, macabre commentary on Freud's "death instinct" and Kristeva's "death drive."

There have been other instances in the twentieth century when annihilation and mutilation of the body and spirit have constituted the chief ends of state: the slaughter of the Armenians by the Turks, the Western front during World War I, Stalin's purges of the Kulaks, Vietnam, Cambodia, South Africa, and on and on. Are such acts rational, motivated by mundane or banal reasons of state? Or is the seemingly routine bureaucratic organization of mass killing a reaction-formation that masks a pervasive sickness and nihilism in the *culture,* a disdain, even hatred, for the being of those labeled as "poison," "impure," "corrupt," "defiled," or "not us," an active embrace of annihilating power as the singular means of dealing with such "otherness"? No matter how "banal" the bureaucracy or the bureaucrats look and sound (Hannah Arendt's argument, for example, in *Eichmann in Jerusalem*), such acts may suggest a deeper alienation and violent psychosis in the culture itself.

In *The Psychotic Core* (1986), Michael Eigen lists four properties characteristic of psychosis: hallucination, mindlessness, lack of boundaries, and moments of intense hate and aggression. Is not racism a kind of hallucination? Were not the ideologies spawned by the Nazi doctors to justify euthanasia and later mass killing peculiarly modern delusional statements, couched in the dry, objective language of a scientific vision? At what point does any public policy take on delusional and psychotic properties; at what point does rage overpower limitation, creating a kind of political mindlessness? At what point do limitations, all shared and consensual understandings, disappear and people become mere calculations in mass orgies of murder and death?

The psychotic self does not match the tame image of madness one sees, for example, in the film *King of Hearts.* To suffer psychosis is to be a human being whose connection with social reality has been totally eroded, whose inner life approaches a madness that inevitably operates on the level of bizarre and violent hallucination. To be psychotic is to suffer terrible acts of violence directed at the self, the death and destruction of "reason," the disappearance of boundaries, and uncontainable hate and rage appearing in delusional power schemes and acts of aggression directed against the body. To be mad, therefore, is to exist in the midst of a nexus of violence and power which annihilates consensual identity. Although psychotic persons undoubtedly are victims of a number of different internal and external "agents," it is still the case that to be dominated by unconscious phantasies is to experience a terribly violent state of being that brings torture, pain, and the experience of power as annihilation.

In a fascinating psychoanalytic approach to the creation of enemies in international politics, Vamik Volkan (1988) examines the relation between internal psychological precepts (images of "badness") and the politics of hatefulness, what he calls the "need to have enemies." Like Kristeva in *Strangers to Ourselves* (1991), he sees certain similarities between intrapsychic dynamics and the psychology of projection, which locates badness "outside," in some hated or denied other, Kristeva's "foreigner." "When kept inside," he notes, "unintegrated bad units threaten the self's cohesiveness: when put out there at a safe distance and used for comparison with good self and object representations, they can enhance the sense of self" (33). To define a group or person or race as hated, polluted, defiled, helps self-identity cohere by placing the self's internal sense of badness and worthlessness "outside". This "externalization" also strengthens group identity, since the hated other can be collectively shared and collectively destroyed.

Volkan continues: "I suggest that shared, durable, bad suitable targets contain the beginning of the concept of any enemy in a social and political sense" (33). The psychodynamic origin of the enemy derives from profound splits in the self or from powerful regressive dynamics that erode the distinction between outer and inner, thereby releasing an intense range of primitive affect. These hated others become *public* "targets of externalization" (32). The right political and historical conditions may lead to "mass group regression" (134); groups may "dehumanize" their enemies and transform them into "nonhuman or inanimate suitable target(s) of externalization" (120). The group comes to see itself as exclusive, possessing a boundary the hated other may never pass or threaten (the Nazi definition of the Jew); the border separates the pure from the impure, the defiled from the cleansed, the polluted from the good. Lifton writes:

> Nazi perpetrators had to see their victims as posing absolute danger, as "infecting" the "German national body," and as (in the last

> three words of Hitler's testament) "deadly Jewish poison." Similarly, "*Kultur*-poisoning Jews" were infiltrating the art world, and the general danger of "inner Judaization" and "racial pollution" was perceived as a fundamental threat to German biological and biosocial continuity and immortality. In addition, Jews—or the concept of "the Jew"—were equated with every form of death-associated degeneracy and decomposition, including homosexuality, urban confusion, liberalism, capitalism and Marxism. Goebbels could use straight medical imagery in declaring, "Our task here is surgical . . . drastic incisions, or some day Europe will perish of the Jewish disease." (476–77)

Volkan points out that this process "paradoxically" binds the group to its enemy: "Psychological borders are established between the group and its enemy to bind their felt and shared anxiety' (120–21). And it is hate that cements the borders, builds the walls, makes them impregnable, and forces identity in an unyielding position. Power is put in the service of hatred. Hatred then develops into a profound force in the linking of identity creation in the self to the regime's or the group's public aims and objectives. Politics is driven by what regression or splitting projects onto the public stage as the other, the enemy, the "target." The psychotic's internal world turns into ideology, or to put it another way, delusion on the individual level and delusion on the group level perform identical functions: both use power to annihilate.

Maureen's self-destruction, for example, her fascination with death and dismemberment, provides a kind of paradigm, a microvision of the terror of retreating from the world of limitation, proportion, sensitivity, and regard for the other—Freud's secondary process. Such "values," which indeed have their psychological correlates, are politically charged as well. A *personal* world of limitation, respect, shared understandings, regard for the body, sensitivity to others, implies a political world of tolerance, respect for rights, and acknowledgment of the right of the other to live, and to live without domination. Psychotic time, however, provokes domination and destruction; it is tragic, like the madness of an Oedipus at Colonus or the torment of a Medea, reflecting the tragedy not only of her family but of an entire society and culture.

Greek tragedy depicted the psychotic as commentary on public life: an explosive blend of hallucination, mindlessness, hatred, and lack of boundaries. For the Greeks, as C. Fred Alford (1993) has so eloquently explained, the tragic figure, no matter how destructive, symbolized the frailty and impulsiveness of human nature, its susceptibility to uncontained violence. In the twentieth century that violence finds itself organized, indeed mobilized, by a scientific vision that overlooks moral distinctions and acts in the name of a nihilism disguised as ideological call to action.

No matter what their cause, regression, splitting, and the accompanying release of violence cause tremendous harm to individuals and states. The lament of Oedipus at Colonus could not be separated from the fate of his city. Similarly with Medea: the breakdown of the polity is interwoven with the breakdown and violence of the self. The underworld of phantasy and rage transgresses what even the gods might tolerate.

Conclusion: Self and State

Plato in book 9 of *The Republic* speaks of the tyrannical nature that "never tastes freedom or true friendship," of "the man who, in his waking hours, has the qualities we found in his dream state" (1964, 576, 576b). He asks, "And may we not infer that the relation of state to state in respect of virtue and happiness is the same as that of the man to the man?" (576c). Using Plato's argument as a philosophical background, is there not a connection between what appears as regression or splitting in the self, the movement away from balance, moderation, compromise, proportion, and limitation—the repudiation of shared histories—and similar dynamics in large group situations? Is it implausible to expect that unconscious projections, as a form of power, might exercise a similar effect on the actions of states and societies? I assume here a psychoanalytic argument, probably not resolvable, over the *source* of unconscious phantasies, whether in the facts of child abuse (Alice Miller), in preoedipal wishes for reunion (Janine Chasseguet-Smirgel, Otto Kernberg), in oedipal attachment and idealization (Freud), in group-dependent unconscious impulses (Wilfred Bion), or in maternal terror and fusion (Kristeva).

In political life, unconscious phantasies take specific sites as their object: nations, races, markets, spheres of influence, territorial domains, and with terrorists, innocent bystanders. The violence of power works itself out on and through human experience: bodies, spirits, and minds.

The tyrant, says Plato, "teems with terrors and is full of convulsions and pains . . . he resembles the condition of the city which he rules, and he is like it, is he not?" (579e). What Maureen felt as compelling need, the wish to mutilate the very container of her being, finds historical and political shape in policies of nations and in the reality of organizational and administrative programs that direct annihilation outward—for example, the Nazis' early euthanasia program and the "final solution" into which it evolved.

Unconscious phantasies, through their projective power, can and do initiate projects of enormous destruction. In both the self and the collective what produces tyranny, appears in an annihilating power, whether that power be directed (in the self) against the body or (in the political regime) against groups defined as outcast, scapegoat, and evil. What this psychoanalytic view strongly suggests is that the political process and its leaders may themselves be susceptible to psychotic acts and perceptions.

EIGHT

The Ego Ideal: Power as Hate and Disintegration

THE question is how to explain the psychodynamic reasons behind the deployment of annihilating power and how to interpret the unconscious phantasies motivating the collusion between leader and audience. If Plato's argument is correct, then psychological processes at work in the collective *may* mirror similar functions in the individual. In this sense the concept of the ego ideal may provide a useful interpretive bridge between the individual and the group.

The concept broadens the reach of Lacanian/Kristevan approaches to understanding the relation between the self and the group. What are the effects of the fascination with death and destruction on the self, and more specifically, what kinds of psychological constructs and values derive from this early preoedipal play of death imagery and death drive? What kind of imprint does the experience of the imaginary leave on the psyche, and how does the psyche spell out these "imprints" in affective and cognitive ideals stimulating action and provoking identification?

It is possible to speak of both an individual ego ideal and a collective one—or so Janine Chasseguet-Smirgel assumes. Her work on the ego ideal and its functions is an important contribution to psychoanalytic theory. The ego ideal helps to explain the configurations of power. It functions as a motivating dynamic, a set of psychological percepts, defining and guiding action. For example, in the group the ego ideal appears as ideological formulation and proclamation. Its effects may be generative and creative or toxic and destructive. According to Chasseguet-Smirgel, it is a critical presence in the self and the group, and it accounts for the way power is experienced and employed and for the status of the objects power defines.

The ego ideal, an internalized psychological presence, imparts direction to the self's growth and disintegration. A healthy ego ideal encourages reciprocity, mutuality, sharing, cooperation, resolution of conflict, and tolerance. If it is pathological, its effects on the self may induce regression toward an idealized maternal fusion (Chasseguet-Smirgel's argument concerning violent group action), what Kristeva sees as "death-bearing symbiosis" with the mother (1989, 250). The ego ideal may induce a repudiation of consensual reality, a retreat to delusion, and the projection of a delusional epistemology as truth—that is, psychosis.

The ego ideal, therefore, is a very important concept in thinking through the relation among self, the exercise of power, and democratic practices. A narcissistically regressed ego ideal can motivate or activate unconscious phantasies leading to tyrannical uses of power and contempt for or denial of consensual reality. By contrast, an ego ideal tempered through transitional spaces and the kind of psychological growth that accompanies integration into larger and more inclusive social relations may have generative effects not only on the self but on the political life of the culture. Ego ideals that embrace consensual reality, that have benefited from the self's successful navigation of transitional spaces (and transitional objects) expand and enhance a participatory, democratic exercise of power. Ego ideals that derive from regressed impulses, from the psychological world of Kristeva's abject, split-off part-objects, remain riveted to narcissistic fixations and fail to navigate the "space" between solipsism and social exchange. Such ego ideals may have disastrous consequences for the self *and* the polity.

The ego ideal, as Janine Chasseguet-Smirgel formulates the concept, is the embodiment of the child's aspirations. It lies at the foundation of the value world itself. Because of its place in the psychological structure, the ego ideal is critical in the development of the self's moral sense, and it binds the infant to the broader social goals that constitute civilization. It therefore possesses profound political significance in the context of large group actions. When its functioning is healthy, the ego ideal is a profoundly civilizing dynamic; it opens the self to an appreciation of otherness as a set of facts that impinge on consciousness. It can enhance a culture's tolerance.

In more traditional terms, the ego ideal may embrace the Aristotelian ideal of participation; it encourages, if not authors, the transition from the primary narcissism of infancy to the interpersonal consensual ties of civil society. The ego ideal, then, in its Aristotelian form, may be thought of as an empathic, educative structure, but only if its functions are developmentally progressive, moving the self toward more complex forms of differentiation, tolerance, and respect for difference—in other words, a democratic self. Chasseguet-Smirgel sees the ego ideal as a *potential* ally of the political values of difference, tolerance, individuality, and democracy.

Since the ego ideal carries with it the elaboration of social value, it allows the isolated consciousness of the infant to forge connections with the external world by imparting form and meaning to the content of the self's functions. It is a mistake to underestimate the power of the ego ideal as an ally of civilization, a deflector of the consciousness of abjection, and a creator of consensual understandings. Nor should we overlook the function of the ego ideal in the infant's preverbal experience of ever-shifting and fragmenting objects, the psychoanalytic term for others or part perceptions of others' emotions. Thus, the ego ideal may work in the interests of civilization—integration into larger, more reciprocal, and shared power—or it may exert a profoundly regressive pull on the self toward Lacan's "primordial masochism," or psychotic time, a yearning for return to an archaic fusion. In its infantile and atavistic or psychotic form, Chasseguet-Smirgel maintains, the ego ideal involves a project that is "grandiose and unattainable" by adults "save perhaps in orgasm, [or] the most profound regression (psychosis) and death" (7).[1]

It needs to be stressed: what keeps the ego ideal involved in social formations, in civilizing functions and respect for otherness, and prevents it from becoming an agent that takes the self back to its psychotic condition (with the accompanying sense of unlimited entitlement) is the interpersonal environment and the struggle of the self to find its place in the world. The ego ideal in its integrative operation allows the self to find value by giving a *social* context to regressive narcissistic drives, the "desire to find a lost perfection once again" (8). In psychotic time, however, this social embodiment of the ego ideal and its limiting boundaries are lost; the facts of identity find themselves tied to the regressive aims of fusion and symbiotic reunion. Narcissistic regression overpowers the transition of the self from isolated internality toward social integration. A psychotic ego ideal, or what Thomas Ogden calls "psychological deep structure" (1989, 145), elaborates the most pathogenic, death-driven aspects of regression. It provokes in Chasseguet-Smirgel's view "a regression towards a more archaic form of 'narcissistic reinstatement', or even towards psychotic megalomania in which the original lack of differentiation between internal and external perception recurs" (1985, 28).

The effect of such regression on a leader's formulation of ideology, for example, or on a group's sense of its place in history or its narrative of the race or the biology of the future may be quite chilling. What is the lost paradise? Where is the "race" or "culture" to find that "symbiotic re-union," the timeless region outside of history? Who has to be destroyed to attain those ends? What myth has to be realized? What does "perfection" mean in a political sense, particularly if specific groups in the culture are singled out as carriers of "imperfection," "filth," and historical "dirt"? As Kristeva says, "The strange appears as a defense put up by a distraught self"; through projection, the other becomes evil, "a malevolent double into which [the anxious collective self] expels the share of destruction it cannot contain" (1991, 183, 184). The ego ideal may move the self away from unconscious phantasy toward the shared experience of law.[2] But, and this is its pathogenicity, it may find itself overwhelmed, even absorbed, by the self's lingering narcissistic impulses. In those instances, the narcissistic pull possesses terribly destructive implications—what Ogden describes as an "unspeakable terror of the dissolution of boundedness resulting in feelings of leaking, falling, or dissolving into endless, shapeless space" (1989, 81). Power is employed against limitation, boundary, and history.

Chasseguet-Smirgel distinguishes this formulation of the ego ideal from Freud's concept of the "level of development of the ego" (28). It is a much more significant structure in her formulation, since with Kristeva she believes the ego ideal begins its development long before the appearance of the linguistic injunctions of the societal superego, the paternal inscription. In infancy, the ego ideal is a compendium of images persistently elaborating the differences between inner and outer; for Freud, the ego ideal attains significance only as a linguistic presence that feeds into the larger aims of superego constraint. It has no preoedipal significance or meaning.

For Freud, the superego, which lay at the foundation of the development of the sense of conscience and value, performed socially valuable functions. It enforced the norms of society. It guided the ego toward the resolution of its most profound and vexing emotional dilemma: the Oedipus complex. Yet, the superego could also be terribly punitive, and Freud (1930) often remarked that the ego was the battleground where id and superego struggled. Yet, in Freudian theory, the superego is acquired relatively late in development. Psychotic time, however, and its disintegrative forms of power, derive from much earlier phases of psychological growth (Spitz 1965; Schulz 1980; Mahler 1968; Kristeva 1982). The concept of the ego ideal, which is present in the preoedipal self as the container of global percepts, thus proves useful in understanding the psychotic origins of persecution and torture, in understanding these phenomena as forms of power totally enclosing the self and body.[3]

Developmentally, the ego ideal *precedes* the appearance of the superego and therefore exercises a more controlling effect on the self's sense of itself as alive or dead, fractured or "whole," isolated or integrated. Persecution and torture, to speak of *perverse* ego ideals, lack the symbolic and linguistic distance that accompanies struggle over superego commands. Conscience, its recognitions and struggle, presumes some distance between the subject and the expression of feeling. A superego injunction might lead to the feeling "I am bad"; it is discernible; consciousness recognizes this judgment about itself. A perverse ego ideal, however, would have a considerably more devastating effect on the self. The perception would not be "I feel bad; why am I feeling so bad?" but Jenny's kind of perception: "I am bad; therefore, I am being murdered; something out there is sticking a knife into me; my head fell off last night; the water is acid; I can't drink it. I am punished for being bad." Victor Tausk's (1948) notion of the schizophrenic self as hooked up to a gigantic influencing machine that controls the body's every action gives some indication of the intensity of the persecutory and harassing elements of power in a psychotic ego ideal. As Ogden puts it, "Collapse in the direction of a paranoid-schizoid mode results in a sense of entrapment in a world of things-in-themselves wherein one does not experience oneself as the author of one's own thoughts and feelings; rather, thoughts, feelings and sensations are experienced as objects or forces bombarding, entering into, or propelled from oneself" (77–78).

For Chasseguet-Smirgel, sickness in the ego ideal demonstrates the triumph of primary narcissism, what Lacan calls primordial masochism, over the reality principle. The perversion may take many forms, but it is not amorphous or without terror. In adults, and this is particularly true of the two cases I will turn to in a moment, a psychotic ego ideal may contain sophisticated cognitive functions and operations. It may appear as a language game that totally preoccupies consciousness but with psychological underpinnings in psychotic time. Politically, it may appear as ideological statement, possessing language, reference, identification, value and, quite often, force (for example, Nazi pronouncements regarding race, culture, biology, and identity). These pathogenic ego ideals deny otherness and rigidly divide the universe between those who live and those who die; they persecute and torture. The Aristotelian values of respect, virtue, and participation have no place within an ego ideal that elaborates itself as a power regime of torture and domination.

The political ego ideal, as Lifton (1986) and Chasseguet-Smirgel (1985) have argued, is capable of horrendous acts of violence against the scapegoat, Kristeva's (1991) foreigner. Ideology replaces a dialectical concept of self/other with a rigidly nondialectical view of the supremacy of self-as-sameness over the vileness of other-as-different. Thus, in the racist forms of this relation (and the language used to enforce it), the vile other needs to be removed, denied, contained, or annihilated; the other/foreigner may be reduced to the status of a thing, an animal, an insect. In the white Afrikaaners' twisted idealization, for example, there is nothing morally wrong about transforming a majority of the human beings who occupy a given geographical space into mere things and computations.

This politically perverse "ideal" operates from closed epistemological assumptions and a logic that admits no other determination than its split-off and radically inverted premises. One would assume that seeing some meaning in the other would make it impossible to deny personhood. For example, blackness (in the Afrikaaner ideology), whiteness, cities, reserves, force, violence, rights, speech—all these politically charged concepts serve specific functions that depend entirely on the closed system of a logic that refuses to acknowledge the (black) other as an equal human being and that elevates a romanticized lost past to the status of a political program.

Clinically, where the ego ideal has become perverse, the self is enslaved and defined by its narcissistic introject, a victim of an internalized form of power. There is, as Ogden puts it, "no within or without" (1989, 74) or, as Winnicott says, no "potential space" (1982) between self and other, no experience "rooted in the dialectical interplay of the sensory and the symbolic" (Ogden 1989, 81). It is a "realm of experience that lies between a world of timeless, strangulated internal object relations [psychotic time] and a more primitive, inarticulate, sensory-based world of autistic shapes and objects" (108). In political terms, the equivalent is the tyrant or tyrannical regime. On neither the individual nor collective level does the perverse ego ideal create what Chasseguet-Smirgel (1985) sees as essential for healthy development. A good sense of "self-esteem will thereby be increased," making the self "more autonomous in relation to 'opinion' . . . and less dependent" on others for the "regulation" of self-esteem (155).

I want to describe two cases characterized not by tolerance and limitation but by the blunt and unforgiving power of tyranny, paranoia, and tyrannical judgment. In these cases the self and its mental functions are overtaken by starkly regressive ego ideals, what Kristeva calls "archaic inscription" (1989, 23), the primal maternal object, whose presence precedes language and the use of symbol. Again, the psychotic levels or moments in these patients demonstrate the microgenesis of forms of tyranny and oppression which in their political incarnations have the power to annihilate. "Never," says Kristeva, "has the power of destructive forces appeared as unquestionable and unavoidable as now, within and without society and the individual. The despoliation of nature, lives and property is accompanied by an upsurge, or simply a more obvious display, of disorders whose diagnoses are being refined by psychiatry—psychosis, depression, manic-depressive states, borderline states, false selves, etc." (221–22).

Pete: Murderous Rage and the Entrapment of Power

Pete was a thirty-six-year-old man with an overwhelming need to punish himself. That punishment took the forms of pounding his leg and head with his clenched fist, a certainty that his body had been poisoned by contact with a prostitute; and a conviction that he was forever condemned to physical torment by incessant itching in his genitalia and what he believed to be persistent discharge from his penis. His therapist noted:

> Study of this patient in a setting where close clinical observation is possible really discloses that much of his thinking is quite bizarre and distorted. For example, the patient once had the fantasy that if he drank a can of Drano, he would be dead eight seconds later, which would allow him to visit with his friend of childhood who had been killed in Viet Nam. On another occasion he entertained seriously the idea that everything that was happening to him was a dream which he could end by blowing his brains out. In addition to this, much of his worry about having AIDS or venereal diseases or unknown processes going on in his body, really has a delusional paranoid character to it. I think a good deal is clarified by thinking of this patient as being within the schizo-affective spectrum. This speaks to the severity of the illness and its chronicity as well.

During the six months in which I spoke with Pete, I became fascinated by his world, its images of perversion, his "fear of rotting, leaking" (Ogden, 1989), and the intensity of his experience of alienation and abjection.[4] He had, his therapist noted, "self-deprecating, despondent, aggressively pessimistic presentation, deeply negativistic system for maintaining a continuous sense of self." Yet, his interactions with me began to be defined by a sadism that placed us in a relationship of torment. I would ask him if he had gotten "better" and say that he "looked" better, when in fact it was impossible to tell, when I knew that such remarks would only make Pete feel worse since *he* knew he felt worse than he had last week. On his side, Pete persistently denigrated my research project, calling it stupid, telling me he enjoyed speaking to his therapist and social worker far more than to me, that I bored him, my questions were ridiculous. Why did I waste my time? His judgments of me and my project were accompanied by sneers and, on one occasion, an outburst of controlled rage which I experienced as physically threatening. It was at that point that I decided to terminate my conversations with Pete. I became alarmed not only at what I perceived to be his potential violence but at the sadistic folie à deux that seemed to be emerging between us.

One more factor of Pete's persona (as I saw it) also contributed to my decision. I came to believe Pete could be perfectly at home as a concentration camp guard and murderer. He seemed to be Kristeva's real and present *de-ject.* I imagined him as an SS guard at Auschwitz. I had recently read a book called *Escape from Sorbibor.* There was Pete: a camp guard murdering Jews. Pete, the tormentor, the destroyer, the annihilator, appeared in my mind whenever I thought about political oppression. I began to think of him as the prototypical Nazi and found myself shocked that people could even speak with him. Newspaper stories about mass murder, death, plane crashes, disasters whether man-made or "natural," brought Pete to mind. I envisioned him dropping atom bombs, engaging in terrorist acts. After conversing with him, I had the impulse to run onto the hall and insist that the nursing staff lock him up or, better, call the police and have him put in jail. His being became *menacing;* I questioned his therapist about how he managed his fear of this patient. How could he endure such torment? Why did he even continue treating such a terrible person? I wondered how the staff could deal every day with this vilest representative of the human species.

The Other as Mirror: Torture and Reciprocal Presence

Pete and I became enmeshed in the imaginative projections of a murderous rage, a dialogue about the worst kinds of power, which was the other side of Pete's intense helplessness and despair. I could not bear the rage and disgust inside myself; nor could I continue to sustain the grim view of the world which so defined Pete's sense of reality. In the final analysis I found it intolerable to subject myself to his punishment and torture, the constant denigration and intense rage he directed at me, and to my sadistic feelings toward him. I was not alone in my dislike for this patient; he managed to induce hate and disgust in everyone he came in contact with, suggesting the extent of his own feelings of worthlessness and self-hatred. I could never bring myself to sympathize with his position. There was not a shred of empathy in this relationship. My revulsion at his being, his spiritual ugliness, and the violence of his soul (for want of a better word) overcame any empathic sensibility.

I still believe Pete could be a good Nazi, that he could murder me or his therapist or his nurses and not feel any remorse, that his anger at the world could take the form of mass destruction. His alienation is prototypical for individuals who could be convinced that destruction and murder are noble ways of life. Pete might find himself in agreement with the sentiments of Paul de Lagarde, whom Lifton identifies as "a distinguished professor of oriental studies and a prominent Christian thinker," who nevertheless in 1886 "could denounce Jews as 'aliens' and 'nothing but carriers of decomposition' and declare that 'with trichinae and bacilli one does not negotiate, . . . they are exterminated as quickly and thoroughly as possible' " (478).

My disgust with Pete brought me too close to his internal world; I dreaded our meetings. I felt on edge all the time, tense, as if each second required supreme effort and patience. Pete's oppressive presence seemed to stay with me, even after our interviews were over. I felt troubled by my antipathy. No other patient had ever inspired such negative feelings in me, nor had I ever found myself judging a patient as I did Pete. I ceased, in fact, to see him as a "patient," a person with overwhelming conflicts, and began to see him as a representation or symbol of a negativity with political equivalents.

Is it that Pete is unlike us, the denied other, or are persons like Pete living embodiments of a self-recognition we choose not to accept? Do we store the Petes of the world away in mental hospitals in order to avoid looking at the full range of human disgust and hatred, the "baseness," degradation, and "abjection" that compose the historical monuments to the destructiveness of human action? From the perspective of formal psychiatry, Pete possesses no significance beyond his illness: he is sick; therefore, he is not "of us." His illness makes him into an aberration rather than a representation or, in Lacanian terms, a signifier of the universality of human hate.

When speaking with Pete became a form of torture, I found myself inside his world, and I had sense enough to step out of it. Such is the danger in listening too closely to the languages of madness. To be in Pete's psychological field, to listen to his narratives, to experience his projections, was to bear a persistent threat of annihilation. I could not sustain that view of self. Nevertheless, in enduring Pete, it was possible to gain some insight into that modality of human and political experience in which torture and hate define the vicissitudes of conscious life.

What, then, were the contents of Pete's internal world? What is one to make of a patient that Ogden (1989) describes in the following terms? "The emptiness of the schizoid patient is not simply the emptiness of loneliness; it is also the emptiness of ungroundedness in anything outside of his own mind. It is the emptiness of a self that is imaginary because it is disconnected from intersubjective human experience, through which the self ordinarily acquires a sense of its own realness through recognition by the other" (1989, 86). Pete's life, a stewpot of accumulated rages and fears, demonstrates, in Kristeva's words, an "integration of negativism, rejection, and death drive" (1982, 196). He mobilized a range of hatreds that "concealed the empty, dilapidated castle of a foul, putrid, crisis-ridden identity" (186).

Filth and Defeat: Pathways of Twisted Desire

Pete's thinking revolved around the belief that he had poisoned himself; he had committed a sexual sin. He understood his "mental illness" as a direct result of what he perceived as an unnatural act. He felt compelled to show God that he had cleansed himself of this crime, and he thought long and hard about how to do so. Yet, God refused to forgive, would not grant absolution for his defilement. Pete was in constant suspense, unable to figure out how to know if God had decided to forgive him. Pete stood in abeyance before God, trembling not with doubt but with rage at himself for being so bad that God would torment him by denying him any indication as to the nature, duration, or cause of his punishment.

Pete's ego ideal circulated around the prospect or, better, nonprospect of God's judgment, which was never a realistic possibility even in imagination, since Pete could not fathom God's intent and was enraged by God's unwillingness to reveal it. Pete's terror, intensified by God's refusal to forgive, worked itself out on his body: he became his own tormenting power. As with Maureen, the power of abjection directed itself against Pete's body: he slugged himself, pounded himself, complained of infection, itching, rotting, soreness, weakness, and so on. Lacking any idea when or if he would be forgiven, cleansed, and released from this terrible fate, he experienced intense anxiety and frustration. His state of mind was not unlike the more dramatic schizophrenic sense of reality—for example, that of the patient who believed that if hot water was put in the tub, it would burn off his penis, or that of the patient who feared wearing clothes because they were poisoned, or that of the patient who constantly walked in circles and hid under his blanket because of the fear he might be killed by unknown and invisible assailants. Pete gave similar powers to a God who sadistically refused a benediction that might have released him from the bondage of his sin.

In Pete's inner world, nothing was good. "He is without access to the mediation of love, he is a stranger to the world of forgiveness" (Kristeva 1989, 203). Defeated, an even more depressing rendition of Dostoevski's underground man, Pete wandered amidst a total nihilism. The world was dirty; he was dirty; I was filthy; his therapist stank; the nurses should be executed; the patients gassed. The constant itching in his genitalia convinced him he had contracted a degenerative venereal disease. He demanded treatment for "pus" coming from his penis, but the nurses found no evidence of infection or discharge. Nothing was worth living for; nothing mattered. Pete could have stepped out of a Samuel Beckett play.

Everything was defeat and rage, "dejection and murder" (Kristeva 1989, 199); playfulness and pleasure had no place in Pete's world. Nothing could replace his incessant macabre repetition of death, meaninglessness, and torture. When he slugged himself in the leg or the head, he seemed to be trying to pound whatever life remained out of himself. I imagined him becoming some sort of inert shell, without being or qualities, a kind of lifeless form whose sole distinguishing feature was his stare, a cold empty "look" that seemed to drip from eyes that were alternately dead or enraged. At those moments I thought Pete could kill, but in fact, as I later discovered, the stare disguised complex internal actions whose imagery was suicidal and self-mutilating.

Pete's ritual "refrain" ran something like the following: "Why do I feel like this; what's happening; why does this have to happen to me; what did I do to deserve this?" His sense of defeat framed his use of language and the symbologies he used to organize his life; he lived in a room without doors; he wanted to commit crimes; he felt knives sticking into his chest, groin, brain; iron spikes tore up his body, ripped it into shreds; whores rubbed their blood and vaginal discharge in his face; his body hurt. He felt his father would hire a private security force that would try to rescue him; they would clash with Sheppard's security guards; there would be a war. "People will be shooting each other to get me out to a VD doctor." Over and over he repeated: "Why has this happened to me? Why is God doing this to me? Why doesn't He help me?" Language lacked any emotion other than rage or despair. Speech embodied his "anxiety of disintegration" (Ogden, 71). And Pete, who saw himself as the most alienated man in the universe, became Pete the protofascist. "I wish I could kill the Jews; if I had my way, I'd burn everyone in the hospital; and then I'd take all the whores, all the filth in the world, and knife them one by one!"[5]

The God who presided over this mélange of twisted desire was not kind or comforting. He appeared as a tormentor, a wielder of sadistic power, lacerating his faithful servant for perversion and desire. Pete understood this oppressiveness in God's will as a kind of test; in order to become "good," Pete would somehow have to atone for his sexual crime. But he could not figure out the proper form of atonement; he had no idea what God wanted of him, merely a vague sense he was being "punished" for having had sex with a prostitute. Therefore he lived in constant pain and negative self-judgment; God, as ego ideal, came to Pete as torturing presence, leaving him no way out, no exit, just pain.

If the models of the ego ideal (in its socializing incarnations) represent an accommodation with the shared world of ends, purposes, and judgment, then Pete had radically reversed the entire process. *His* ego ideal, wrapped up in God's will and judgment, pulled him away from social reality toward a primitive archaic world filled with torture, poison, and filth. A judgmental, harsh, sadistic God, a self eternally poisoned—what "life" could Pete expect? He lay trapped in the misery of his imaginative projections. In Lacan's words,

> In madness of whatever nature, we must recognize, on the one hand, the negative liberty of a Word which has given up trying to make itself recognized, or what we call an obstacle to transference, and, on the other hand, we must recognize the singular formation of a delusion which—fabulous, fantastic or cosmological; interpretive, re-

> vindicating or idealist—objectifies the subject in a Language without dialectic. (1968, 42–43)

Think of Pete's inner world or, for that matter, psychotic perceptions in general as a "language without dialectic," without the consensual validation of others and without socially dependent ends. For Pete, moral points of view consistent with Aristotelian civility had no meaning. He simply could not escape the powerful "symptoms" that entrapped him, and his ego ideal evolved into what Lacan calls a "primary language," repudiating the language of civility, the Aristotelian world of ends about which Pete's God had been absolutely silent. Lacan notes that "words themselves can undergo symbolic lesions and accomplish Imaginary acts of which the patient is the subject" (65). For Pete such words came to represent the "pure state of the death instinct" (81) or Kristeva's death drive, a narcissistic project tapping the most atavistic elements of self.

In *The Interpretation of Dreams* (1900), Freud likened dreams to a window allowing the observer/psychoanalyst entry into the deepest recesses of the "mental apparatus." Similarly, the psychotic symptom, the *verbe* of this nondialectical language, and its existence in a peculiar time without boundaries, might be a clue to the nature of the psychological processes that influence value and perception. Pete's felt universe, his utter disdain for those he murdered, mutilated, and killed in his imagination, his fantasies of annihilation and destruction, his lack of compassion, sentiment, remorse, and empathy, his pervasive nihilism (reinforced through God's imagined judgment) may be considered a "window," in Freud's terms, into personality types easily at home in movements such as the Afrikaaner, National Socialism, or contemporary fascisms, whether state supported or the product of terrorists. Perhaps such types might be thought of as psychotic personalities who appear normal, who do not fit the classic caricatures of madness or dementia or schizophrenia but are nevertheless capable of doing enormous damage to the bodies of persons defined as "other." This type of personality has the power to provoke what Bion (1961) calls "nameless dread," or Ogden calls "experiences stripped of containment and meaning" (1989, 39).

Yet, I want to stress that to see the Petes of the world as windows into fascist or tyrannical personalities is not to deny the equally compelling and not necessarily antagonistic argument that groups composed of so-called normal people may be capable of psychotic acts. Pete may indeed be an archetype of the fascist personality. It is still the case, however, as Bion and Lifton have said, that the group persona or identity is capable of initiating horrifying and annihilating projects even though the members are relatively "normal" (nonpsychopathic).[6]

Marge: Internal Texts and Self-torture

Psychosis feeds on the twisted ego ideals of persons and ideologies that cast destruction and exclusion as the primary aim of political and public life, for whom power operates primarily as a fragmenting, oppressive force. Such "ideals" may very well take possession of persons and communities and, through their regressive force, take the self or community "back" to more primitive and absolute (authoritarian or narcissistic) perceptions and desires. Such regressions or splits in the self appear as self-torture and in groups as torture, the exclusion and domination of the hated other. Psychosis, with its power to disintegrate boundaries, to mutilate bodies, to induce hate and build visions that have the force of hallucination, is the critical variable. What unites the micro-level (Pete) with the macroview (the Afrikaaner, the Nazi, the jingoistic Victorian) is the power of regression or splitting to dissolve boundaries and to mobilize visions in the service of brutality. But such visions, no matter how horrendous, require language for their expression. Again, in Lacan's terms: "The Word is in fact a gift of Language, and Language is not immaterial. It is a subtle body, but body it is. Words are trapped in all the corporeal images which captivate the subject; this can make the hysteric pregnant, be identified with the object of *penis-neid,* represent the flood of urine of urethral ambition, or the retained faeces of avaricious *jouissance*" (1968, 64).

Nowhere is this material, embodied quality of language more powerfully represented than in the ritual power connected to words. To look more closely at this representation, I want to turn to Marge, a twenty-four-year-old woman hospitalized because of her inability to live, to move, to exist. Her symptoms, as her therapist noted, covered so wide a spectrum as effectively to incapacitate her:

> This is a patient who presents with a collection of *DSM-III* [Diagnostic and Statistical Manual of Mental Disorders, third edition] diagnoses. On Axis I she meets the criteria for major depression in partial remission. The patient also meets criteria for obsessive-compulsive disorder and bulimia. It is important to note that while some of her obsessional content is about food, she obsesses more generally about the notion of sinning and Satan and God. This religiosity and obsessionality is so intense that it makes one consider even more disturbing underlying problems, such as schizophrenia. There is also evidence that the patient meets the criteria for obsessive-compulsive personality disorder.

Marge was not classically demented, nor had she any of the outward signs of an uncontrollable madness. It would not be accurate to describe her as schizophrenic, but she did display psychotic symptoms and reflections. Her language world evolved around set-piece rituals that celebrated God's power to punish and Marge's belief in her predilection to sin and attraction to Satan. Marge was yet another example of Kristeva's notion of the abject or the psychological state of abjection.

Her obsessional actions involved "checking" to see if certain actions were performed correctly (she also made voluminous lists)—for example, closing doors, shutting drawers, and so on. Marge, her therapist noted, might have the "idea that she should do jigsaw puzzles from left to right [and] this may be Satan helping her to do the jigsaw puzzle." If she could stop at five checks, she knew Satan was influencing her, since five and six were bad numbers. Further, Satan's presence confirmed her sinfulness: why else would she stop with five checks and not four or seven? All forms of what Freud called the life instinct took on the properties of sin. Eating, sex, pleasure, life—all were equal to sin and filth.

"Virtues" were organized around punishment: obedience to ritual, self-inflicted pain, acquiescence to God's will, accepting pain as God's intention. While God was the object of Marge's desire, His presence in her life denied all forms of human desire. Yet God, or the ego ideal based on God, performed a vital function: He replaced the overcontrolling actions of a mother who in Marge's childhood had instilled a pathological fear of the world and a hatred of all strangers and otherness. Marge's rituals reenacted her mother's commands. They replayed a psychological environment defined by the mother's will (as subject) imposed absolutely on her daughter (as object). The God-demand (as twisted ego ideal) supplanted the mother-demand, and Marge experienced her guilt as "a visitation from God."

Countless rituals, list making, and checking, occupied every moment of Marge's day—from putting on her slippers and shoes, to her hair brushing, teeth washing, eating, getting ready for bed, closing and opening of doors, and on and on. Each ritual consumed consciousness and required all her energy; what emerged was an almost pure culture of the master-slave relationship. "Master" took the form of God as ritual; Marge's will and desires became the enslaved object. Or as Kristeva paraphrases this "paralysis of action": "I do not act, or if I do it, it is abominable, it must be reprehensible" (1989, 81).

Existence for the Other: The Power of Internal Enslavement

"In order to exist for oneself," Jessica Benjamin writes, in order to achieve autonomous selfhood, the Hegelian sense of being free, "one has to exist for an other"; to desire an other therefore means one wants to be recognized. "If I destroy the other, there is no one to recognize me." What the self gets back in return for this "loss of sovereignty" is "the pleasure of sharing, the communion with another subject" (1988, 53). Marge lacked these interpersonal capacities. For her, the effective field for being free was not the other and the other's desire but the projected images of a hallucinatory and often delusional imagination. The Hegelian concept of freedom moves the self outward, toward ever-increasing spheres of inclusion and experience. With Marge the movement was just the opposite: away from experience and inward, excluding the other, perceiving experience as the enemy; fixed rituals became the defining elements of action and perception, power employed against the self. Ogden (1989) describes this inward movement in an interesting way:

> To the extent that the bodily system is closed off from mutually transforming experiences with human beings, there is an absence of [what Winnicott calls "potential space"] . . . between oneself and the other

> (a potential psychological space between self-experience and sensory perception). This closed bodily world is a world without room in which to create a distinction between symbol and symbolized, and therefore a world in which there is no possibility for the coming into being of an interpreting subject; it is a world in which there is no psychological space between the infant and the mother in which transitional phenomena might be created/discovered. (60)

The self totally enclosed in its own projections takes itself as both subject and object. There is no distinction between inside and outside. Power in this context can only have a self-destructive effect.

If Marge kept herself firmly entrenched in or fused to her mother's view of life as dangerous, filthy, and threatening, she protected herself from fatal intrusions by the "outside" or "others." Her flight into ritual firmly anchored and shut off whatever identity she had, and ritual enactment became Marge's holding environment, her sphere of "freedom." The path of her therapy, therefore, was persistently obstructed by Marge's unwillingness to accept the indeterminacy of the interpersonal world, particularly the sense of reciprocity or shared experience. "If she has any kind of pleasure, she will have to 'undo' this with a great deal of self-punishment," her therapist noted. As her psychologist observed, "Others, human or divine, are to be placated; she cannot be sure what will fill the bill. . . . She continually waits for the expected rejection." The Hegelian project of self-recognition that embraces shared rituals was subverted and destroyed; Marge lived in the prison of her own internality; she locked herself in badness, worthlessness.

The whole picture of Marge's perverse ego ideal and her denial of otherness, persistent phenomena in psychosis, was complicated by her obsession with perfection, a power that tormented her. The belief that any action, any choice, has to be perfect instilled terror; it paralyzed her. It was impossible for her ever to undertake any action, lest it be imperfect, a confirmation of her deeply felt sense of worthlessness. Properties Kristeva attributes to "feminine depression" describe what Marge frequently projected as immobility, being stuck, lack of being, "a total paralysis of psyche and body, an irremediable dissociation between herself and everything else . . . implacable helplessness . . . an absolute impotence . . . prostrate, mindless, motionless, passivity" (1989, 72, 73).

Perhaps the most devastating description of all identifies such a woman as "the inaccessible citizen of the magnificent land of Death" (74).

Marge could never be "good enough." As her therapist described it: "She has been focusing on her extreme uses of impossible ideals of herself; when she does not meet these impossible ideals, she feels crushed and defeated." Any sort of action became a horrifying project since the ideal, by definition, can never be matched.

Not only did Marge face the impulse to perfection and the inevitable defeat, she found herself in a psychological place in which the torturing mother of her past had become the rigid and strict God of her present. It was a radical derailment of desire and its object. This unfree self, haunted by forms of power that lacerated her being, moved amidst images that kept her in a state of almost total domination. Otherness was transferred to the plane of hallucination and delusion: the fear of landing on a bad number; the tyranny of the inner ideal of perfection; the dread of the outside, the phobias against touching, verging on the paranoid, which her parents had instilled in her. The "outside," beyond the walls of her house, she had been told over and over as a child, kills, maims, and rapes. Her parents' injunction: "Stay away from the consensual, shared world; it will burn you to death."

Marge was first hospitalized for psychiatric illness when she was nineteen. For several years previously, her mother had been caring for her grandmother. Marge's mother had told her that if Grandmother were to die, Mother would die too. Grandmother died during Marge's first psychiatric hospitalization. Of course, Marge's mother did not die; Marge asked her why. Her mother replied, "You were sick so I didn't have to die." The message: "As long as you, Marge, remain sick, I, Mother, will not die. My life depends on your sickness." That message had been reinforced by a childhood in which Marge found herself surrounded by images of annihilation. Her parents had told her that men lurked outside, waiting to kidnap and rape her; therefore, she should not go out. If she went out, someone might place a nickel in her hand coated with acid; she would be scarred for life.

In the words of her therapist: "If she becomes well, she feels she will become isolated and separated from her mother, and then have no personality left. The notion is very frightening to her. On the other hand, if she stays sick, she will remain fused with her mother." Marge's subjectivity, if indeed she even knew herself as a 'subject,' suffered severe limitation. She found herself trapped in Ogden's "paranoid schizoid pole . . . characterized by imprisonment in a nonsubjective world of thoughts and feelings experienced in terms of frightening and projective things that simply happen, and that cannot be thought about or interpreted" (1989, 46).

It was Marge's belief, both conscious and unconscious, that if she were to become "well," if she were able to participate fully and effectively in the world of others, she would lose her "self" and dissolve into nonbeing. The only being she knew was punishment and self-punishment. Punishment told her she was alive; pain and the exercise of masochistic power acknowledged her selfhood. Sin and punishment confirmed her reality and theory of meaning. To cease being a slave, then, would be to lose or relinquish the only selfhood she understood *emotionally*. She *trusted* punishment and pain; they were the only constants that framed her life. Nothing "was" except pain, loneliness, and suffering. She saw no way out; she believed that by God's wish she was fated to pain.

Further, Marge was convinced that if she found herself free, in that Hegelian sense of growth and self-recognition, all the impulses that tormented her as a child, particularly eating and rage, would no longer be contained by God's power. She risked fragmentation and self-implosion if she escaped the mastery of God and ritual; she could not tolerate the prospect of this entropy, what from a consensual perspective would be understood as "freedom." Given this set of circumstances, Marge's "political" slavery found itself elaborated in the nonbeing of a kind of spiritual annihilation. Freedom in the Hegelian sense would for Marge bring fragmentation, disintegration, and death. It would mean nonself. Thus, perversely, Marge denied the world of otherness for the world of slavery. It was the ritual, the pain, the power of God's commands that framed her sense of identity and served as the objects of her desire. Since she could not bear the prospect of nonidentity (nonbeing), she remained trapped in the hallucinatory and sometimes delusional world of domination. It was a terrible sadomasochistic dilemma; her psyche as power devoured her body. Nothing was left but Marge's terrified and enslaved sense that what desire signified and what "otherness" meant was domination.

Marge kept the content of most of her rituals to herself; she hid it even from her therapist. But she summed up the intensity of the rituals and their association with God's judgment: "My greatest worry is that I won't lead the kind of life God wants me to." And once she asked me to leave our interview because, in her words, "You're keeping me from vomiting."

NINE

Identity and Power: The Disintegrating Self

WHY should we be concerned with disintegration, with the concept of identity? Because identities are what political regimes are founded upon; because the exercise of power, as Alice Miller and others have argued, molds the structure of the self. Explanations of political reality and motive must involve more than a consideration of "interests" or "reason" or the structure of historical intention. There is the self and its identity, its internality and the presence, creation, and cohesion of identity in groups and cultures. Disintegrating identities may invoke defensive power (regression, splitting), which in political contexts may take on fascist forms: the call for domination, racism, jingoism, fanaticism, and absolutism—the effects of tyrannical power.

In its human incarnations, disintegration of identity, induced by tyrannical power, is ugly, painful, and rejecting; it is not supportive of democratic or participatory ends because disintegrating selves are not inclined toward the negotiation, respect for difference, and autonomy that democratic regimes and selves require. It is quite the opposite: disintegrating selves and states may embrace absolutism, racism, and nihilism. Such phenomena are striking in schizophrenics, for whom the delusional universe is an endless array of totalitarian, absolutist, and racist fantasies. Democratic forms of participation require a sense of wholeness, a cohesive identity in the self; absent that, democracy itself becomes subject to an enormous range of influences, which, appealing with promises to counteract and "fix" disintegration, replace shared, reciprocal realities with fixed, authoritarian ones.

I suggest that democratic forms of participation involve an understanding of power and relationship which resists the disintegration of identity. The fall into terrifying psychological places is unlikely to enhance the respect for human dignity and rights which lies at the heart of democratic theory. Further, the breakup of the self is much more than an intellectual proposition; to "break up" the self means, from a psychoanalytic point of view, to assault the self's boundaries and its stabilizing structures. Relationship and its operation are disrupted, and breakup invariably involves some form of regression or splitting in which the self is thrown back to earlier (in a psychological sense) modes of functioning.

One of the most dangerous consequences of regression is to be thrown back to a paranoid-schizoid state of human experience. The clinical effects of this kind of regression are quite compelling—certainly different from the redemptive or romantic styles of madness one sees in recent films (for example, *The Fisher King* and *What about Bob?*). Real live disintegrated selves are not pretty, nor do such selves experience themselves as Nietzschean transcendent forces, modern-day Zarathustras, dancing their way to knowledge. Quite the contrary: if such persons are not howling, weeping, cutting themselves with whatever they can get their hands on, smearing feces on the wall, mumbling incoherently, or shouting profanities, they lie in bed staring at the ceiling with a deadness that is not revelatory but defeated.

I have great difficulty seeing the benefits in shredding identities, in advocating the nothingness of an identity-less existence. Free falls of whatever kind are not fun; you end up as a pile of crushed bones. In a psychological sense, that is exactly what happens to people without identities: the abuse of self, the destruction of language, and the annihilation of meaning and hope—or, in Bion's terms, psychosis and insanity. To be a *good* democrat one must possess a sense of self situated in a resilient identity bounded by shared, reciprocal power. The terror of free fall or nothingness does not contribute to a firm sense of human or communal purpose. Disintegrating selves possess no sense of community, reciprocity, or reality as a continuing historical experience and little, if any, self-respect or dignity.

Having observed the tragedies of madness, I find it inconceivable that anyone might celebrate the social potentiality of severe psychological breakdown. Disintegration is a tragedy, as the Greeks understood quite well. So did Shakespeare, Marcel Proust, Franz Kafka, and in the modern context, Toni Morrison, Hélène Cixous, Luce Irigaray, Jacques Lacan, and Julia Kristeva, just to name a few. The postmodern rush to embrace disintegration as an ideal ignores this repository of knowledge. Euripides' Bacchae, Shakespeare's Richard III and King Lear, Toni Morrison's Pecola in *The Bluest Eye,* the French feminists' critique of patriarchy reveal the connections between disintegration in selves and disintegration in culture and the relation between disintegrating political and psychological environments and the brutal effects of personal and political power.

It should also be noted that cognitive interests and enlightened rationality, while certainly important, are insufficient basis for a theory of the democratic self. As Mark Warren puts it, "The self is not just what we can articulate linguistically as its identity. It is also constituted by inarticulate strivings, desires, needs, compulsions, and sentiments, as well as connections to the world that escape language, such as nonverbal communications and sensuous, aesthetic, and spatial relations" (1992, 15). A theory based only on rational considerations, on the rational evidence of discourse, misses what may be more pessimistic readings of dangers to the democratic self, which arise out of psychoanalytic theory—particularly the Kleinian/Kristevan view of the unconscious and its productions.

Melanie Klein's concept of regression to a paranoid/schizoid internality and Julia Kristeva's concept of abjection describe in the self a breakup of identity that can be extraordinarily damaging. In both personal and political life, as I have shown, the self's retreat to primitive forms of mental functioning threatens democratic processes of exchange and transformation, in addition to plaguing consciousness with tyrannical and delusional forms of power. The paranoid self is certainly no democrat, nor is the schizophrenic, who searches for absolutist resolutions. Nor is schizoid detachment, which brings on cold, lifeless, and empty or emptied-out readings of power and life, conducive to democratic participation.

Power is the central problematic in political reality, and how power is internalized and shaped determines whether one engages in democratic or nondemocratic political practices. Shared power obviously tends toward democracy; absolutist power, veers away. What, however, is the effect of power on identity? Is one's identity as a human being, the sense of one's bounded self, related not only to how one exercises power but to how one grasps or feels its presence? And does the question of identity have anything to do with the self's organization of its internal object relations? If so, how the self conceives of power may be intimately related to how power was exercised on the self, and how the self internalized, experienced, and phantasized forms of power encountered in its life-space at critical psychodevelopmental moments.

If the self understands power according to the radical emotional oscillations of the paranoid-schizoid stage, then a yearning to return to that form of power may arise, an unconscious phantasy (for example, Kristeva's view of maternal fusion) that lingers in the self. Chasseguet-Smirgel (1985) speaks about this phenomenon as a phantasy, a wish to return to or capture an oceanic oneness based in an omnipotent identification with the mother. This is a dangerous form of power because it is exclusionary; it rests on a wishful, narcissistic symbiosis with a force greater than oneself, a delusion, rather than a progressive effort to diminish the presence of such forces within the self. The wish for or phantasy of fusion is hardly a creative or democratic form of power. Selves drawn to paranoid and schizoid resolutions can hardly be said to respect shared, reciprocal forms of power.

If D. W. Winnicott is right in his theory of transitional objects (and I return to this theory in more detail in the next chapter), the self moves from primary narcissism to an engagement with social reality in a process largely determined by the presence of transitional objects and transitional spaces. The transition is characterized by a certain mobility and plasticity. "It is a living part of the dynamic stream of rearrangement that is the growth of the personality" (Lewin and Schulz 1992, 66). This fundamental socializing dynamic draws the self from its narcissistic state of nature into emerging social relations, but if the self becomes terrified in posttransitional space, if the process is "arrested in a form that does not change in keeping with changing adaptive demands both from within and without" (66), if the self engages in actions that repudiate its sociality and shared reality, then power as a drive becomes tied to paranoid and schizoid psychological dynamics. And power in this *form* degenerates into pathology, sickness, violence, and terror.

The self caught up in narcissistic grandiosity or a desire to fuse with some force "greater" than itself poses a considerable threat to democratic process and the *civitas* necessary to respect and maintain rights. All too often in the twentieth century, power has appeared as cruelty, indifference, and a sadistic willingness to drive the other or the group into states of distraction and madness.[1]

The Value of the Psychoanalytic Position

Much recent criticism of Freud and psychoanalysis sees the psychoanalytic project as a monolithic reading of what the self is. This view misunderstands the psychoanalytic frame. While there is much to admire in Alice Miller's work, for example, her often harsh attacks on contemporary psychoanalytic thinking ignore vital aspects of what the theory *explains*. In *Banished Knowledge* (1990a), she repudiates with great bitterness much of the psychoanalytic influence on her earlier work and maintains that psychological suffering derives primarily, if not exclusively, from abusive families and the experience of children in such families. It is almost as if she retreats to a single-cause explanation. In my view, her theory is simply not comprehensive enough; there are other psychoanalytic approaches to understanding the political behavior of groups.

Psychoanalytic theory does not deny the reality of childhood abuse, but it posits a phantasizing component of the self which can be as strong (given the right circumstances) as forms of actual physical abuse. We may abuse ourselves psychologically for reasons not of our own choosing. Phobias, borderline rages, schizoid withdrawals, narcissistic disorders may derive from unconscious mental processes and the phantasies that accompany repression and splitting. Psychoanalysis as a response to human suffering sees the self as a complex bundle of emotions and feelings deriving both from hidden unconscious processes and from actual concrete experiences in the world.

Miller writes:

> With his drive theory Freud has inflicted great harm on humanity. Instead of taking his personal plight seriously, he sought shelter from it behind theories. By going even further, by founding a school and dogmatizing his theses, he institutionalized the denial that endowed the lies of pedagogy with alleged scientific legitimacy. For the Freudian

> dogmas corresponded to the widespread notion that the child is by nature wicked and bad and must be trained by adults to be good. (1990a, 57)

Not exactly Freud, but what kind of psychoanalysis is Miller referring to? Because psychoanalysis posits phantasy as an ingredient of neurotic and psychotic conflict, she believes it must be denying actual child abuse, and that denial delegitimates psychoanalysis for her. This reasoning distorts the psychoanalytic project: even if we disregard the many psychoanalytically trained therapists who treat actual cases of child abuse, it is not true that the abuse theory and the phantasy theory are in conflict. They describe two radically different orders of experience, which are clinically distinguishable. Only the most dogmatic analyst would consider narratives of child abuse by father or mother to be figments of the imagination or elaborate stories that disguise a wish for sexual relations with the parent. And there is certainly enough room in the different variations of psychoanalysis to account for emotional pain as a product of *both* actual abuse and the phantasies that build on that abuse or that derive from unconscious wishes having nothing to do with child abuse.

Psychoanalysis is a therapy, a process of understanding the self, a revelation in language allowing for the description and potential demystification of repressed, denied, or split-off areas of the self. It encourages a knowledge of self through other. The analyst-analysand relationship (a "formal" psychoanalysis) is complicated; it is hardly fitting for a victim of child abuse. I know of no psychoanalyst who would prescribe psychoanalysis proper as treatment for the psychological effects of child abuse. Miller, then, in this aspect of her argument, has attacked a straw man of her own creation. Who is abusing whom here?

Similarly with E. Fuller Torrey's *Freudian Fraud,* a scandalous, political-historical assault on Freud, as if psychoanalysis and Freud are identical, as if this "90-year-old grandfather," as Miller puts it, lacked intellectual grandchildren and great-grandchildren who have transformed and enriched the tradition. There is little if any mention of the *tradition* itself: Melanie Klein, D. W. Winnicott, Jacques Lacan, Heinz Kohut, Otto Kernberg, Janine Chasseguet-Smirgel, Erik Erikson, Julia Kristeva, and so on. It would be like arguing that Marx and Marxism or Locke and liberalism are identical.

Fuller Torrey (1992) contends that science has not demonstrated the truth value of Freudian precepts, that psychoanalysis has little therapeutic value, that its usefulness to society has been demonstrated to be ideological and polemical. As a means of understanding the severe mental illnesses, he argues, it has been a dismal failure; chemical and biological dysfunctions have nothing to do with the Freudian notion of childhood phantasy or oedipal conflict.

In assuming that psychoanalysis is Freud, critics like E. Fuller Torrey make a terrible mistake; Freud, it is true, was dogmatic, but the tradition of psychoanalysis is as complicated as any other philosophical history. It is absurd to speak of it as if it were an intellectual monolith, as Fuller Torrey does. And because the oedipal theory, theories of infantile sexuality, the psychosexual stages of development have not been "scientifically" quantified, he dismisses their explanatory value. The theory of psychoanalysis is not subject or even amenable to formal proof by the method of the natural sciences (scientific method as prescriptive function). Emotions, feelings, repressed or split-off memories and affect cannot be quantified like test scores on a computerized sheet. Nevertheless, there are criteria of proof which Fuller Torrey does not entertain: the place and role of myth and mythology; the self-reports of patients; the retro-dictive posture of psychoanalysis, which recovers the past from the present (in contrast to the pre-dictive scientific method); the methodology and techniques for uncovering mental processes and defenses; imagery from literature and art (see Kristeva, *Black Sun*); autobiographical narratives (Marie Cardinal, *The Words to Say It,* for example).

Fuller Torrey does not consider psychoanalysis as a process, as an evolving theory of the self and an explanatory framework for human behavior. He tends to see it primarily as a predictor of whether specific disturbances in orality and anality will affect adult behavior—a very limited view of the domain psychoanalysis seeks to explain. He summarizes twenty-six research studies into toilet training and anal personality traits and concludes that none of the studies confirms Freud's theory, as if this kind of analysis sums up what psychoanalysis accomplishes as an inquiry into disorders of the self. Such experiences as mourning, grief, loss, attachment, separation, fusion, regression, splitting, and so on simply do not enter into his calculations. Nor does he evaluate any of the recent French contributions to psychoanalytic theory.

It is not that psychoanalysis is "right." What theory purporting to explain human motivation can be "right?" But psychoanalytic theory and practice are, as E. V. Wolfenstein (1993) and C. Fred Alford (1991) demonstrate, a living, changing, transforming tradition that responds to suffering and takes psychological pain quite seriously. Psychoanalysis has traveled a great distance since its founding. It is not a thing in itself. It is not Freud. It is certainly not a mirror of its founder.

The Psychotic Substratum of Self Experience

I would like to turn to one concept in modern psychoanalysis which may shed light on identity, democracy, and the effect of power on shared democratic purpose. This is Wilfred Bion's (1984) concept of holding and the holding environment, the other as holder or container for unwanted aspects of self, particularly those aspects that appear in the exercise of power.

Bion's formulation of holding is useful because of its political implication and meanings and for what it reveals about shared or reciprocal power. There are two poles to this notion: container (holding and holding environment) and contained (emotions or feelings with possible toxic effects). Each is essential to the stability and resiliency of the self and to how the self experiences its polarities: as psychotic and therefore split off and not held or as integrated, unified, and whole and therefore held and contained—what might be called the "normal" or sane state of ambivalence and conflict tolerance.

This framework, says Bion derives from infantile experience. The mother holds unwanted or intolerable (psychotic) aspects of self, metabolizing or transforming unbearable rage or hate into bearable anxiety. The mother as container allows the infant to remain within a social relation without exploding either the self (literally) or the mother (in phantasy). Against the backdrop of this concept, psychoanalytic theory becomes extremely useful in understanding the relations among self, identity, and democracy and the dangers posed by disintegrating identities. A democratic self or identity is capable of both holding and projecting into the other anxieties whose toxicity remains below the psychotic threshold. That capability requires an openness and a willingness to sustain the other's bad self-representations without feeling overwhelmed or annihilated by the inevitable anxiety.

It is not an easy task, for holding presumes trust, reciprocity, and a willingness to tolerate the other's narcissistic retreats into omnipotent power, the psychotic part of who and what we are. Most important, it requires a willingness to defuse the toxicity and potential violence of psychotic power. Successful projective identification in a therapeutic sense (holding) means the psychotic part of the patient, as the patient experiences it, does not destroy the therapist. Similarly, holding permits the therapist to place those "psychotic parts" back in the patient, but modified so they can be sustained and lived with. Or to put it another way, an identity that works dialectically with others is an identity that will not be destroyed by the other's psychotic part-self or by the annihilating power held within the psychotic self. Selves capable of democratic participation metabolize psychotic phantasies through projective identification. The democratic self, then, is sensitized to contain the other's rage and to find others to metabolize and hold its rage, narcissistic impulses, and phantasies of omnipotence. Holding and containing, as a dialectic linking self and other, keep psychosis within the bounds of a civil self, and prevent a fall into disintegration which *may* lead the self back toward a paranoid-schizoid resolution of anxiety which is antidemocratic, absolutist, and risks identification with omnipotent power.

Roger Lewin and Clarence Schulz amplify Bion's concept:

> By holding we mean an action, literal or symbolic, that has the effect of supplementing the existing psychic infrastructure so as to render what might be an overwhelming situation less overwhelming, thus providing the patient a degree of increased security that allows for continued developmental effort and experimenting with new ways of experiencing that may have not only more adaptive promise but more promise in terms of self-realization. (1992, 116–17)

And regarding projective identification and the concept of the container or holder of unwanted parts of self, they write:

> The recipient of the projection is asked to function as a sort of safe deposit box for what does not yet have a secure place in the projector's self. Ultimately, his job is to hold onto the disavowed in such a way as to contribute to its possible return to the sender. The extent to which the recipient can perform this function depends on how safe, or at least "safely unsafe," he is able to feel with what the pressures from

> the projector evoke in him. . . . This correspondence is an active, if mostly unconscious process. It has a back-and-forth quality, almost as if letters were traveling back and forth, but written in a language that neither party yet knows quite how to read. (119)

Clinical Aspects of Holding: Bion's View

Before drawing out the political dimension of the theory, I would like to explore Bion's psychoanalytic formulation at greater length. He writes:

> When the patient strove to rid himself of fears of death which were felt to be too powerful for his personality to contain he split off his fears and put them into me, the idea apparently being that if they were allowed to repose there long enough they would undergo modification by my psyche and could then be safely reintrojected [that is, taken back into the patient's self]. On the occasion I have in mind the patient had felt . . . that I evacuated them [unwanted, hateful feelings] so quickly that the feelings were not modified, but had become more painful. (1984, 103)

The patient became increasingly paranoid; he thought Bion was refusing to accept parts of his personality. "Consequently he strove to force them into me with increased desperation and violence. . . . The more violent his phantasies of projective identification, the more frightened he became of me" (104).

Holding is impossible in this context; therapy as a dialectical process of transformation appears to be breaking down. The patient experiences Bion as unwilling to internalize and therefore modify increasingly desperate anxieties and fears. The patient becomes more desperate, more insistent, more absolutist in his demands. In this instance the failure of the holding function creates a more violent regime, a more destructive exercise of power inside the self and between patient and therapist.

For Bion, holding as a therapeutic function actually means containing the self's psychotic wishes and fears, its precivil being, its narcissistic yearnings for merger with an all-powerful object, its annihilating impulses, and its fears of being annihilated. But what is also fascinating about Bion's analysis is that holding and containing are not only therapeutic functions but also human psychological processes present from the very moment of birth. Containing and holding distinguish the human psyche from the animal one: "selves" are connected through what each one of us projects, as unwanted or unbearable parts of who we are, into the other. That is how we survive, how we live, how we interact, and how we deal with, live, and sustain the other's and our own repressed or split-off psychotic self-representations.

The closer or more intimate we find ourselves as human beings, the more open we are to receive the split-off or repressed psychotic core of the other. The farther apart we are, the more objectified or distant from our neighbors' lives, the more likely we are to create and implement social or political institutions to hold and contain or embody split-off psychotic aspects. Underlying the bleak humor of the Danny de Vito comedy *The War of the Roses* is a vision of how powerful and destructive psychotic elements of self can become when they are unhinged from their containing/container frameworks, no matter how defensive the constructs. For example, psychotic children are often created by caretakers who simply do not acknowledge this side of infantile emotional reality, who refuse to hold and contain the infant's rage, instead returning it unmediated and filled with terrifying phantasies. Uncontained rage is not integrated into the self structure and exists as a kind of loose cannon in the self, possibly provoking arrested psychological development or borderline or schizophrenic resolutions. (For Alice Miller, rage invariably works itself out on the body in actual physical assaults on the child.) Bion's great contribution was to demonstrate how real and present is this psychotic side of who we are and how rooted it is in infantile development.

> I felt that the patient had experienced in infancy a mother who dutifully responded to the infant's emotional displays. The dutiful response had in it an element of impatient "I don't know what's the matter with the child." My deduction was that in order to understand what the child wanted the mother should have treated the infant's cry as more than a demand for her presence. From the infant's point of view she should have taken into her, and thus experienced, the fear that the child was dying. It was this fear that the child could not contain. He strove to split it off together with the part of the personality in which it lay and project it into the mother. An understanding mother is able to experience the feeling of dread, that this baby was striving to deal with by projective identification, and yet retain a balanced out-

> look. This patient had to deal with a mother who could not tolerate experiencing such feelings and reacted either by denying them ingress, or alternatively by becoming a prey to the anxiety which resulted from introjection of the infant's feelings. (104)

The mother who performs effective containing, what Winnicott called "good-enough" mothering, is capable of holding those aspects of the self's insides which threaten to destroy it, the power turned against the self in the form of dread, anxiety, fear, rage, hate, envy, and greed. What is vital is that the *other* be there and present as container if psychological development is not to be dominated by split-off parts of the self. If the mother throws the projected pieces of self (its hate or rage or murderousness) back to the infant without digesting and detoxifying them, these "parts" will remain in the self structure as leading or driving emotional dynamics.

To contain the infant's murderousness is to hold the ancillary urges to murder and annihilation (hate, rage, and dread) in a whole or totalized self structure. The self's tendencies toward reciprocity, therefore, its capacity to move outward without being impeded by split-off emotional parts, will be stronger than the narcissistic pull induced by splitting. A self in which reciprocity and shared realities dominate, in which language and participation modify rage and hate, such a self structure will have integrated its hated aspects and will feel capable of tolerating and holding those of others.

The essential issue here is what is being held and what allows this holding to happen. According to Bion, "The link between patient and analyst, or infant and breast, [or self and other] is the mechanism of projective identification" (105). What prevent or impede holding and containing are what Bion calls "destructive attacks" on this link, efforts to destroy the projective process and thereby to shatter the dialectic between self and other. When that link is not established, as in the example of the mother who refuses to hold the infant's projections, a holding environment is impossible and the self is "split" into pieces that come back to haunt consciousness as hate, rage, and destructiveness.

> If the infant feels it is dying it can arouse fears that it is dying in the mother. A well-balanced mother [Bion has in mind tolerance, understanding, compassion, and empathy—the affect critical to any par-

> ticipatory environment] can accept these and respond therapeutically: that is to say, in a manner that makes the infant feel it is receiving its frightened personality back again but in a form that it can tolerate—the fears are manageable by the infant personality. (114–15)

The tragedy of the psychotic self is that it has externalized these fears. Their intensity makes it impossible for them to be integrated into the self's perception of its own being and limits. It is not "I am frightened; something is bothering me, scaring me, terrifying me." Rather, the psychotic self thinks the spaceship or the underground atom bomb holds the danger. Bion continues: "If the projection is not accepted by the mother the infant feels that its feeling that it is dying is stripped of such meaning as it has. It therefore reintrojects not a fear of dying made tolerable, but a nameless dread" (116).

Consequences of Attacks on Linking

"Linking" is a way of sustaining emotions or affects, particularly hate and aggression, so that we can tie or link ourselves to the emotions or affects of other human beings in such a way that the threats of fusion, annihilation, or fragmentation (of self) are avoided. Bion regards the attack on linking (which may push the self psychically back toward identification with omnipotent power) as "the central feature of the environmental factor in the production of the psychotic personality" (1984, 105). In the adult the rupture of the link releases entropic emotional currents, mobilizes hate and aggression, and destroys the holding/containing aspects of human subjectivity. The consequence may be a retreat into solipsism, with an ego ideal psychically projected as absolute power or narcissistic fusion. From the political perspective, the democratic process fails, and the nation finds itself dominated by vicious emotional currents whose destructive potential is enormous.

On the individual level there are certain internal dispositions or characteristics, what I have been calling phantasies, which play an important role in "producing attacks by the infant on all that links him to the breast, namely, primary aggression and envy" (105). Bion deduces this phenomenon by examining how his patients' attacks on links to *him* clearly frustrate his capacity to "introject the patient's projective identifications" without appearing to the patient to be going mad or suffering a breakdown. This phenomenon, he argues, is analogous to the infant's "hatred and envy of the mother's ability to retain a comfortable state of mind although experiencing the infant's feelings" (105). Or to put it another way, we want others to feel and be as miserable and hateful as we are. To attack the link between self and other (the capacity of the other to sustain the self's projections without going mad), therefore, is to attack an essential ingredient of democratic participation and a means of defusing or detoxifying tyrannical power.

The ability to sustain conflict, to tolerate difference, to respect shared power, and to retain composure despite seriously disturbed and disturbing feelings, signifies a psychological capacity to retain boundaries and limits in the face of intense emotional aggression. "Attacks on the link," Bion continues, "are synonymous with attacks on the analyst's, and originally the mother's, peace of mind" (105). What is being "attacked" is the crucial psychological mechanism that allows the self to defuse annihilating power, to use the other as a calming presence, the ability to trust the other *enough* with feelings the self cannot handle or transform on its own.

Attacks on linking seriously jeopardize the self's capacity to integrate and tolerate ambivalent and frustrating experiences. For example, in the patient-therapist relationship, the "patient's envy and hate" may transform into "greed devouring the patient's psyche" (106). The transference link between the patient's affect and the therapist's receptivity is severed. Analogously, in the infant (Bion establishes retro-dictive inferences from the clinical situation to infantile psychic reality), establishing the link through projective identification "makes it possible" for the infant "to investigate his own feelings in a personality powerful enough [or, in the case of the therapist, resilient enough] to contain them" (106). The "container" (the actual mother or the mothering person) provides a psychological environment with boundaries and limits, the very boundaries and limits the self is unable to construct and sustain for itself. Rupture of the link breaks the communicative and containing channels that transmit and modify affect between self and other, leading to emotional and psychological disaster.

> Denial of the use of this mechanism, either by the refusal of the mother to serve as a repository for the infant's feelings, or by the hatred and

> envy of the patient who cannot allow the mother to exercise this function, leads to a destruction of the link between infant and breast and consequently to a severe disorder of the impulse to be curious on which all learning depends. The way is therefore prepared for a severe arrest of development. (106–7)

The role and function of illusion (and, for the infant, transitional objects) as the agent for social change, facilitating transitions to more sophisticated and abstract forms of reasoning and play, is muted, if not retarded altogether. I have a great deal to say about this catastrophe in the next chapter.

Since for Bion psychological development possesses—or, more accurately, *may* possess—an Aristotelian component that tends toward an increased sense of autonomy, participation, and capacity to endure ambivalence, attacks on linking not only inhibit intellectual development but also have enormous impact on the self's relation to the larger community. Because of the arrest in development, the self's participatory and therefore democratic potential is injured. "Feelings of hatred are thereupon directed against all emotions including hate itself, and against external reality which stimulates them. It is a short step from hatred of the emotions to hatred of life itself," a nihilistic antidemocratic impulse (107).

Bion believes the damage done to the self by attacks on linking creates highly destructive internal percepts (the technical term being *introjects*). For example, the infant may experience the mother's efforts to "understand it" as hostile and full of hate. With the links severed, there is no possibility of any interpersonal dialectic, and unconscious phantasies of envy and hate may come to dominate the infant's perceptual universe. Bion sees resonances of this phenomenon when the effort of the therapist to understand the patient is experienced by the patient as an attempt to drive the patient insane.

To summarize: the attack on linking comes from tyrannical power, an internal or psychological "object" that hates pleasure, life, and the awareness that derives from participation and tolerance. "The patient's psyche contains an internal object which is opposed to, and destructive of, all links whatsoever from the most primitive . . . to the most sophisticated forms of verbal communication and the arts," as Bion puts it (108). In the extreme of this state of mind, which Bion sees as psychotic or at least as imbued with psychotic potential, "emotion is hated; it is felt to be too powerful. . . . it is felt to link objects" (that is, to establish relationships) (108). In schizophrenic states, the self chooses not to feel at all, since whatever reservoirs of feeling it retains are so full of rage that to "feel" this current threatens annihilation. The failure to develop linking mechanisms means that at least part of the psyche resides in a very hateful and cold universe, and this hate and coldness define not only affect but perception and value. This kind of split psyche finds its reason or rationality influenced in large measure by an emotionality with deadly and hateful components. The percepts regarding others which survive in the self "are perverse, cruel, and sterile" (109).

When these "perverse, cruel and sterile" remnants become politically charged, when such hatred takes concrete projective form in political or ideological calls for action, the result can only be a destruction of democratic, participatory reason. That is why the linking function, psychoanalytically understood, is so vital: it maintains a sense of reciprocal or shared power within the self. Attacks on linking have a tremendously important political effect. They encourage the release and expression of extreme rage or hatred, usually taking up residence in specific groups, scapegoats, targets of opportunity. Or they permit a complete indifference to the fate of others, specifically in matters relating to killing and massacre.

The Political Theory of Linking Objects

We split off the psychotic part of ourselves and place it in our politics. It is a collective act; the bridge between the psychotic and nonpsychotic part of the personality is not available. As a culture, we have no interest in communicating with that part of who we are which may be psychotic. We therefore split off our "unacceptable" or hateful selves, but we recover that split, we heal the break through public political acts that impose significant harm on others. We communicate with the psychotic part of our self by locating that communication in our politics. If Bion is right, we never escape who we are: psychotic and nonpsychotic. We only hide or repress or split off the unacceptable side of who we are and project outward, as collective phantasies, toxic emotions that take shape in political programs, acts, and ideologies.

This is a much different argument from Alice Miller's; for Miller, it is the collusion between an audience's repressed experiences of child abuse and the leader's political program responding projectively to these memories which generates the terrifying projects of destruction. For Bion, the psychotic substrate of human experience is far more extensive, far more a product of internally held phantasies projected as political policy, than derivative of actual experiences of repeated child abuse. What generates these phantasies in groups is a shared terror, a collective regression to a psychological place of omnipotent power or fear that constitutes itself as group action. The leader does not create a program; the group initiates a program and then chooses a leader who possesses the requisite psychopathological traits to institute it. Bion is less sensitive to the role of the leader as creator of destructive inspiration than is Miller, since for Bion the leader is almost an incidental choice of the group. The founding impulses to actions of destruction or flight begin in the group, and the group identity chooses the leader, not the other way around.

The public realm, in addition to being a repository of political organization and the locus of occasional democratic participation, may also be a place where society collectively enshrines annihilating impulses. Actions that may be considered delusional, psychotic, or "criminal" in the private realm may in fact be acceptable in public forums, constituting a legitimate part of national "policy," reasons of state, political imperatives. Further, the political capacity to institutionalize psychotic acts makes it possible to live in our public life in a kind of insanity (or, certainly, moments of psychotic unleashing), held together by what power projects as public "reason" or "rationality."

Consider, for example, the enormous bureaucracies Nazi Germany developed to deal with Jewishness, to govern everything from the manufacture of gases to deciding just how much "Jewishness" determined one to be a Jew. Were not these a kind of insanity, but with structure and science: reason in the service of psychosis? The engineers who built the death camps, the chemists who devised the chemicals for extermination, the doctors who supervised the selections—were not these scientists in the service of psychosis? We cannot be psychotic with one another; after all, to live the lives we do we have to be civil (Hobbes clearly understood this aspect of social life). We are constrained to act civilly, even if such action requires massive social denial, a kind of collective repression or splitting. We have to accept the limits of our own reason; otherwise we might find ourselves outcasts, thrown out of the civil framework, as, for example, are many "insane" persons.

But we surely can act uncivilly in our politics; there, we permit ourselves to demonstrate our barbarism, what Bion calls our "psychotic sanity," and that part of ourselves Bion believes is unbridgeable and split off on an individual level. Psychosis, however, *is* bridgeable on a group level. While the group is acting both insane and psychotic, the individual may retain the appearance of "reason" and "sanity." Adolf Eichmann was a good family man; he couldn't stomach barbarity in his own neighborhood; he had difficulty watching mass executions; but as participant in a group with a collective will and project, his actions became barbaric and insane. What is psychotic and what is not may be kept apart in the individual but reunited in the group as a form of tyrannical power.

Psychosis is natural, not aberrant; it is there; it is not pretty; it is destructive; it is the product of annihilating power and isolation from others, for example, the severing of linking objects in the self. The political question is, where do we place that psychotic core? How do we come to grips with that part of ourselves which not only the individual but the culture has a vital interest in keeping separate and apart? It may be that psychosis and the self are reunited, from time to time, in public life, in the *civitas*. It may be that the public space allows psychosis to work itself out and through in collectively accepted forms—what Bion defines as "psychotic sanity." The psychotic sane, unfortunately, are capable of imposing enormous political damage.

From time to time, I sponsored internships with students who wished to explore the psychological environment of the wards at Sheppard-Pratt. Part of the project was to talk with patients and keep journals. An observation from one of the interns reminds me in retrospect of Kristeva's (1991) view that "our fleeting or more or less threatening encounter with uncanny strangeness" gives us insights or clues "to our psychotic latencies and the fragility of our repression" (1991, 186–87):

> When I leave the unit I'm usually glad to get out of there. But midway on my ride back to College Park, I want to turn around; I want to return. I think about having dinner in the cafeteria, or finishing a

> conversation with a patient; the urge is real enough. I do not want to go home. I feel compelled to be on the unit, in the midst of all that strangeness, the feelings, despair, pain. I have no idea why; but I think it may have something to do with the strangeness inside myself and my need to look at it, again and again. I'm not sure what I'll find, but I'm dead certain it's not comforting or soothing. . . . Being in that place, Sheppard-Pratt, just hanging out, listening, talking, watching, I feel overwhelmed with curiosity and excitement, like a place I had known all my life, but never known at all. Does that make sense?

I think I understood what she was driving at. Psychosis does exercise a fascination, a pull; it is attractive in its ugliness, because it speaks to sides of the self structure which individuals and the culture spend a great deal of time and effort disguising, projecting, and hiding. This attraction may explain the appeal of artists and writers who find themselves obsessed with the cruel, perverse, and fantastic dimensions of human exchange and relationship. After all, psychosis is the *other* side of who we are, the largely unexplored side not only of the self but also of the culture and its political life.

Democracy, as both a personal and political aspect of human relationship, guards against the fall into psychotic forms of behavior. Whether on the individual or the collective level, it protects because it strengthens the links between internal percepts and external objects. It is not bound together by an all-or-nothing view of the world, by absolutist phantasies or delusional introjects. Democratic participation requires an effort to adapt illusion to reality and to listen to what others say, no matter how distorted. Self structures capable of holding and being held enhance the democratic processes of negotiation, compromise, respect for rights, and tolerance. Participation is made psychologically available, but in individuals where the links between outer and inner have been destroyed, it is far more likely that the personal level of their lives will be characterized by hatefulness, indifference, and cruelty. Such is the importance Bion assigns to linking.

What I want to emphasize is that these links take on terribly important political meaning. If we as a culture are able to contain hateful aspects of self action, if we develop collective ways to detoxify hate, envy, and greed and to avoid projecting them into autonomous political agendas, then as a society we accomplish essentially what the "good-enough" mother attains for her infant: we tolerate the hatefulness of what and who we are, our "divided" selves, without letting that hatefulness find its way into split-off, autonomous regions of public life, where it develops a toxicity and power that threaten the very foundation of human cooperation.

TEN

Psychodynamic Preconditions for the Democratic Exercise of Power

D. W. WINNICOTT recognizes limitations in the arrogance or delusional grandeur of the self proclaiming its freedom from history, meaning, and value. But his argument has a stronger claim, one he does not make, but which I believe can be inferred from his psychological theory. It is a political argument, a defense of democratic participation, an attack on annihilating power, an appreciation of otherness and tolerance, rooted in a firm respect for individuality, and motivated not by property and possession but by the appreciation of difference and the willingness to reach solutions through participatory social projects.

Winnicott advances the object-relational psychoanalytic view that the self, from the very beginning, is enmeshed in relations with others and these relations define affect, perception, and consciousness. What, however, holds these relations together is the power of illusion to bind individuals through a set of shared assumptions which actively protects the self from regression to the impulses of unconscious phantasy and the dominion of psychotic time. It is a humane argument, without, however, the phallocentric center of classical humanism.

What is a self without illusion? To be without belief, without historical pattern, to live absolutely within the obsessional terms of psychotic time, is almost impossible to imagine without being there, without actually being psychotic. Maybe this is what Jacques Lacan means by the real, but to see the real without illusion is to gaze upon death: the only illusionless state. Even the most "postmodern" self would have great difficulty adapting to a social world without the habits created by illusion. It would be like living one step away from death. Nietzsche (1873) writes:

> So what is truth? . . . truths are illusions one has forgotten are such, metaphors which have become habitual and lost their sensory force, coins which have been effaced and which from then on are taken to be, not pieces of money, but metal. . . . To be sure, man forgets that things are like this for him; so he lies unconsciously in the required manner and in accordance with age-old custom—and, precisely because of this unconsciousness and this forgetting, he arrives at a feeling of truth. (182)

Nietzsche's criticism here works on hard intellectual or ideological truths, but if he means those practices and beliefs that guide the self through its day-to-day existence, then there is a harshness here, a demand for lucidity that in the end would mean either death or madness. How does one live without habit? Schizophrenics live without habits; delusions free consciousness from metaphors that make sense of life. But at what cost?

To lie unconsciously, to make up as-if stories, even to deceive oneself—such actions, even if they allow the self to move through a day, still rivet consciousness in the deadly environs of delusional knowledge. When the lies turn into voices, when the self begins to act in peculiar ways, others may notice that something is terribly wrong; when the lies take on the imagery of delusional power, then action begins to reflect the radical estrangement or isolation of the inner self. In these kinds of psychological spaces, it is not a matter of curing oneself of the lies, ripping them out of being, but of making intolerable lies conscious (the function of therapy) and diminishing their terror and power. To free oneself of habitual metaphors that guide the self, metaphors that have not attained a pathological valence, is to tear being from its position in a given historicity. To live completely without illusion is to be Nietzsche's *Übermensch,* but it is a dry existence and a frighteningly lonely one.

If, however, one witnesses such "liberated" souls in the flesh, one sees psychosis; the true ahistorical self, the self without any social metaphors or illusions, the self absolutely liberated from causality, is the schizophrenic. The laughing dance of Nietzsche's Zarathustra is the dance of madness.

The danger to self, to its autonomy and energy, lies not so much in illusion, those subtle bonds of belief which coalesce communities, but from the presence of what I have been calling delusional or psychotic time. Delusion severs the connection between self and others; self and community (Sullivan, 1952). When habitual (that is, historically transmitted and sanctioned) metaphors break down, illusion may become delusional. The result, in both the self and the community, is tragedy.

It is Winnicott's belief that illusion, what grows from the experience of shared power, defends the self from delusional regression and narcissistic withdrawal. On the individual level, illusion facilitates the self's engagement with ever-growing communities and representations of power, breaks down or disperses power, allows the self to exercise power not as an omnipotent extension of narcissistic grandiosity (a twisted ego ideal) but as a set of reciprocal exchanges and arrangements enhancing both self's and other's respect for difference. Illusion creates in the self the first stirrings of reciprocal obligation and responsibility.

Winnicott's psychoanalytic observations on illusion add useful but not entirely unproblematic perspectives to thinking about traditional political concepts such as obligation, citizenship, and responsibility. (I look at some contestable issues in the Conclusion.) His theory allows for a more complete psychological explanation of the *foundations* of obligation and civic responsibility and the psychodynamic preconditions for democratic participation. He discusses dangers to shared participation, particularly the danger posed by regression to tyrannical forms of power; he outlines psychodevelopmental steps that assure and bind participation in a definite, historically framed community; and he describes psychological factors necessary to support a theory of power possessing democratic promise.

I am thinking here of the political functions of what Winnicott calls the transitional object and how it relates to the world of political consent and the reciprocity accompanying shared power. Winnicott, over and over, stresses the importance of *illusion* in the transitional stage; and a politics of consent, liberty, participation may have a great deal to do with illusion—not delusion but illusion—that acquires a certain *power* over consciousness and choice: the illusion, for example, of progress, liberty, participation, possibility, and so on. In democratic communities people act together (a "politics") because they believe in something: democracy, rights, justice, and liberty. Even though such beliefs may seem illusory in the face of harsh political regimes, they are nonetheless real and "there" for what they speak about human life, shared power, and its promise.

Equality, justice, mutuality enhance the political qualities of what Freud (1923) called Eros. Domination, tyranny, destruction of rights enhance tendencies toward disintegration, toward the appearance of absolute or omnipotent power in the human community. To have faith in democratic participation, then, is to believe in the efficacy of a certain kind of illusion. It is also to deny the power or legitimacy of delusional imagery that appears as ideology. And in democracy, as I have maintained, delusion means closing off possibility, retreating to solipsism in the form of hermetic explanation (racism, jingoism, fanaticism—all-or-nothing beliefs that eschew the tentativeness of illusion). A cult, for example, might be considered delusional; yet, there is a clear distinction to be made between the fanaticism of a cult and its belief structures (for example, the Branch Davidians) and those religious illusions that find themselves represented in the culture through practice and institution.

There is an enormous gap between illusion and delusion, between what Freud in *The Future of an Illusion* (1927) calls a mass "neurosis" and psychotic projection. Illusion encourages the democratic potentiality of politics; delusion kills it. Winnicott's "transitional object" and the self's navigation of that psychological phenomenon serve illusion and its attendant political benefits. To attach to the transitional object implies a defense against delusion (regression or splitting), since illusions allow the self to become involved in realities greater than its own internality, its own solipsistic reflection. An illusional politics depends on consent and obligation; it protects the general conditions for sustaining the group, as the bearer of specific interests, without denying the individual's place within it.

How, then, does the psychoanalytic notion of a transitional object contribute to the concept of an illusional or consensual politics? How do transitional objects and the concept of "transitional space" protect against annihilating power, against ideologies that frame the world in psychotic terms? I want to distinguish between fanatical faiths and binding illusions or, to put it another way, to contrast fundamentalism in cultures, religions, or races to the belief in "democracy" broadly understood. Fanaticism, whether in individuals or in an entire populace, possesses psychotic or psychoticlike dimensions.

Transition: Embracing the Outer

Winnicott maintains that the transitional object facilitates the movement of the self away from its internal preoccupations (the solipsism and omnipotence of infancy) into a form of relationship. It is the primary element in creating or facilitating the infant's use of symbol formation and therefore the critical element leading the self into cultural life: "In between the infant and the object is some thing, or some activity or sensation. In so far as this joins the infant to the object (viz., maternal part-object), so far is this the basis of symbol-formation. On the other hand, in so far as this something separates instead of joins, so is its function of leading on to symbol-formation blocked" (1965, 146). Further, if this process is blocked, if the transitional object fails to move the infant psychically away from its omnipotent connection with the all-powerful mothering presence, that failure may be traced to deficiencies in the mother's "adaptation to the infant's hallucinations and spontaneous impulses" (146). The adaptation, in Winnicott's terms, is not "good enough." That failure may remain in the self as a split-off part self, retaining enormous power over how consciousness experiences the surrounding world, the "environmental provision." It is this split-off part self, suffering, incomplete, fearful of external reality, which defines the self's actual location in relation to community, to others, to the very meaning of life. For example, cognition, the use of language, may develop normally in the individual, but emotionally the self retains this infantile orientation, this utter fear of being with others: "Failure of early basic environmental provision disturbs maturational processes, or prevents their contributing to the individual child's emotional growth, and it is this failure of the maturational processes, integration, etc., that constitutes the ill-health that we call psychotic" (257).

To make the "transition" is to leave the world of delusion and accept the reality of illusion; it is also to create the emotional preconditions for mediating belief (illusion) with what Winnicott calls "external reality." Acceptance of external reality moderates illusion with tolerance, ambivalence, acceptance, empathy, and understanding—all states of mind which presume some appreciation of the stance and position of the other. Psychosis or delusion precludes such mediations because of the absolute, all-or-nothing quality of delusional projection and definition. To move, then, from the isolation of infancy and phantasies of omnipotence to "being with" others is to find oneself in a political world, a world of mediation, compromise, otherness, relationship, mutuality, and so on. This transitional stage, which begins in infancy, is a complex process that keeps the self attached to a form of community outside its own phantasized or delusional preoccupations.[1] "It is hoped," Winnicott writes, "that psychoanalysts will be able to use the theory of transitional phenomena in order to describe the way in which good-enough environmental provision at the very earliest stages makes it possible for the individual to cope with the immense shock of loss of omnipotence" (1982, 71).

Transition is a continuing process because human beings do "regress" and may find themselves struggling with deep, primitive fears that force the self back onto itself, encouraging withdrawal and retreat to fixed delusional positions. Not only individuals but societies constantly face the prospect of sliding back in developmental time to more primitive, regressed states. If early development has been successful, the danger is less: "It is necessary to explore the possibility that mental health in terms of lessened liability to schizoid states and to schizophrenia is laid down in the very earliest stages, when the infant is being introduced gradually to external reality" (1975, 221). In Winnicott's terms, the psychotic self remains locked inside the omnipotence and hermeticism of infancy, rejects "being" for permanent isolation: "The non-communicating central self, for ever immune from the reality principle," remains "for ever silent" (1965, 192).

The period of transition, then, is crucial, and the transitional object, in whatever form, is a significant movement toward the external world. Yet, from a political perspective, what is compelling about Winnicott's argument is that the process of transition, establishing social and psychological contact with external reality, never ends. This competition among closed systems of belief, delusional readings of reality, and acceptance of illusion or belief as forms of external reality constantly repeats itself. It is always an effort to avoid moving backward into solipsism and the reenactment of infantile omnipotence as enslavement to a perverse ego ideal.

Let me restate the basic contours of Winnicott's argument: the transitional object, whether it be a teddy bear, a blanket, a piece of clothing as a stand-in for the mother, takes the infant out of its environmental and psychological isolation; a failure in this "good-enough active environmental adaptation, however, enforces isolation, and may provoke a psychotic distortion of the environment-individual set up" (1975, 222). This is experienced by the self as the loss of the sense of coherence. It seeks refuge in psychotic time, and solipsism or omnipotence becomes the defining frame of existence. Politically, regression leads away from democratic norms toward more absolutist forms of social and political identification. For the individual, the failure in environmental provision, the inability to navigate the transitional space, may reappear in later years as schizophrenia or psychosis, a serious breakdown of emotional and cognitive organization, a "loss of reality contact [and contact with objects] . . . reality sense, disintegration and depersonalization" (1975, 162).

Transitional Objects and the Danger of Regression

Let us consider in somewhat more detail Winnicott's concept of the transitional process and some of its pitfalls, what transition means in the life of the self and in the construction of a respect for shared beliefs, values, and the foundation of a democratic politics that resists the tyranny of power. In his essay "Psychosis and Child Care" (1952), Winnicott argues that the infantile self connects with the environment by moving outward from its psychological isolation; consciousness accepts and mediates "impingements," the demands of external reality. This is normal and healthy development, what might be considered the prototype for development of the self and of concepts of reciprocal power. Pathology arises when impingement produces a "reactive response," and the self retreats, returning to its original isolation and omnipotent relation to power. It may happen that the self learns cognitively how to relate to social objects, to manipulate social operations, but affectively remains regressed, infantile, struggling with the transitional world. Or as Ned, a twenty-eight-year-old manic-depressive patient, put it: "I can't stand it; I can't communicate with anybody; I feel so locked up in myself; why can't anyone understand what I say? Why do I live in an iron cage so shut off from everyone?"

Even though Ned was proficient with language, even though he wrote lucid and intensely metaphoric poetry, he remained locked into himself, isolated. The illusions of the shared world, Winnicott's universe of sociality, were not sufficient to combat the pull of delusional power, the projections of the inner world. When Ned proclaimed that he sometimes went "up with God," what he was saying was that his real communication, his significant communication, lay in those moments when he spoke by himself to God and received His messages on how to live. Ned went up to God through an opening in the surrounding world that only he knew. Similarly, he received true knowledge when he spoke with Thomas Jefferson in the graveyard. He and Jefferson shared a world no one else understood. This psychological projection performed some of the functions Ned attributed, when he was five, to the basement furnace, the "only place in the house where I felt close to something, where there was some sense of certainty, where I knew what would happen, from one morning to the next. That furnace, and its turning on and off, became the only reliable presence in my house. It was the only place I felt safe."

Ned never attained that Winnicottian position of hope where the child begins to see beyond the despair brought on by environmental failure and moves toward a sense of "I AM, I am alive, I am myself" (1982, 56), a capacity to trust, to strive after *shared* realities, without being overwhelmed by disappointment. Hope and the consciousness of the outside begin in the "intermediate" area, the world of the transitional object and space. "Environmental failure" increases the danger that the transitional phase may never be emotionally transcended (or, better, never achieve the Hegelian overcoming, *Aufhebung*), leading to the possibility of severe regressions in adult life. *Pre*-transitional object "being," the realm of psychotic time, remains sealed off from interpersonal experience. The outer world, external reality, brings threat; sociality and life in the external world are experienced as unbearable. Efforts are undertaken (in psychosis) to preserve whatever shreds of self remain, to protect the cut-off core of the inner self and "the threat of its being found, altered, communicated with" (1965, 187). Suffering from a "failure of basic provision," the psychotic self retreats to that depleted, crippled center, that cut-off, hidden area of life which creates its own meaning and orientations. For Winnicott, the *founding* of the self in transitional space is essential: "After being—doing and being done to. But first, being" (1982, 85).

It was not that Ned was completely lost in the autism of a regressed emotional world; he was at least linguistically able to participate in a shared reality. Yet, I want to emphasize that as a knowledge form, his delusional phantasies were a more powerful force than the shared illusions and belief systems of the social and historical world. He forsook a sense of shared power (which involves an other) for "going up with God" or whatever delusional power occupied his consciousness. He found true or reliable knowledge not in the belief structures of history and society (where democracy draws its meaning), but in the hermetic projections of his own imagination. Is that not analogous to what happens, frequently, in political life? Was not Ned describing a competition (between two forms of knowledge, delusion and illusion) that frequently appears in politics, in the public organization of reality (for example, the collusion Alice Miller finds between Hitler's unconscious phantasies and repressed or split-off memory in his pan-European audience)?

Winnicott, in his essay "Transitional Objects and Transitional Phenomena" (1953), speaks of the "positive value of illusion . . . the first possession" as transitional object (242). For a period the infant dwells in this "intermediate area" (239) of illusion, but eventually, the self comes to distinguish more clearly and definitively between subjective reality and external reality. At this point, when illusion finds itself subject to the tests of the outer world, the self comes to understand the shared bases of experience. What is politically interesting about Winnicott's observations is the social *and* participatory quality he assigns to the place of illusion in culture. Culture and the products of culture, including political culture, derive from the illusional bases of psychological development.

Illusion, then, in Winnicott's theory provides the psychological foundation for the political process of consent, the self's participation in worlds greater than its mother's and the accompanying phantasies and delusional projections. Did not Ned, in rejecting that intermediate area, in failing to find relief in shared illusions, and instead dwelling in the solipsism of his cut-off world, reject social process, the consent structures of culture and its corresponding obligations? Ned's rejection of the communal world, because of the debilitating effect of his illness, may have reenacted an earlier infantile refusal, an inability or an unwillingness to traverse illusional, transitional space.

These ideas are speculative, but I want to suggest a working hypothesis for thinking about the transitional object as important in the "founding" of the *sense* of democratic participation. If Winnicott is right, Ned's persistent delusional identifications, his distrust of the shared world, and his retreat to interior psychological spaces signified a self that had yet to consent to participate in a politically defined world. In a literal sense, Ned remained outside the polity, excluded from participatory norms. Periodically, he engaged in social rituals, but emotionally, he lived in an unreachable universe of fear and crippling anxiety, not the world of shared illusion and action but one of hermetic isolation and its delusional imagery of power.

The Politics of Limitation

Winnicott speaks of "lingering" too long in the intermediate area, of too much illusion, possibly akin to what Hobbes in *Leviathan* calls "too much appearing passion." At some point, illusion may become delusional. The artist, for example, may become so psychologically obsessed with the object of art itself or the language of description (Proust comes to mind here) that the imagery takes on its own kind of madness—in Nietzschean terms, Dionysian madness represented through Apollonian art. It is the peculiar torment and trouble of the artistic mentality. Religion presents similar troubles—for example, Hobbes's argument in *Leviathan* on the Kingdom of Darkness: "Phantasms" have the power to take over mind and consciousness, to dissolve or disintegrate political and public understanding (see Glass 1985, 124ff.). Yet, in its mediated sense, where illusion sustains itself as a shared presence in the life of the self and the community, the illusionary belief may be a defense against the unlimited and unbounded power of psychotic time. Illusion provides a buffer between the delusional phantasms of the self, Melanie Klein's paranoid/schizoid position, and the consent structures of external reality.

The *madness* of illusion appears when its meaning structures find themselves unencumbered by restraint, by recognitions in the external world, the autonomy of an "otherness" that represents or signifies a shared and bounded historical world. Illusion belongs to history; delusion belongs to the timelessness of unconscious phantasies and imposes havoc on history. A patient such as Ned lives inside a withdrawn, isolated subjectivity, where the "other" becomes secondary to the internal projections and private knowledge systems never scrutinized by the test of the "environmental provision." To remain too long in the intermediate area of illusion becomes a "special indulgence," tolerable for the infant but pathological for the adult—Narcissus, for example, riveted to his image in the pool. The pathological illusion ("narcissism") prevents movement toward or engagement with external reality, it eventually encases the self and becomes elaborated as delusional presence. Or as Winnicott describes it, "If an individual claims special indulgence in respect of this intermediate area, we recognize psychosis."[2]

Let me return to the microdynamics of this process for a moment. I am saying that transitional objects operate in the world of politics with as much effectiveness as they do in the world of the infant. Illusion is what binds democratic communities together; delusion destroys democratic process and function. Similarly with the infant: failure to navigate the transitional stage may create fissures or splits in the self that later come back to haunt the adult as serious, even psychotic disturbance. In Winnicott's view, this terrible psychological consequence is almost certain to follow failure to become an interdependent self, connected with the external world. Winnicott finds this "basic" split at the core of the psychotic process itself: "In the extreme case of splitting, the secret inner life has very little in it derived from external reality. It is fully incommunicable" (1975, 225).

Now, what does this split signify; what is its impact on the self? In the individual, the split means the beginning of a *false* life and self, by which Winnicott means, first, a life dissociated from reality and, second, a life dissociated from community or without trust in the shared reality of power. Ned, for example, was totally and tragically unable to conceptualize power as reciprocal exchange. The false self maintains the cognitive or conscious connection to external reality, the appearance of being, *semblance,* but at some point the false self dissolves and the madness underneath disintegrates whatever fragile threads consciousness maintained with the external world. All "semblance" in this condition, the "masks" of being, evolve around compliance. "The false self, developed on a compliance basis, cannot attain to the independence of maturity, except perhaps a pseudo-maturity in a psychotic environment" (1975, 225). Or to put it another way, the secret inner self creates a delusional organization, a solipsistic knowledge without foundation either in the intermediate world of illusion or in the more testable and verifiable impingements of external reality. "The false self has one positive and very important function: to hide the True Self, which it does by compliance with environmental demands" (1965, 146–47). To be penetrated, to be communicated with ("the violation of the self's core, the alteration of the self's central elements by communication seeping through the defences") holds life-threatening possibilities (1965, 187).

The false self system indicates a serious illness in the core self. Inwardly, in this split condition, the core self feels empty, depleted, dry, barren; its appearance or adaptation may simulate aliveness, but the core experiences itself as dead. It therefore turns to delusion, the knowledge form of this kind of "death." That knowledge and its origins in unconscious phantasies is kept secret, hidden. If existence is understood secretly in these terms of unreality, deadness, lack of being, what do such feelings imply for complex social actions such as reciprocity and participation? As Ned put it: "I am my own community; I need no one else; I have all I need; when I need advice I go up with God." It may be that the pretransitional object self (the paranoid/schizoid self) caught up in withdrawal and dread, the fear of annihilation, has repudiated or never even forged those fragile attachments to otherness implied by the acceptance of the illusional or transitional space. For the delusional self lost to history, whose inner organization takes on psychotic dimensions, the sense of otherness has little meaning. To be part of a community requires an agreement that goes beyond the self; it demands engagement, acceptance of external reality as other-than-self, Winnicott's "not-me" possession. But even more important, consent also requires the emotional *need* to attain consent: to be a participant in something outside of oneself, in a community, a shared reality.

It is a terrible dilemma: the regressive power of paranoid/schizoid tendencies inhibiting the movement toward transition and reciprocity. In an adult, the dilemma is an incessant struggle to maintain sanity, contact, connection, to avoid transforming the self's "primary isolation" into an existential regression. Ned believed he totally controlled reality; this feeling of omnipotence was noticeable during his manic phases but also certainly present in his more withdrawn or depressed moments: "I am the best therapist in the hospital, but I'm lying low now because I think other patients on the hall need to try to make it by themselves." He kept his knowledge of his own power "hidden"; it was something he believed others intuited. Everyone knew Ned to be the most powerful person on the unit; yet, it was not something he wanted to "reveal" all the time. Frequently, he "put on an act," but he wanted me to know he was the "most powerful of all." Whereas Ned's self may have appeared to be "normal" or "together," emotionally he inhabited a world as cut off from reality as the infant's solipsistic wanderings through extreme despair, rage, and frustrated desire. It was as if Ned psychically recaptured the omnipotence and terror of power characteristic of infancy. In Winnicott's terms: "The infant lives permanently in his or her own inner world which is not, however, firmly organized" (1975, 227). For Ned, the shared, participatory, *democratic* world became the threat.

Transitional Areas and the Understanding of Consent

In Winnicott's view, the transitional area exists as a "resting place for the individual engaged in the perpetual human task of keeping inner and outer reality separate yet inter-related" (1975, 230). Its effects appear in art and religion and, as I have been arguing, in belief systems and in the psychological preconditions determining reciprocity and the acceptance of shared realities. It can be seen in the infant's relation to inanimate objects; it possesses distinct psychological significance; it is manifested, socially, in illusion. The transitional object and the notion of the "transitional space" support the world of illusion as opposed to that of delusion.

I would at this point like to suggest a typology in which the notion of the transitional object demarcates the major epistemic difference between systems of domination and democratic (political) systems of tolerance and respect for rights (Table 3). A democratic politics and a theory of power firmly tied to reciprocity depend on the extent to which illusion has been liberated from a *pre*transitional object politics, an in-dwelling in psychotic time which lacks the consent necessary to exist in and to tolerate the external world with its competing demands. A

Table 3. A Psychotypology of political form

	Psychotic	Nonpsychotic
Political form	tyranny/dictatorship	democracy, respect for difference
Epistemic foundation	delusion appearance in ethics, actions against out-groups, violent repression, ideological proclamations	illusion → illusion as mediated belief appearance in institutions, rituals, laws
Psychodynamics	unconscious phantasy as: paranoid/schizoid all-or-nothing black or white thinking all-good/all-bad dichotomies	reciprocity as: transitional object → external reality ambivalence → development of conscience testing through shared experience → appreciation of tolerance, empathy, obligation

psychotic politics, together with its tyrannical forms of power, remakes reality according to its own closed systems. It is clear, however, that the precondition for the presence of a democratic politics premised on reciprocity is the navigation of that area of experience Winnicott calls "transitional." Without the mediation between inner and outer, development finds itself blocked and the self suffers severe pathological distortion.

A political ideology, then, that finds itself mired in closed systems of thought, in cultlike behavior, in racist and unyielding concepts of reality replays what on an infantile-developmental level might be understood as the paranoid/schizoid position and its immersion in omnipotent power. A political/ideological formulation that mirrors *pre*transitional percepts, nondialectical thinking, an in-dwelling in psychotic time lacks the capacity to exist in and to tolerate the external world with its competing demands. A psychotic political program and its tyrannical forms of power remakes reality according to its own closed systems of perception; it denies consent, just as a democratic politics encourages it. Similarly the individual suffering from a basic split in the self has not affectively consented to be in the social world, but remains locked into a hidden, cut-off universe (psychotic time) that lacks consensual validation. Further, the ingredients of a viable consent, a respect for autonomy, a belief in compromise, a willingness to entertain the position of the other, derive from psychodevelopmental phases that have successfully assimilated or transcended schizoid adaptations.

For Winnicott, the coherence of the self appears not in its rigidity or its rationality but in its capacity to regulate experience that has the potential to be regressive and fragmenting. Self-knowledge builds on psychodevelopmental stages, and to move from pretransitional *space* to transitional objects to relational stages is to internalize a knowing that possesses an increasing valence for self-regulation and social organization. Yet, it is not the regulation and control of patriarchy; it is not the order of domination and submission but the effort to *regulate* experience in such a way that the possibilities of human exchange, the dialectics of empathy, will be enhanced and contained. It thus embraces relationships of love and care and also anger, rage, hatred, greed, and envy—an emotional world Winnicott only partially succeeds in demystifying (more on this in the next chapter). The transitional object provides the psychological foundation that allows the self to sustain the stress of what it means to live within a myriad of relationships that bring happiness, sadness, disappointment, exultation, and despair; relationships that protect the self from falling into the isolating coldness of psychotic time, the terror of detached and disembodied power.

The experience of grief or mourning is vital to psychological growth, central to what it means to be human. If mourning or grief is impossible or blocked, the self's capacity to change or transform will be inhibited. Giving up objects, losing attachments, suffering disappointments—these kinds of experiences, which schizophrenics find quite difficult, are central to the human and political project. Mourning moves the self toward new integrations; the process is facilitated by the capacity to reexperience transitional objects, to forge attachments and to internalize illusions, which heal the shattering and despair. Without the capacity to mourn, the self remains fixed in frozen and terrifying places.

It is Winnicott's contention that it is precisely the developmental line, the self's historical development through transitional objects to differentiated object relations, which provides the essential inward resiliency to endure loss and to forge connections that provide historical meaning and context. What is so tragic about psychosis is that delusional power defines experience in a perpetual present; the actions and symbologies of delusion, are always present to consciousness; nothing remains of a past and therefore a set of remembrances to mourn. Nor does a sense of the future and therefore hope guide the kind of power representations of delusional symbologies. Jenny, for example, lived completely in the present; she was unable to mourn. In her inability to experience loss, grieve for absence and then attempt to ground a present in the knowledge and feelings of loss, Jenny's entrapment in projections of delusional power became even more absolute.

For Winnicott the capacity to endure and sustain grief and the ability to build solid social relations depend on each other. The transitional object symbolizes a dimension of loss. The infant is giving something up, giving up its idealized merger with the mothering presence, but also gaining the ability to navigate more complex forms of social integration. Winnicott and object-relations theory generally move us to a defense of political liberty, toleration, and moderation, precisely because such political conditions mirror the mature capacities of the individual self to grieve and to give and receive pleasure from the relations of reciprocity without destroying the self in the exchange.

If the transitional object is in individual psychological life a bridge between inner and outer, such objects may repeat themselves in politics and history through the projection of shared as opposed to autistic belief systems. To think about this concept politically is to think about the *affective* or emotional foundations of consent. What kind of internal self structure is required to validate the respect for rights, liberty, and personhood at the heart of modern democratic values, the psychological position of ambivalence?

To entertain a democratic politics it may be essential to think about a self capable of containing and metabolizing affect that splits and polarizes (recall Bion's theory of container/contained). It is not a matter of seeking to justify a therapeutic or "therapizing" society. The relation between self and collective is an issue not of "therapy" but of the impact of unconscious and interpersonal dynamics on the world of both feeling *and* thought.

Nor is the use of psychodevelopmental concepts reflective of what Michel Foucault (1980) calls the intersection of power/knowledge or what Gilles Deleuze and Félix Guattari (1977) see as the bourgeois ideology of psychoanalysis. Nor do I understand the political values of liberty, tolerance, and moderation to be bourgeois inventions whose only function is to protect property. To "be" in the world, as Winnicott suggests, is to be able to sustain the self's essential aloneness, its primary isolation, yet to live among others and to receive gratification from the humanness of reciprocity. To be able to experience the pleasure of reciprocity, transcend despair, and regard the other as an autonomous, sentient being (a "being" with definable rights)—these psychological adaptations, not the least of which is passing from the world of the inner to that of the outer by learning how to contain toxic aspects of self-experience, are essential for a democratic politics. There may be a great deal to learn about psychosis in *politics* by studying *individuals* who are psychotic. To say that biology, genetics, and chemistry affect psychotic states is not to deny Winnicott's critical observation that psychosis implies a basic disorder in "being."

Limits in the Rationalist Approach

Finally, to what extent is a participatory democratic politics dependent on a theory of political consent that presumes the assimilation of the binding and shared properties of illusion? Is illusion as opposed to delusion the essential backdrop to the intellectual or rational properties of justice, equality, rights, obligation, responsibility, and care? What are the constituents of a political will that grants respect to various belief systems that make up the polity?

It is a distortion of political will to see it only as a bundle of cognition, a strictly "rational" process, a function of games or the rational appraisal of choices and alternatives (for example, the position of rational choice theory). It is a more complex process.

Modern rationalism, particularly theory in the line of John Rawls (1971) (and the rationalism of his methodology), falls short in thinking about what consent means, what it implies as a function of psychological development. Even critics of the Rawlsian contractarian position (for example, Michael Sandel) ignore the implications of consent and its relation to internal psychological dynamics.[3] For example, Sandel writes: "[I]t is important to distinguish two different senses of 'agreement.' The first involves agreement with a person (or persons) with respect to a proposition, the second agreement to a proposition" (1982, 129). Agreement obviously has a great deal to do with consent and with percepts that accompany participation; however, it may be that agreement in the conscious sense intended by both Rawls and Sandel has nothing to do with the emotional or affective foundations of consent. Whether the individual—or, better, the "self"—consents to be in a polity or not may have been determined in a developmental phase prior to the appearance of "reason" or cognition. To put it another way, agreement to be part of a polity and its assumptions regarding shared power may be founded on psychodevelopmental phenomena that fall far outside the range of rational appraisal or verification. Consent is a factor in John Rawls's theory of justice: justice depends on agreement, on the willingness to conceptualize the relative advantage or disadvantage of the other. Justice, then, implies a degree of empathy, the capacity to put oneself in the position of the other, although Rawls talks about this difficult concept only abstractly, in a language bereft of an understanding of the self's "object relations."

Both Rawls and Sandel begin from the assumption of rationality; their differences are not so much over psychology as epistemology. For example, Sandel comments:

> For Rawls, the consequences of taking seriously the distinction between persons are not directly moral but more decisively epistemological. What the bounds between persons confine is less the reach of our sentiments—this they do not prejudge—than the reach of our understanding, of our cognitive access to others. And it is this *epistemic* deficit (which derives from the nature of the subject) more than any shortage of benevolence (which is in any case variable and contingent) that requires justice for its remedy and so accounts for its pre-eminence. (1982, 172)

Sandel, however, makes allowance for a more complicated self than appears in the pages of Rawls's *Theory of Justice;* he speaks of attachments and aspirations, but he never asks the question of *origins:* where do such attachments come from? What is the relation between attachment and the self's object relations? What is the influence of psychological states such as paranoia and schizophrenia on "reason," perception, choice and consent? Might schizoid tendencies in the self have some effect on the development of the rational faculty and the deployment of power? As Sandel notes, "To be capable of a more thoroughgoing reflection, we cannot be wholly unencumbered subjects of possession, individuated in advance and given prior to our ends, but must be subjects constituted in part by our central aspirations and attachments, always open, indeed vulnerable, to growth and transformation in the light of revised self-understandings" (172).

I want to suggest that these "self understandings" may be composed of complex developmental factors (internal object relations) that produce a particular kind of consciousness. What we normally call "reason" may be as dependent on early developmental influences, including the navigation of the transitional object stage, as any formal instruction in learning or any assimilation of cognitive skills. It is not intellect that is the issue here, but the genesis, structure, and function of passions that take root in the self at a very early age. Further, as psychoanalytic theorists such as Winnicott suggest, the psychology of regression affects the structure of perception and intellect. A psychically regressed self may be quite intelligent, "perceptive," but may very well see the world in much different terms from those of the sophisticated, almost translucent self that appears in the writings of the rationalists. For example, where is a consideration of narcissism in modern rational choice theory?

Sandel continues: "And in so far as our constitutive self-understandings comprehend a wider subject than the individual alone, whether a family or tribe or city or class or nation or people, to this extent they define a community in the constitutive sense" (172). But what is the relation between the individual and the community in these terms? Might there be some psychodynamic factors, such as transitional objects, regressions, the effect of splitting on perception, which determine this "constitutive sense"? What provides cohesiveness in a community? Might it have something to do with the reality of *shared* illusions?

Sandel and the rationalists generally never address the *affective* constituents of a healthy participatory community, the fragility of psychological processes, the presence and operation of false self systems and what such systems create in politics. Both rationalists and communitarians are insensitive to the power of regression to disrupt the democratic process and to the function of primitive atavistic identifications (the consequence of splitting) on "reason" and political judgment. Sandel speaks of "a common vocabulary of discourse and a background of implicit practices and understandings" (172–73). But where is consideration of the psychological capacity for such understandings and discourses (Little, 1985), the relation between political value and character, the effects of child care, child abuse, and unconscious phantasies on the development of the self?

Psychotic factors influence politics, much as they influence the self; groups, societies, and states periodically find themselves subject to the regressive pull of the boundlessness and mindlessness of psychotic disintegration and psychotic time. A democratic politics, however, provides a defense against regression; and illusion, contained within supportive and tolerant frames, works in the interests of developmental processes that in an individual would be considered mature and "healthy." Winnicott's prototype for healthy individual development—the environmental provision, empathy, the importance of transitional objects—may, as well, create a certain stability and containing effect in politics. His inquiry and analysis may provide a prototype of the psychological underpinnings of a democratic politics. It may also be that the "transitional object" and transitional phase set the emotional preconditions for the concept of liberty and the exercise of consent; that as a concept, transitional objects and spaces may explain something of the origins of belief systems and provide a way of distinguishing healthy from pathological belief systems.

Most important, Winnicott fleshes out the abstractness of the stick figures in rationalist psychology. He sees individualism and the prerequisites for rationality as more than an exercise in cognition. Rather, for Winnicott, the democratic self, with an appreciation of otherness and shared, as opposed to omnipotent, power implies a complex developmental course that has successfully avoided the psychic entropy inducing regression and splitting. Emotions are considerably more than sentiments or preference rankings, in his view. For example, the concept of the split self implies a deep unconscious alienation from the external world which may be manifested in sentiments or what Winnicott calls "adaptations." Or sentiments may be used to defend against such a massive alienation. In any case, Winnicott is certain that sentiments are not what they seem.

The Winnicottian view of the individual, in addition to object-relations theory and its origins in the work of Melanie Klein, requires a close look at the function of phantasy (both conscious and unconscious) in delineating the structure of perception. It envisions a self sensitive to such processes as symbiosis, fusion, projection, and projective identification, to the psychodynamics of paranoia, schizophrenia, and manic-depression. In this sense, the psychotic process may be understood as a "model" or formulation for examining aspects of political life. Psychosis is a central fact of human experience; it does not disappear with infancy but may linger in the individual. Psychosis, as Bion has demonstrated, affects the group's relation to the external world. It is illusion, however, in addition to reason, that binds communities, that provides a defense against the pathogenicity of delusional introjects. Reason provides the forum for dialogue, the mechanisms of dispute and contention. Reason defines the rules of the game; illusion constructs the context in which the game is possible. Illusion forms the cohesion of community by literally constituting its belief structures and respecting the limits of the individual self. What unite the group in this respect are *dialectical* illusions, founded in a tolerance for reciprocity, in the endless ambivalence of the human position and the willingness to respect the limits and difference of the other.

Sandel writes: "Of any society it can always be asked to what extent it is just, or 'well ordered' in Rawls' sense, and to what extent it is a community, and the answer can in neither case fully be given by reference to the sentiments and desires of the participants alone" (1982, 173). Yet, well-ordered individuals and the well-ordered polity do have something in common, and disordered communities reflect symptoms of disordered elements in the self. It is essential, therefore, to look at the psychopathology of "desire," the derailment of self by unconscious phantasies, to ascertain not only the force that binds communities but the divisiveness that attacks them, including the divisiveness of reason. What is the self's "original position," to borrow a term from John Rawls, if not an amalgam of inner and outer, phantasy and reality, a confused dialectic between internal psychological structure, sometimes split off, sometimes repressed, and the vastness of the interpersonal world surrounding the self. It is this dialectical understanding of self, group, and power that is missing not only from modern discussions of consent and obligation but from the very methodological assumptions of the rationalist ethos and its justification of liberal democracy.

ELEVEN

Conclusion: Psychosis, Political Value, and Democracy

To understand the extremes of the political process, it may be necessary to examine the extremes of human regression and, even more important, to listen for the origins of those extremes in the self's intrapsychic history. Selves have histories just as nations do. It may therefore be useful to look for the reasons motivating states and polities in the dynamics of psychological development and the vicissitudes of psychosis.

And psychotic groups, for example, the SS or the Afrikaaners or the Ku Klux Klan, may indeed be reflected in psychotic selves. In groups and in selves, regression and splitting attack the functioning of secondary process defenses and make accessible to consciousness archaic or primitive drive structures, Chasseguet-Smirgel's primary narcissism. On the individual level, the psychotic self appears to be consumed by torture, self-destruction, and internally held images distinguished by violence and domination. On the public level, psychotic ideologies attack individuality and tolerance and cast the world as an otherness that needs to be destroyed, purified, or returned to a lost past. Sensitivity, then, to the psychotic individual may lead to a keener awareness of the extent to which psychosis pervades more collective and group-based structures.

Sensitivity to psychotic time and its linguistic correlates certainly gives rise to a healthy skepticism regarding rationality and those theoretical and political formulations for which a rationalist perspective defines elements of choice and decision. For example, Rawlsian rationalism and rational choice theory ignore important psychodynamic factors in the psychotic dimension or core of human life and in aspects of human and political experience which precede the cognitive elaboration of rational perception—what, for example, psychoanalysis calls the unconscious. The psychotic narrative, or, in Julia Kristeva's terms, the "psychotic text" in the modern world, is very real; it causes extraordinary damage.

Lifton elaborates with a terrifying clarity in his analysis of the Nazi doctors (1986). These seemingly most "rational" of professionals engaged in acts and justifications that clearly pushed science beyond a humane rationality into a grotesque madness in which sophisticated "tools" were used to "rationalize" mass killings. At what point does science itself become psychotic? Do ideologies, movements, and nations use "science" for ends that push beyond the limits of reason and reasonableness into that primary process, nondialectical language of psychosis? At what price "experimentation"? Rationalism of the type Rawls espouses, which seems very much in vogue in modern philosophy (cognitive science, for instance), ignores this core of human experience which derives from the self's primary narcissism and the perversion of the ego ideal. Postmodern philosophy, as well, pays little attention to the destructive potential of the boundlessness of psychotic forms of identification (Glass, 1993).

The danger posed to the self by the invasion of power, no matter what its form, should not be underestimated. Even though the superego, in its presence as conscience and limitation, may be an ally of reasonableness, when it is assimilated or annihilated by the ego ideal, it becomes pathogenic. When groups act according to the narcissistic dictates of the ego ideal, when they seem focused only on a set of assumptions that reinforce closed systems of belief, groups have the potential of becoming psychotic. To put it another way, the collective regresses toward more absolutist forms of thinking. Chasseguet-Smirgel (1985) calls this phenomenon the group "delusion," which is an effort to restore through program or ideology aspects or "states" of a lost narcissism. If the group becomes the victim or agent of a regressed state of mind expressed ideologically, if it finds itself acting out a collective *de*lusion, it has reached the point of sealing off its language-validating properties. What is "outside," in Volkan's terms, becomes "enemy." Thinking ceases to be dialectical or consensual and retreats to the fixed positions of psychotic time. The values and perceptions produced by this nondialectical language energize the group psychotic state.[1]

In such states, it is possible for the *individual* not to be psychotic (the opposite, for example, of my analysis of Pete) but to be overtaken by the collective ego ideal, which in the context of what the group demands of its membership, the group's *understanding,* may be psychotic. Thus one explains the paradox of Nazi doctors engaging themselves in insane group actions, yet on an individual level not exhibiting any specific, idiosyncratic psychotic symptoms or believing what they were doing was crazy. The group's illusions—or, better, delusions—transform reality; the group establishes its own perceptual and moral norms, for example, the Jew as poisoner or corrupter of the culture and therefore a danger to the Aryan/German race. To be within the sphere of the group's influence, what Lifton calls "doubling," to internalize its ideals as one's own, that process of internalization or introjection transforms the so-called "normal" individual into an agent of the psychotic group delusion. Bion (1961) understood this process very well.

Yet, unlike the psychotic individual, the group trapped by its unconscious phantasies finds itself defined by nondialectical languages, by its own self-validating system of thought, which takes on the character of torture and persecution. Certain groups—Bion's basic assumptions groups, for example—may contain a psychotic substructure, which, if harnessed to specific ends, induce galvanic currents releasing intense spurts of energy and destructiveness. Whether in the group or in individuals such as Pete and Marge, nondialectical language severs the transitional links between inner and outer, the imperatives of consensual reality. Inner percepts or fixed beliefs take over, and the structure of value, in the case of politics and ideology, depends on the regressive tyranny of the ego ideal.

Michael Eigen writes: "The human subject is the discontinuity that inaugurates him" (1986, 132). When *discontinuity* or disconnection becomes the determining element of experience, however, and not the effort to define oneself as separate and autonomous, when discontinuity induces a retreat into psychological hermeticism, nothing is left but the subject's own mental productions, imagination projected as *both* reality and truth—for example, Pete's sense of himself as filth. The effort to recapture a lost narcissism may produce mindless delusions bounded only by their own structure and energy. It is such limitlessness within the self, coalescing as ego ideal, degenerating into psychotic time, which provokes so much of the destructiveness of psychotic power. For ultimately, psychosis manifests itself as a series of linguistic frames that enclose reality. It is a language of nonbeing and, in the case of politics, an *action* of nonbeing, and it is a mistake to think that either this language or action lacks logic and meaning. Quite the opposite: psychotic projections are filled with perverse theories of meaning, dimensionality, and reference. Witness, for example, the state-supported Nazi research into race and the biological and physiological differences between Jew and Aryan. Psychotic frames lack appreciation of otherness, empathy and respect for difference; psychosis is distinguished by the dread of the other, the fragmentation of the interpersonal, the disintegration of care and touch; *and,* particularly in the case of political life, the idealization of master-slave relationships.

It is a paradox: psychosis frees the self or the group from the constraints of consensual reality or normalizing society, but it is a delusional freedom, because even though the narcissism of psychosis produces imaginative creations of horrendous proportions, these "creations" are born in terror and live to torture and persecute. Whether it is the self-torture of Pete and Marge or the torture of repressive political regimes, the pivotal feature of psychotic *nonbeing* is torture and its presence in human experience as perverted power. Psychosis allows the self to create its own perfect world *and* perfect power, and in such a world, anything, including annihilation, is possible. The self possesses omnipotent power; therefore psychosis creates a limitless field for the actions of these internal products, and if the "products" of power are perverse and nihilistic, so will be the consequences of its actions.

What, then, can limit or even block the political effects of psychotic action, power, and identification? I have said that democracy possesses this political potential; that its operation inhibits and contains the psychotic substructure of human experience. I have used the psychoanalytic theory of D. W. Winnicott in support of this position.

I would like to close, however, by pointing to some real difficulties in employing Winnicott's theory in a political defense against psychosis. I think this cautionary note is useful not because I in any way want to "disprove" Winnicott or to subvert the utility of his concepts in exploring the psychodynamics of democratic theory. His theory is an insightful defense of the democratic self and the values of tolerance and participation. Nevertheless, it may be helpful to look at what Winnicott leaves out or neglects when he articulates the relationship between the self and the unconscious. In this respect, the work of Julia Kristeva becomes vital, indeed essential, in developing a resilient psychodynamic defense of democratic process.

Democracy and the Status of the Unconscious

I am not unmindful of problems in using the theory of Winnicott. He may be too sanguine, may overidealize the good-enough mother. Winnicott, and there is merit to this argument, takes out of the Kleinian and Lacanian concept of the unconscious much of what is undesirable, nasty, and violent in human experience.

Cynthia Burack takes a somewhat different tack. She maintains that social theorists—and her target here is Jessica Benjamin's *Bonds of Love*—generally underestimate the importance Winnicott attributes to aggression and hate, "to the enduring quality of destruction, and to its affective grasp" (1993, 443). In fact, she says, Benjamin may place too much emphasis on reparation and not enough on the destructive dynamics of hate. The argument between Burack and Benjamin (1993) points up real, contestable issues in the interpretation of Winnicott's psychoanalytic theorizing, although Burack herself may overemphasize Winnicott's approach to destruction. The exchange between the two, somewhat bitter on Benjamin's side, is interesting and worth looking at. Jane Flax (1993) has noted, as well, serious problems in what might be called, generally, a defanging of the unconscious.

It is not that Winnicott is wrong; individuals are capable of reciprocity and change and tolerance. The social *subject* does forge exchange structures with surrounding reality. But as Klein, Lacan, and Kristeva keep reminding us, we must take seriously the cautionary note that all subjects are divided, full of conflict, and plagued by unconscious phantasies that drastically affect perception and action. Reciprocity, the linchpin of Winnicott's psychodynamic support for democratic theory, is not the whole story, and Winnicott may diminish the importance of the conflicted or conflictual self with considerable evidence, although Burack argues strenuously in the other direction (1994, 87ff.). He assumes we can transcend or move beyond what he calls "destruction," that the affects or passions of destruction can be integrated or absorbed into the self through the use of transitional objects. The destruction of objects (particularly intense in infancy) is literally folded into the self; the other and the self survive destruction; growth goes on. It is a persuasive argument, as I have tried to demonstrate.

But this is precisely what Kristeva and Lacan say may not be possible. It is a crucial disagreement with Winnicott, and it should be addressed.

How is one to account for the self full of hate, the divided subject? Are we to take Lacan as a closet Hobbesian, warning us of the "war of all against all," a champion of political authority? I don't think so. Accepting Lacan's thesis does not require a retreat into the repressive structures of a stern, paternal Hobbesism. Nor does it mean the rageful, ugly self can be contained only by being dominated. Entertaining Lacan and Kristeva's interpretation of the drives plaguing the subject need not imply enthusiasm for a Hobbesian view of political sovereignty. Quite the contrary: a Lacanian/Kristevan position requires that a true democratic theory must take into account what is being contained, the divisiveness of the subject, and how to accomplish the act of containment without idealizing or mystifying the unconscious or negating its presence through a faith in transitional objects as instruments of socialization.

Lacan and Kristeva contend that the unconscious may be more powerful than the ameliorating presence of transitional objects or spaces. Further, it may be that the regressive potential of the self is not at all diminished in the posttransitional phase. Rather, it is kept under control with varying degrees of success. For Winnicott, transitional objects suggest a somewhat teleological social process; the emotional attachment to the object might detoxify regressive potential, the yearning to return to more archaic phases of psychological functioning, and might thereby contribute to the self's developing ego resiliency and its place amid social objects. Lacan and Kristeva have much less faith than Winnicott in the *social* functions of transitional objects, in socialization, in fact. They believe that the archaic dimension of the self, remaining always close to the surface, retains its destructive and disintegrative power.

The upshot of Winnicott's theory of the unconscious—or so it is possible to argue—is that nasty, destructive impulses can be assimilated, tamed, "repaired"; the self's movement toward integration implies healing, reparation, growth. But his project may involve mystifying much of what drives the self. In Kristeva's terms, he wants to repress or deconstruct the "uncanny other" inside the self, what the Kleinians call introjects or bad object representations and what Kristeva from time to time calls the internal foreigner (or self as "alien" to itself). These are not pleasant or generative aspects of who we are, these split-off or borderline rages and hates that constitute much of human experience, the residues of Kristeva's abject governing human drives, the "badness" (Klein) of the self concretized in violent and hateful passions that simply cannot be wished away. There is a certain naïveté to Winnicott's argument, although Burack (1993) makes a strong and intelligent case for Winnicott's *recognition* of the self's destructive passions.

To understand the constitution or construction of the self, we must give thought to these very unpleasant and dangerous aspects of what and who we are—dangerous in their regressive and explosive potential. And it is a myth or a mistake to think the self can become whole, that we can somehow purge out of ourselves these messy and mess-making parts by positing an idealized "wholeness" or otherness based on the good-enough mother. It is, in a psychological sense, impossible to get this other/mother out of me, to expurgate my entropic unconscious phantasies, to dismiss the narcissistic ugliness of my being, to forget about it, to send it back to the netherworld of the unconscious. It doesn't matter if I'm male or female. Abjection, narcissism, masochism, sadism—these parts of what human beings in fact are, from infancy onward, simply cannot be assimilated or argued away. They weigh too heavily on the self.

Certainly there is a need for cultivating reciprocity in the self's object relations. Lacan, like Winnicott, acknowledges as much; so does Kristeva. And accepting this "uncanny other" is not inconsistent with a commitment to reciprocity and tolerance. Both Lacan and Kristeva believe we can make the "uncanny other" less toxic, less fatal. To do so, we must acknowledge it, represent it, not run from it, *and* we must contain it within political structures whose dynamic leads to an understanding and *toleration* of conflict and helps to prevent struggle from spilling over into scapegoating, mindless violence, or the persecution of out-groups.

The crux of the argument is the perspective on the concept of wholeness. It is possible to live in a democratic environment, to support democratic ends and aims, and yet not necessarily to conceive of the democratic self in terms of a wholeness that ignores the conflicted and divided quality of human experience. It is possible, then, to criticize this side of Winnicott's theory without rejecting it altogether if we draw out and accept the Kleinian/Lacanian position that what pushes the self may not be so sanguine or healing as the transitional object, that the Kristevan abject drives much in human experience. Democratic institutions require a great deal of sensitivity to the very hateful projections of this abject and to the danger abject projections pose to a democratic culture.

One may be divided and conflicted as a human being and still maintain a democratic posture, as long as the reasons behind that "conflict" are acknowledged and accepted as part of what it means to be human. Democracy from this perspective, indeed what it means to be human, requires a hypersensitivity to conflict and not to wholeness or togetherness or community. What needs to be asked is how to sustain conflict, deal with it, accept it as part of the human project without totalizing experience at the expense of someone else, some other group or project. Conflict, as a form of communication, need not be debilitating; it may potentially be creative, supporting the ends of tolerance, as long as the public or political realm understands that conflict (and occasionally ugly emotions) motivates human action and identification, that this "uncanny other" in the self cannot be healed "out," and that the place where these nasty emotions are contained is in the public/political realm. Containment of the uncanny other becomes, simultaneously, the purposive and creative end of democratic institutions.

There is a difference between celebration of fragmentation and celebration of division. Acknowledgment of division is acknowledgment that the unconscious is not going to go away, that conflict cannot be purged out of human experience but is essential to what it means to be human and to live within the universe of will, desire, and need. Conflict sustains division. Fragmentation, however, is the destruction by conflict of its containing framework; fragmentation shatters experience, destroys recognition and tolerance, immobilizes the ego, and annihilates identity. Division implies the acceptance and recognition of boundaries and culturally defined spaces that require both acceptance and representation. Division enhances identity by pushing awareness to grasp the divided, yet communicable parts of the self. What Lacan asks is that we acknowledge the unconscious as the subject, rid ourselves of the conceit that somehow our rational or even consensual selves can control this frightening part of what we are, that reason has the power to detoxify the heavy paternal wishes and demands behind the "law of the father" or the values and norms of the "symbolic," or that rationality, in Kristevan terms, can somehow tame the psychohistorical forces of abjection.

It may be true that the faith in illusion (Nietzsche's Apollonian) is a flaw in Winnicott's theory. Given the often exclusive claims of cultures and their material desires in contemporary political life, conflict and sometimes pretty ugly manifestations of its power just will not meekly walk away. For Freud, as well as Lacan and Kristeva, the unconscious is too explosive, too powerful a legacy of oedipal and preoedipal experience and phantasy for the soothing and socializing effects of transitional objects to vanquish. These theorists keep reminding us that what provokes the unconscious *precedes* the socializing function of the transitional object, that transition or healing or synthesizing does not tame or tranquilize archaic imagoes embedded in the self. In fact, the Lacanian/Kristevan position suggests that transitional objects and spaces in their teleological operation, bringing the self to higher and more sophisticated levels of social cooperation, may lack the power to detoxify the unconscious and its constituent phantasies and self-representations. Throughout development, the unconscious strenuously influences action and identification, and it may take indirect or displaced routes to emerge in the individual as symptom of pathology and in the public as violence, depending on the capacity of political institutions to contain the public manifestations of hate, rage, and aggression.

For both Lacan and Freud, the unconscious is the true subject writing the laws of consciousness. Understanding ourselves as divided, as products of division, may lead to more tolerance, and the self, learning to tolerate what is intolerable, may become more flexible, more accepting of human imperfection and the very messy emotions impelling human behavior. Therefore, the true democratic self may not be one of resolution, of Winnicottian reconciliation, consensus, illusion in the service of reciprocity. The other piece of the puzzle, equally important, is learning to live with the conflict and rage accompanying human desire and not to ignore or underestimate these passions, substituting false illusions or myths about consensus or the natural bases for human cooperation. The conflicted or divided subject becomes the occasion for learning about conflict in the political world. If we can live with a conflicted self, if we can tolerate and contain the "uncanny other" inside of us, if we can detoxify through the containing and limit-creating potential of public institutions the all-too-human tendency toward psychosis and psychotic identification, then it is indeed possible to learn to live with conflict in the external political world, without allowing it to annihilate human purposes and reciprocity.

It is conceivable that the Winnicottian view can itself become totalitarian, that it might become aligned with the communitarian phantasy of unity and transcendence. Winnicott's view of illusion might even support myths or ideologies that try to forge unities at the expense of conflict and division, the illusion, for example, of wholeness brought to a political context or argument. It may not be consensus that drives the democratic process so much as endless conflict, contained through participatory mechanisms and forums, not conflict spilling out of institutional or constitutional limits but conflict acknowledging and respecting the other without assimilating otherness into an idealized (ideolog-ized) view of human possibility and action.

Kristeva and the Foreigner Within

Kristeva acknowledges the power of internal self-representations impelled by destructiveness, violence, fear, and exclusionary impulses, terror, dread, maternal power, the "return of the repressed in the guise of anxiety, and more specifically of uncanny strangeness" (1991, 184). Kristeva calls this strangeness the foreigner in the self: "Foreignness, an uncanny one, creeps into the tranquility of reason itself [and] irrigates our very speaking-being. . . . we are foreigners to ourselves" (170). For reasons we are unaware of (because they are unconscious), we find ourselves, in political and social relations, hating, excluding, defiling, and tormenting others; it is the fear of this foreignness and the efforts to repress, deny, or split it off which motivate much in human action. This foreigner is the personal and political source of much of our "distress" and "unsociability."

In Kristeva's reading of Freud, "the unconscious . . . the strange in the psyche" is part of what human life is all about, "an *otherness* that is both biological *and* symbolic . . . an integral part of the *same*" (181). And to be human is to be divided against oneself; it is to live with a conflicted internal self, and this internal division possesses political implications.

"Freud," Kristeva comments, "noted that the archaic, narcissistic self, not yet demarcated by the outside world, projects out of itself what it experiences as dangerous or unpleasant in itself, making of it an alien *double,* uncanny and demoniacal" (183). And if this otherness or foreignness is found to be "out there" as a "race [or] a nation [or] glorified as a secret *volksgeist*" (181), these massive projections indicate an effort to steer the debate away from the self, from the knowledge that what we see out there as scapegoat, hated or reviled other, are, in effect, pieces of ourselves we choose not to acknowledge or accept. So we take these pieces, place them in out-groups, nations, or entities and then move to destroy or otherwise persecute them. It is not the other who is evil; it is we: "Uncanny, foreignness is within us: we are our own foreigners, we are divided" (181). And because of that division, individuals and nations often commit crimes.

Kristeva's conception accounts for the feeling of difference and unsettledness in living with the "foreigner," the immigrant, the different. This feeling is, in fact, a symptom of the "ill-ease in the continuous presence of the 'other scene' within us. My discontent in living with the other—my strangeness, his strangeness"—derives from a "perturbed logic . . . constituted by the unconscious" (181–82), internal, psychological scripts, self-representations constantly disrupting reason, tranquility, and cooperation. Internal emotional conflict and, by implication, externalized forms of *political* violence never disappear, but in Kristeva's reading, psychoanalysis possesses the capacity to show us how to become reconciled to this otherness, this "foreign component of our psyche," how to "play on" my own otherness-foreignness "and live by it," without destroying others or ourselves in the various enactments of unconscious phantasies (182).

Kristeva holds out a profound heuristic function for what psychoanalysis reveals about the self, for its potential to unravel the strangeness of the other and diminish the fear attached to acknowledging and living with strangeness (although she never fully addresses the problem of how psychoanalysis is to find its way into the institutions, into the deliberations of leadership). Psychoanalysis, in her view, has the capacity to teach consciousness to construct an ethic of tolerance respecting otherness. In addition, a psychoanalytic understanding of otherness, at least on the individual level, inhibits, if it does not altogether prevent, dealing violently and indifferently with the other: "Psychoanalysis is then experienced as a journey into the strangeness of the other and of oneself, toward an ethics of respect for the irreconcilable. How could one tolerate a foreigner if one did not know one was a stranger to oneself?" (182).

To recognize this foreignness is not only to face the psychological suffering caused by the uncanny and its dread; it is also to sensitize consciousness to what suffering induces in others as alienation, confusion, and despair. "By recognizing *our* uncanny strangeness we shall neither suffer from it nor enjoy it from the outside. The foreigner is within me, hence we are all foreigners. If I am a foreigner, there are no foreigners" (192). Perhaps this is Kristeva's idealism: psychoanalysis implies both an ethics and a politics. To demystify the internal foreigner is to establish new understandings for human exchange. An ethics "far removed from a call for brotherhood," supporting "a cosmopolitanism of a new sort . . . cutting across governments, economies, and markets, might work for a mankind whose solidarity is founded on the consciousness of its unconscious—desiring, destructive, fearful, empty, impossible" (192). What distinguishes Kristeva's vision from a more traditional humanistic reading of human cooperation is her belief in the reality of division, a fractious human nature, dangerous and ugly passions that cannot be wished away. Her faith in the sustainability of difference, while vague in its structural components, nonetheless offers some hope for democratic approaches to conflict resolution. If we are the foreigner, then it makes utterly no sense to destroy or harm the other. It is not the scapegoat provoking the violence; it is our own fearful inability to look at and accept the "strangeness" within ourselves.

Afterword

THIS is the final volume in a series that has explored the relationship between psychological dislocation and social and political theory. It has taken a long time, this project, some seventeen years, the better part of my professional life. The research has focused on what symptom clusters in schizophrenia, borderline personality, manic depression, and multiple personality signify for broader social, political, and philosophical issues. I have concluded the clinical research for two reasons.

First, listening to these stories, especially the horrifying narratives of women with multiple personalities, has been exhausting and personally draining. In addition, I have completed an investigation into a set of political and philosophical problematics that over time kept this research alive and drew me to the wards in the Sheppard and Enoch Pratt Hospital, though there is obviously a great deal more to say about the structure of the self, the relation between self and public, and the reality of psychotic and borderline psychotic states. It has been an extraordinary experience, these dialogues with patients and observing the day-to-day life on a psychiatric ward, and I leave the hospital's clinical world with memories and images I shall never forget.

The patients whom I met and spoke with revealed truths about what it means to live and suffer which I have attempted to describe. But I can find no language sufficiently dramatic to convey the intensity and sadness of hours spent listening to narratives of alienation, words and images of estrangement and degradation, and moments of utterly immobilizing despair in patients such as Mary, Jenny, Chuck, Nora, Kimberly, Louis, and many others. These patients were mirrors for a multiple set of truth reflections, always changing and transforming, permitting a glimpse into what Julia Kristeva (1986) calls the "True/Real." Their stories and words had taken root not in letters but in suffering bodies. The expressions of pain and the all-too-frequent wishes to die came from bruised and emaciated bodies, faces twisted by years of inner torment, muscles atrophied by incessant self-reflection, medication, and a desperate need to escape the pain. These human beings were not disembodied texts; it was as living, breathing texts that they had so much importance. They brought through their bodies a presence to language, made immanent the devastating stories and parables of emotional disintegration.

The second major reason I have concluded my project is the demise of long-term *hospitalized* psychiatric care. I was fortunate to establish my research project at Sheppard-Pratt. As an institution, the hospital provided empathic and sensitive treatment through programs devoted to untangling complex psychological puzzles, to providing forums and space for the representation of mental illness, environments distinguished by their flexibility and dedication to treating severe emotional and psychological distress. In witnessing the pain of mental illness and the response of the staff to its manifestations, I found myself less sympathetic to the antipsychiatric and antiasylum arguments of theorists such as Michel Foucault and Gilles Deleuze and Félix Guattari (for reasons I have explained elsewhere [Glass, 1993]).

I want to emphasize that many patients experienced Sheppard-Pratt as a refuge, and many of its practices demonstrated just the opposite of the ideological attributions antipsychiatry critics hurled at institutional care. But then again, Sheppard-Pratt was not a conventional hospital—particularly not a conventional state or public mental institution. It was Sheppard's governing assumption that the fear, terror, anguish, and alienation "normal" people never know as part of their daily conscious life requires a containment possible only in the context of an asylum (asylum understood as a place of safety and refuge; see Glass, 1989), in addition to therapists who refuse to objectify the patient in a physiological and chemical gestalt that dehumanizes suffering and excises the psychological self from a knowledge of suffering.

Many therapists (although certainly not all) saw themselves not only as medical practitioners but as seekers after truth. They listened to the anguish of the human spirit day after day, thought about it, and explored mental illness as terrifying contradictions in human adaptation and meaning, not as narrowly defined medical dysfunctions to be administered and solved. If there is a repository of knowledge and understanding about the self, it lies in the experience and perspectives of these therapists, who regard the *contents* of self as a back-and-forth interplay of metaphoric, physiological, and public realities.

It does no service to the history of human suffering to disparage the efforts of practitioners who approach human pain and despair with enormous seriousness and dedication. In any mental hospital there are therapists and staff members who do things well and those who do not; yet it is important to keep in mind what psychoanalytically informed psychotherapy as a practice can accomplish in healing, containing, and treating. Of course, there has been plenty of evidence of what institutional care cannot accomplish and of its insensitivity to suffering. My research at Sheppard-Pratt convinced me, however, that the possibilities of learning from psychosis and from therapists who work with psychotic and borderline patients are significant. Psychiatry, psychoanalysis, and psychotherapy are as good or bad as their practitioners and the holding environments they support. I found talented and intuitive mental health workers and nurses, just as I encountered individuals who should not have been working on a mental ward.

Long-term care for serious mental illness is finished, a dinosaur, a relic of a past with more resources, more latitude. When in 1976 I first started research on schizophrenia at Sheppard-Pratt, there were at least five units with patients who had been in the hospital more than eight months. The psychiatric residency program required residents to work on the long-term units for two years. Psychiatric case evaluations by senior psychiatrists and residents were fascinating excursions into philosophy and medical treatment, and at their center was an interest in the context of self in a history of suffering and misunderstanding. I cannot emphasize too strongly that psychiatric residents chose Sheppard-Pratt because it offered a chance to explore the self and not techniques for distancing illness. The hospital staff, for the most part, resisted the complete medicalization of illness, the categorization according to the physiology and chemistry of psychiatric disturbance. This teaching venue was much different from that of other hospitals, whose residents, even in the old days of long-term care, received very little instruction in psychotherapy or psychodynamic processes such as projective identification and countertransference, critical forms of human interaction.

Narratives, stories, symbols, metaphors, feelings, and experience were the stuff of case evaluations at Sheppard-Pratt. I attended countless psychiatric supervisions and evaluations. It was an education to watch this disentangling of language, the tentative search for meaning, the frustration when the truth of the self could not be grasped, interpretations that seemed to go nowhere, that turned back on themselves, pieces of truth emerging from time to time only to be lost, and the persistence in identifying some coherence in what the psychotic and borderline self speaks, means, and feels.

When I finished the clinical side of my research in the early nineties, psychiatric residents no longer had the opportunity to do any long-term work; the maximum stay, in almost all cases, had declined to thirty days. Many of the patients I spoke with during the 1970s and 1980s had been at the hospital for at least a year. The insight into the mind, into the self's fissures, cracks, interstices, and history which can be achieved in the long-term relationship—that kind of experience *and* knowledge is part of the past. Psychiatric residents now treat what might be called the "thirty-day self," but such treatment is superficial and insufficient and makes a mockery of understanding. It amounts to management and suppression of symptoms. Therapy in this modern psychiatric environment has ceased to be a shared encounter in pursuit of meaning through the discovery and elaboration *in language* of the reasons behind pain. It has become instead a management by objectives with medication as the primary therapeutic intervention. Understanding and insight, too, have become dinosaurs.

The clinical receptiveness of Sheppard-Pratt provided a multitude of different avenues into the self. Not only psychotherapy but the ancillary therapies (which, if not cut from the hospital's program, have been seriously scaled back) aided the patient's effort to ameliorate crippling emotional pain. The dance, art, and occupational therapies elaborated the self and its movements and expressions from points of view which aided the psychotherapist, providing information about the self's emotional position that psychotherapy could not see or elicit.

In the refuge provided by Sheppard-Pratt, the language and gestures of psychosis were not regarded as the enemy to be sealed over or managed with the intent of maintaining a calm ward atmosphere. On occasion, nursing or psychiatric staff would argue for more (or less) medication, but therapeutic approach never found itself defined *only* by insurance limitations or the patient's proclivity for emotional outbursts. Disputes about treatment guidelines and therapeutic method and consciousness of countertransference reactions were all part of the unit's atmosphere. What mattered was unraveling and understanding the patient's internal world and the projective processes governing exchanges and actions on the unit.

With stays of less than thirty days, it is not possible to encourage a therapeutic environment where months could pass before the self even offered a glimpse of any of the keys capable of unlocking its secrets. Long-term care provided a place in the society "safe enough" to encourage, interpret, and demystify psychotic expressiveness. Therapy outside the hospital setting is limited in its resources, and psychotic stories, much less their interpretation, may have to be repressed or sealed over, since neither the therapist nor the society can *afford* the time or patience to listen to and decipher the complex messages of linguistic and psychological dislocation.

It is a sad state of affairs. A vast number of persons with debilitating mental illness require careful listening, empathy, and holding, but society and its agents systematically discourage these practices for the more "cost-effective" methods of administering the self and defining treatment as the medical suppression of the symptomatology of the internal world. What has been lost is a tradition, a search through language for a knowledge that moves beneath the surface, that looks for and tries to decipher the self's relation to the edges of social life, the threat psychosis poses to psychological and consensual borders, and the effect of this isolation on family, friends, and public associations. The self now has almost no place to go where these stories may be told over an extended period of time, their common structures uncovered, their symbols interpreted, their often annihilating power demystified through a painstaking collaboration among persons who have had the experience of *listening*. It is a human and social tragedy of great proportion.

NOTES

Introduction

1. Psychosis may be thought of as a state or condition that repudiates consensual reality and projects delusional images of power as the self's central frame of reference. What exist prior, in terms of psychological development, to the linguistic construction of self, to secondary process defenses, are feelings and sensations that possess a delusional meaning. These sensations or feelings, embodied in often peculiar and extraordinary images of domination and victimization, constitute a part of the self which is hidden and often split off in the case of borderline conditions or entirely fragmented in schizophrenia.

2. Jacques Lacan (1993) regards the delusional world that holds these images of power as thoroughly detached from consensual reality, what he calls the realm of the "symbolic." As Carolyn Dean notes, Lacan views delusion (psychotic hallucination, Dean calls it) as an "impossible symbolism . . . a set of signifiers with no stable referents." Psychosis (in Dean's exposition of Lacan) "express[es] the psychotic's suspended relationship with language and culture—with the symbolic order [and] offers an 'open testimony' of the unconscious . . . made transparent" (1992, 116). In Lacan's words, psychosis has the power to "threaten the entire edifice . . . of symbolization" (1993, 85). "The psychotic," Dean continues, "becomes a rift in the symbolic order . . . [and] is thus a metaphor for what is impossible, unknowable, and yet most true about the self: what Lacan calls the other par excellence—the real" (118). Or in Julia Kristeva's (1989) terms, "If *repudiation* (*Verwerfung*) were to prevail over negation the symbolic framework would collapse and erase reality itself: that is the pattern of psychosis" (46).

1. Psychotic Unhinging

1. In her discussion of abjection in *Powers of Horror* (1982) Kristeva relates the concept to borderline patients. She uses the psychiatric term "borderline" in more or less

the same way as object-relations psychoanalytic theorists such as Otto Kernberg, James Masterson (1976), and Clarence Schulz and Roger Lewin. Yet, it seems to me, her notion of abjection is also descriptive of certain psychotic states of mind and identifications. The schizophrenic, possibly the paradigmatic ab-ject, lives out the emotional terror of abjection. Central to much in delusional thinking is the fear of being poisoned, the sense of defilement, abomination, horror, dread, the conception of the self as filthy, polluted, and so on. The concept of abjection, therefore, enhances understanding of the experience and phenomenology of psychosis *and* psychotic time. For Kristeva, as for object-relations theory generally, the symptomatology of abjection derives from profoundly disturbing preverbal internalization associated with maternal presence, "the maternal as unclean and improper coalescence, as undifferentiated power and threat, a defilement to be cut off" (1982, 106). Kristeva's fascination with the legacy of maternal power (and its negative properties) links her closely with the theories of Melanie Klein.

2. *Psychotic Time*

1. For Minow-Pinkney, "Woolf's skepticism towards the sequentiality of time, narrative, life, is, in short, a protest against the symbolic order" (1990, 171). The self persistently finds itself in a " 'perpetual warfare . . . [a] shattering and piecing together . . . the eternal renewal, the incessant rise and fall and fall and rise again' " (from *The Waves* [1978], quoted by Minow-Pinkney, 173). Compare also Tina Chanter: "Successive, or linear, time is teleological, a time of progress" (1990, 65); women's time, monumental or feminine time, as Chanter calls it, embraces emotional intensities that place the self or consciousness beyond the constraining effects of historical recognition. It is a time, in Kristeva's words, "without cleavage or escape, which has so little to do with linear time (which passes) that the very word 'temporality' hardly fits" (1986b, 191). Because of the emotional reality of women, particularly those passions associated with maternity and maternal affect, Chanter maintains, the meaning and nature of time veers sharply from what it signifies as a male-*dominated* form of measurement.

Compare Chanter's relatively favorable interpretation of Kristeva's feminism with the following: "Winnicott's view of the bad mother seems benign compared to Kristeva's way of blaming women for every oppressive position they find themselves in: as inhabitants of the harem, as wives of Don Juans, as depressives, and, finally, as single parents. . . . The Kristevan mother is silent or hysterical, suicide or terrorist" (Doane and Hodges 1992, 67, 77).

3. *Jenny*

1. Otto Kernberg calls this process projective identification, which, he says, "in contrast to projection, consists of the projection into another person of split-off parts of the ego or self or of an internal object. Rather than simply dissociating itself from that projected part, the ego, under the effects of projective identification, aims to forcefully enter into the external object [in this case, staff] and control it" (1980, 27).

2. Or in Kernberg's terms, "The tendency to perceive objects as either ideal (all good) or persecutory (all bad) is the consequence of the early defensive operation of splitting. Splitting is the active separation of good from bad experiences, perceptions and emotions linked to objects. Only at later stages of development, when splitting mechanisms

decrease, is a synthesis of good and bad aspects of objects possible and the coming into existence of ambivalence toward whole objects" (1980, 25). Unfortunately, Jenny never attained this state of mind.

4. *Tragedy*

1. Kristeva derives this fear of being poisoned, assaulted by food, from an archaic identification: the sense of sustenance, the mother's milk, as "defilement, sewage, muck." She notes: "Food loathing is perhaps the most elementary and most archaic form of abjection. When the eyes see or the lips touch that skin on the surface of milk—harmless, thin as a sheet of cigarette paper, pitiful as a nail paring—I experience a gagging sensation and, still farther down, spasms in the stomach, the belly; and all the organs shrivel up the body, provoke tears and bile, increase heartbeat, cause forehead and hands to perspire. Along with sight-clouding dizziness, *nausea* makes me balk at that milk cream, separates me from the mother and father who proffer it" (1982, 2–3).

2. Otto Kernberg says that Melanie Klein conceptualized "hypochondriacal delusions as related to unconscious fantasies of a total destruction of the objects of the inner world; fantasies of destruction of the external world would reflect projection of the fantasied destruction of the internal world" (1980, 32).

3. It might be useful to think of this passage in the context of her fear of discharge and her feelings of abandonment.

4. In the "hate Jenny" phase of her treatment on Hall A, while in seclusion, Jenny had soaked her bathrobe in her own urine and tied it around her neck, squeezing as hard as she could before a nurse saw what was happening and prevented her from choking herself.

5. This is a commentary on her transfer from Hall A to Hall B, or at least the nurses construed it as a reflection on her sense of place.

5. *Maureen*

1. J. Doane and D. Hodges (1992) write of Kristeva that she believes "Western civilization as a totalized, melancholy entity . . . is itself in the grip of a death drive" (69).

2. For a fascinating analysis of the psychodynamics and pathology of gender, see Robert J. Stoller, *Presentations of Gender* (1985).

6. *Power and Its Construction*

1. Theorists such as Lacan and Kristeva, not to mention Freud, are correctives to arguments that diminish the importance of psychic reality, unconscious phantasy, and preoedipal identity-forming imagoes. Whether psychic reality, the unconscious as a protest to or a "negative" of the normalizing functions of society, creates or may create a protective barrier between self and society, however, I am not so sure. Nor am I inclined to hinge a resistance to the normalizing power of social convention on a Lacanian adaptation of Freud's concept of the unconscious, although Kristeva may achieve that theoretical aim in her effort to ground the impact of the maternal *chora* in feminine identity. Freud quite strenuously acknowledges the *destructive* potential of the unconscious; this argument is at

the heart of *Civilization and Its Discontents,* and it appears from time to time in Kristeva's theory of abjection and the preoedipal mother.

2. For example, consider the following observation from the creator of the punch-card computer, Willy Heidinger, managing director of what was in the 1930s IBM's German subsidiary: "We are recording the individual characteristics of every single member of the nation on a little card. . . . [It is] a task that provides the physician of the German body politic [Hitler] with the material he needs. We have firm confidence in our physician and will follow his orders blindly. Heil to the German people and their leader!" (quotation from an exhibit in the U.S. Holocaust Memorial Museum, *Washington Post,* April 23, 1993). Zygmunt Bauman writes: "The most horrifying evil in human memory did not result from the dissipation of order, but from an impeccable, faultless and unchallengeable rule of order. It was not the work of an obstreperous and uncontrollable mob [LeBon's theory of group behavior], but of men in uniforms, obedient and disciplined, following the rules and meticulous about the spirit and the letter of their briefing. It became known very soon that these men, whenever they took their uniforms off, were in no way evil. They behaved much like all of us. They had wives they loved, children they cosseted, friends they helped and comforted in case of distress. It seemed unbelievable that once in uniform the same people shot, gassed or presided over the shooting and gassing of thousands of other people, including women who were someone's beloved wives and babies who were someone's cosseted children. It also was terrifying. How could ordinary people like you and me do it?" (1991, 151).

3. Among Oest's suggestions for childhood instruction is the following: "For this reason I would suggest that children be cleansed from head to foot every two to four weeks by an old, dirty, and ugly woman, without anyone else being present; still, parents or those in charge should make sure that even this old woman doesn't linger unnecessarily over any part of the body. This task should be depicted to the children as disgusting, and they should be told that the old woman must be paid to undertake a task that, although necessary for purposes of health and cleanliness, is yet so disgusting that no other person can bring himself to do it. This would serve to prevent a shock to their sense of modesty" (from a 1787 text, quoted by Miller, 47).

4. See James Miller's fascinating discussion of this entire issue, particularly in the context of the relationship between Foucault's life and work, in *The Passion of Michel Foucault* (1993).

5. To be good is to obey; disobedience means slander against parental authority. This state of mind, Miller concludes, has disastrous psychological consequences. Parents fear "misbehavior" so strenuously "that on occasion they feel thoroughly justified in using any means to prevent it" (1984, 41). Psychologically, in the face of such power, the self may come to understand itself as bad, worthless, damaged, or impaired. Power *threatens* in poisonous environments; it is not cooperative, spontaneous, reciprocal or generative; it is dangerous, forbidding and hateful. But the child has little knowledge of what is happening; it is not in the parental interest to stimulate awareness. "Thou shalt not be aware of what your parents are doing to you" (61). Psychological blindness is encouraged; little if any attention is given to the fact that authoritative command may deflect drives or needs in ways harmful to the child's interests.

7. *Psychosis in the Collective*

1. For example, regarding the fight/flight group, Kernberg writes: "Splitting, projection of aggression, and projective identification prevail, and the search for nurture

and dependency characteristic of the dependency group is replaced in the fight-flight group, by conflicts around aggressive control, with suspiciousness, fighting and dread of annihilation" (1980, 214).

2. It might be interesting to contrast Bion's theory of the basic assumption and its psychotic substrates to Rousseau's (1950) concept of the general will. Unlike Rousseau, Bion (1961) defines the basic assumption as fundamentally a psychological phenomenon: "Group mentality is the unanimous expression of the will of the group, contributed to by the individual in ways of which he is unaware, influencing him disagreeably whenever he thinks or behaves in a manner at variance with the basic assumptions. It is thus a machinery of intercommunication that is designed to ensure that group life is in accordance with the basic assumptions" (65). Much distinguishes these two formulations. The general will acts to realize the community's conscious aims; not so the basic assumptions, for unconscious aims often differ radically from the group's task orientation. The general will has an almost legislative or juristic component. It works for the "good," the "virtue" of the community; it binds; it is cohesive. The basic assumptions, by contrast, embody or represent "badness" (in the sense of bad part-objects). They are divisive and induce hostility and conflict. For Rousseau the general will enhances individuality; for Bion, basic assumptions obliterate it. For Rousseau, the group mentality lies at the foundation of the will of the people; for Bion, the underlying unity of the basic assumptions, their valency, may work harm on the community and do irreparable damage. Whereas Rousseau tends to idealize community and the group, Bion points to some of the more terrifying dangers that may be embodied in group process and action.

8. *The Ego Ideal*

1. It might be useful here to recall the importance D. W. Winnicott attaches to the process of transition from primary narcissism to engagement with the social world. For Winnicott (1953), objects or others accomplish the transition; for Chasseguet-Smirgel the models that compose the ego ideal perform some of these transitional functions, moving the self toward autonomy, differentiation, and respect for otherness, although her view of the disintegrative drives and narcissism is much closer to Lacan than to Winnicott. Or, as Thomas Ogden (1989) describes the process: "Transitional phenomena have a dialectical structure. Oneness and separateness, reality and fantasy, me and not-me coexist with one another, each creating, preserving, and negating the other. Reality does not supersede fantasy any more than the conscious mind replaces the unconscious mind in the course of development. Rather, reality enters into a mutually defining and enriching relationship with fantasy" (1989, 117). It is this interaction, a dialectic between inner and outer, that allows the self to forge a dynamic creative relationship with the surrounding consensual world and to build bulwarks against psychotic time and annihilating forms of power. "It is only in the space between reality and fantasy created in this way that subjectivity, personal meaning, symbol formation, and imagination become possible" (117).

2. In a passage that shows the influence of Winnicott's concept of transition, Chasseguet-Smirgel observes: "The originality of the ego ideal is, in fact, that it represents a link-concept between absolute narcissism and object relatedness, between the pleasure principle and the reality principle, because it is itself a product of the severance of the ego from the object" (1985, 28).

3. In an interesting swipe at Lacan, Kristeva writes: "The resources of narcissism and idealization imprint their stamps upon the unconscious and refashion it. For the unconscious is not structured like a language but like all the imprints of the Other, including

and most particularly so those that are most archaic, 'semiotic,' it is constituted by preverbal self-sensualities that the narcissistic or amorous experience restores to me" (1989, 204–5).

4. Pete's father was the president of a large industrial company. He bore his son's suffering as if it were Pete's stigmata. He felt that his own suffering, both personal and financial, showed just how tough he was, able to bear the shame of having a son who had fallen so short of expectations. The therapist noted: "It is interesting that the patient perceives both his father and me as grim, harsh, and fundamentally unpleasable."

5. In *Powers of Horror* (1982), Kristeva presents a disturbing account of the French author Louis-Ferdinand Céline's anti-Semitic texts (mostly written in the 1930s and early 1940s). In "the crushing anarchy or nihilism of [his] discourse . . . an *object* appears—an object of hatred and desire, of threat and aggressivity, of envy and abomination. . . . That object, the Jew, gives thought a focus where all contradictions are explained and satisfied. . . . his anti-Semitism . . . appears as the simple outcome of a fully secular rage; anti-Semitism would be a diehard secularism sweeping away, along with its number one enemy, religion, all its secondary representatives: abstraction, reason, and adulterated power, considered emasculating" (178).

6. For a fascinating analysis of this phenomenon, see Christopher R. Browning's *Ordinary Men: Reserve Police Battalion 101 and the Final Solution in Poland* (1993). Browning looks at the behavior of a small police battalion, recruited from Hamburg and put to work by the SS murdering Jews in the forests around Lublin. Browning contends that the members of this battalion were not in any characterological sense extraordinary. Yet, these policemen, ordinary citizens, easily became killers, even though they had many opportunities to refuse this kind of "service." In Browning's view, the murdering and concentrating of Jews for transportation was undertaken, more often than is recognized, by these "ordinary men," individuals without strong ideological or psychopathological leanings who were nonetheless capable of horrifying acts of mass murder.

9. Identity and Power

1. Toni Morrison's novel *Beloved* describes a good example of this perversion of power from the perspective of the victimized, the sufferer. For a fictional account that takes a look at the internal self-structure of a budding fascist and the paranoid, narcissistic modality of his thinking, see Evan S. Connell's *Diary of a Rapist*.

10. Psychodynamic Preconditions for the Democratic Exercise of Power

1. Winnicott notes: "What I have called the 'subjective object' . . . becomes gradually related to objects that are objectively perceived, but this happens only when a good-enough environmental provision or 'average expectable environment' . . . enables the baby to be mad in one particular way that is conceded to babies. This madness only becomes true madness if it appears in later life" (1982, 71).

2. When illusion becomes fixed and immovable, when it takes on a delusional cast in the phantasies of military officers, in politics, in the closed world of executive actions and "special operations," is psychosis claimed? Is not a president who ignores the historically sanctioned consent of Congress in undertaking certain actions, who revokes consent by disregarding it, not speaking a certain kind of political madness? Is this not a form of political regression?

On an individual level, psychosis is found in "special indulgences," but rarely is it acknowledged in politics. Instead, disregard for the shared political reality or community, for consent, is taken as health or "reasons of state," "part of the game," or protection of national interest, when in fact it is a serious repudiation of a set of political beliefs that embody some form of collective reality, some historical connection. The Iran-Contra hearings described in vivid detail the consequences of a type of thinking that ignored consent and elevated phantasy or closed systems of belief to the position of reasons of state.

3. Sandel depicts individuals as compositions of perceptions and sentiments—sentiment being analogous to preference. His is a radically different concept of feeling from the psychoanalytic notions of affect, defense, pleasure, and so on.

11. Conclusion

1. Discussing Didier Anzieu's (1971) view of groups and their actions, Chasseguet-Smirgel writes: "Temporally the group has a tendency to regress to primary narcissism; topographically, the ego and the superego can no longer exercise their control. The id takes possession of the psychic apparatus with the ideal ego which '*seeks to realize a fusion with the omnipotent mother and the introjective restoration of the lost primary love object.*' The group becomes, for the members, the substitute for this lost object. . . . Anzieu shows therefore that a group that operates by itself (without any controlling organism having the function of reality testing) '*would naturally function within the order of illusion*' [or, even more probably, delusion]" (1985, 81; Chasseguet-Smirgel's emphasis).

REFERENCES

Alford, C. F. 1989. *Melanie Klein and Critical Social Theory: An Account of Politics, Art, and Reason Based on Her Psychoanalytic Theory.* New Haven: Yale University Press.

——. 1991. *The Self in Social Theory: A Psychoanalytic Account of Its Construction in Plato, Hobbes, Locke, Rawls, and Rousseau.* New Haven: Yale University Press.

——. 1993. *The Psychoanalytic Theory of Greek Tragedy: Humane Anti-Humanism.* New Haven: Yale University Press.

Anzieu, D. 1971. "L'illusion groupale." *Nouvelle Revue de Psychanalyse* 4:73–93.

Arendt, H. 1976. *Eichmann in Jerusalem: A Report on the Banality of Evil.* New York: Penguin.

Bauman, Z. 1991. *Modernity and the Holocaust.* Ithaca: Cornell University Press.

Benjamin, J. 1988. *The Bonds of Love: Psychoanalysis, Feminism, and the Problem of Domination.* New York: Pantheon.

——. 1993. "Reply to Burack." *Psychoanalysis and Contemporary Society* 16:447–54.

Bion, W. R. 1961. *Experiences in Groups and Other Papers.* New York: Basic Books.

——. 1970. *Attention and Interpretation: A Scientific Approach to Insight in Psychoanalysis and Groups.* New York: Basic Books.

——. 1983. *Transformations.* New York: Jason Aronson.

——. 1984. *Second Thoughts: Selected Papers in Psychoanalysis.* New York: Jason Aronson.

Browning, C. R. 1993. *Ordinary Men: Reserve Police Battalion 101 and the Final Solution in Poland.* New York: Harper Perennial.

Burack, C. 1993. "Love, Rage, and Destruction: Donald Winnicott and Social Theory." *Psychoanalysis and Contemporary Society* 16:429–46.

——. 1994. *The Problem of the Passions: Feminism, Psychoanalysis, and Social Theory*. New York: New York University Press.

Cardinal, M. 1984. *The Words to Say It: An Autobiographical Novel by Marie Cardinal*. Trans. P. Goodheart. Cambridge: Van Vactor and Goodheart.

Chanter, T. 1990. "Female Temporality and the Future of Feminism." In *Abjection, Melancholia, and Love: The Work of Julia Kristeva*, ed. J. Fletcher and A. Benjamin. New York: Routledge.

Chasseguet-Smirgel, J. 1985. *The Ego Ideal: A Psychoanalytic Essay on the Malady of the Ideal*. Trans. P. Barrows. New York: Norton.

Connell, E. S. 1988. *The Diary of a Rapist*. San Francisco: North Point Press.

Copjec, J. 1990. "Male/Female or Not Reconciled." In *The Woman in Question*, ed. P. Adams and E. Lowie. Cambridge: MIT Press.

Dean, C. J. 1992. *The Self and Its Pleasures: Bataille, Lacan, and the History of the Decentered Subject*. Ithaca: Cornell University Press.

Deleuze, G., and F. Guattari. 1977. *Anti-Oedipus: Capitalism and Schizophrenia*. Trans. R. Hurley, M. Seem, and H. R. Lane. New York: Viking Press.

Doane, J., and D. Hodges. 1992. *From Klein to Kristeva: Psychoanalytic Feminism and the Search for the 'Good Enough' Mother*. Ann Arbor: University of Michigan Press.

Eigen, M. 1986. *The Psychotic Core*. Northvale, N.J.: Jason Aronson.

Erikson, E. H. 1964. *Insight and Responsibility*. New York: Norton.

Felman, S. 1985. "Beyond Oedipus: The Specimen Story of Psychoanalysis." In *Lacan and Narration: The Psychoanalytic Difference in Narrative Theory*, ed. R. C. Davis. Baltimore: Johns Hopkins University Press.

——. 1989. *Writing and Madness (Literature/Philosophy/Psychoanalysis)*. Trans. M. N. Evans, S. Felman, and B. Massumi. Ithaca: Cornell University Press.

Flax, J. 1993. *Disputed Subjects: Essays on Psychoanalysis, Politics, and Philosophy*. New York: Routledge.

Foucault, M. 1965. *Madness and Civilization*. Trans. R. Howard. New York: Random House.

——. 1977. *Language, Counter-Memory, Practice: Selected Essays and Interviews*. Trans. D. F. Bouchard and S. Simon. Ithaca: Cornell University Press.

——. 1979. *Discipline and Punish: The Birth of the Prison*. Trans. A. Sheridan. New York: Vintage.

——. 1980. *Power/Knowledge: Selected Interviews and Other Writings, 1972–1977*. Trans. C. Gordon, L. Marshall, J. Mepham, K. Soper. New York: Pantheon.

Freud, S. 1900. *The Interpretation of Dreams*. *Standard Edition* 4-5:1–697. London: Hogarth.

——. 1920. *Beyond the Pleasure Principle*. *Standard Edition* 18:3–64. London: Hogarth.

——. 1921. *Group Psychology and the Analysis of the Ego*. *Standard Edition* 18:65–143. London: Hogarth.

——. 1923. *The Ego and the Id. Standard Edition* 19:3–66.
——. 1924a. *The Loss of Reality in Neurosis and Psychosis. Standard Edition* 19:183–87. London: Hogarth.
——. 1924b. *Neurosis and Psychosis. Standard Edition* 19:149–53.
——. 1927. *The Future of an Illusion. Standard Edition* 20. 3–56 London: Hogarth.
——. 1930. *Civilization and Its Discontents. Standard Edition* 21:59–145.
——. 1937. *Constructions in Analysis. Standard Edition* 23:255–69. London: Hogarth.
——. 1939. *Moses and Monotheism. Standard Edition* 23:3–137.
Frosch, S. 1983. *The Psychotic Process.* New York: International Universities Press.
Fuller Torrey, E. 1992. *Freudian Fraud: The Malignant Effect of Freud's Theory on American Thought and Culture.* New York: Harper Collins.
Galston, W. A. 1991. *Liberal Purposes: Goods, Virtues, and Diversity in the Liberal State.* New York: Cambridge: Cambridge University Press.
Gay, P. 1982. "Liberalism and Regression." In *The Psychoanalytic Study of the Child* 37. New Haven: Yale University Press.
Girard, R. 1986. *The Scapegoat.* Baltimore: Johns Hopkins University Press.
Glass, J. M. 1985. *Delusion: Internal Dimensions of Political Life.* Chicago: University of Chicago Press.
——. 1989. *Private Terror/Public Life: Psychosis and the Politics of Community.* Ithaca: Cornell University Press.
——. 1993. *Shattered Selves: Multiple Personality in a Postmodern World.* Ithaca: Cornell University Press.
Goffman, E. 1961. *Asylums.* New York: Doubleday Anchor.
Jacobson, E. 1964. *The Self and the Object World.* New York: International Universities Press.
Kernberg, O. 1975. *Borderline Conditions and Pathological Narcissism.* New York: Jason Aronson.
——. 1980. *Internal World and External Reality: Object Relations Applied.* New York: Jason Aronson.
Klein. M. 1935. "A Contribution to the Psychogenesis of Manic-Depressive States." *International Journal of Psychoanalysis* 16:145–74.
——. 1946. "Notes on Some Schizoid Mechanisms." *International Journal of Psychoanalysis* 27:99–110.
Kohut, H. 1971. *The Analysis of the Self.* New York: International Universities Press.
Kristeva, J. 1980. "The Novel as Polylogue." In *Desire in Language: A Semiotic Approach to Literature and Art,* ed. L. S. Roudiez, trans. T. Gora, A. Jardine, L. S. Roudiez. New York: Columbia University Press.
——. 1982. *Powers of Horror: An Essay on Abjection.* Trans. R. Diaz. New York: Columbia University Press.
——. 1986a. "The True/Real." Trans. S. Hand. In *The Kristeva Reader,* ed. T. Moi. New York: Columbia University Press.
——. 1986b. "Women's Time." Trans. A. Jardine and H. Blake. In *The Kristeva Reader,* ed. T. Moi. New York: Columbia University Press.

———. 1989. *Black Sun: Depression and Melancholia*. Trans. L. S. Roudiez. New York: Columbia University Press.
———. 1991. *Strangers to Ourselves*. Trans. L. S. Roudiez. New York: Columbia University Press.
———. 1993. *Nations without Nationalism*. Trans. L. S. Roudiez. New York: Columbia University Press.
Lacan, J. 1968. *Language of the Self: The Function of Language in Psychoanalysis*. Trans. A. Wilder. Baltimore: Johns Hopkins University Press.
———. 1978. *The Four Fundamental Concepts of Psychoanalysis*. Trans. A. Sheridan. New York: Norton.
———. *La Seminaire*, Book II. Quoted in S. Felman. 1985. "Beyond Oedipus: The Specimen Story of Psychoanalysis." In *Lacan and Narration: The Psychoanalytic Difference in Narrative Theory*, ed. R. C. Davis. Baltimore: Johns Hopkins University Press.
———. 1993. *The Seminar of Jacques Lacan*. Book 3: *The Psychoses, 1955–56*. Trans. R. Grigg. New York: Norton.
LeBon, G. 1960. *The Crowd: A Study of the Popular Mind*. New York: Viking.
Lévi-Strauss, C. 1969. *The Savage Mind*. Chicago: University of Chicago Press.
Lewin, R., and C. G. Schulz. 1992. *Losing and Fusing: Borderline Transitional Object and Self Relations*. Northvale, N.J.: Jason Aronson.
Lifton, R. J. 1986. *The Nazi Doctors*. New York: Basic Books.
Little, G. 1985. *Political Ensembles*. New York: Oxford University Press.
Macpherson, C. B. 1979. *The Political Theory of Possessive Individualism*. New York: Oxford.
Mahler, M. S. 1968. *On Human Symbiosis and the Vicissitudes of Individuation*. New York: International Universities Press.
Masson, J. M. 1984. *Assault on Truth: Freud's Suppression of the Seduction Theory*. New York: Farrar, Straus, and Giroux.
Masterson, J. 1976. *Psychotherapy of the Borderline Adult: A Developmental Approach*. New York: Brunner/Mazel.
Milgrim, S. 1974. *Obedience to Authority*. New York: Harper and Row.
Mill, J. S. 1951. "On Liberty." In Mill, *Utilitarianism, Liberty, and Representative Government*. New York: E. P. Dutton.
Miller, A. 1984. *For Your Own Good: Hidden Cruelty in Child-Rearing and the Roots of Violence*. Trans. H. and H. Hannum. New York: Farrar, Straus, and Giroux.
———. 1990a. *Banished Knowledge: Facing Childhood Injuries*. Trans. L. Vennewitz. New York: Anchor Books.
———. 1990b. *The Untouched Key: Tracing Childhood Trauma in Creativity and Destructiveness*. Trans. H. and H. Hannum. New York: Anchor Books.
Miller, J. 1993. *The Passion of Michel Foucault*. New York: Simon and Schuster.
Minow-Pinkney, M. 1990. "Virginia Woolf 'Seen from a Foreign Land.' " In *Abjection, Melancholia, and Love: The Work of Julia Kristeva*, ed. J. Fletcher and A. Benjamin. New York: Routledge.
Morrison, T. 1988. *Beloved*. New York: New American Library.
Nietzsche. F. 1873. *Das Philosophenbuch*. Part III: "On Truth and Lies in an Extra-

Moral Sense." Trans. J. Forrester. In H. Lawson and L. Appignanesi, eds. 1989. *Dismantling Truth: Reality in the Post-Modern World*. New York: St. Martin's Press.

Ogden, T. 1989. *The Primitive Edge of Experience*. Northvale, N.J.: Jason Aronson.

Plato. 1964. *The Republic*. Trans. P. Shorey. In *The Collected Dialogues of Plato*, ed. E. Hamilton and H. Cairns. New York: Pantheon Books.

Rawls, J. 1971. *A Theory of Justice*. Cambridge: Harvard University Press.

Rousseau, J. J. 1950. *The Social Contract and Discourses*. New York: Dutton.

Sandel, M. 1982. *Liberalism and the Limits of Justice*. New York: Cambridge University Press.

Schulz, C. G. 1980. "The Contribution of the Concept of Self Representation/Object Representation to the Understanding of the Schizophrenias." In *The Course of Life: Psychoanalytic Contributions towards Understanding Personality Development*, ed. S. I. Greenspan and G. H. Pollock. Vol. 1: *Infancy and Early Childhood*. Washington, D.C.: National Institute of Mental Health.

Schulz, C. G., and R. K. Kilgalen. 1967. *Case Studies in Schizophrenia*. New York: Basic Books.

Searles, H. 1960. *The Non Human Environment*. New York: International Universities Press.

——. 1965. *Collected Papers on Schizophrenia and Related Subjects*. New York: International Universities Press.

Spitz, R. 1965. *The First Year of Life*. New York: International Universities Press.

Stoller, R. 1985. *Presentations of Gender*. New Haven: Yale University Press.

Sullivan, H. S. 1952. *Schizophrenia as a Human Process*. New York: W. W. Norton.

Tausk, V. 1948. *On the Origin of the "Influencing Machine" in Schizophrenia*. In *The Psychoanalytic Reader*, ed. R. Fleiss. New York: International Universities Press.

Volkan, V. 1988. *The Need to Have Enemies and Allies: From Clinical Practice to International Relationships*. Northvale, N.J.: Jason Aronson.

Warren, M. 1992. "Democratic Theory and Self Transformation." *American Political Science Review* 86:8–23.

Winnicott, D. W. 1952. "Psychosis and Child Care." In *Collected Papers*. 1975. New York: Basic Books.

——. 1953. "Transitional Objects and Transitional Phenomena." In *Collected Papers*, 89. New York: Basic Books, 1975.

——. 1965. *The Maturational Processes and the Facilitating Environment: Studies in the Theory of Emotional Development*. New York: International Universities Press.

——. 1975. *Collected Papers*. New York: Basic Books.

——. 1982. *Playing and Reality*. London: Tavistock.

Wolfenstein, E. V. 1993. *Psychoanalytic Marxism: Groundwork*. New York: Guilford Press.

Woolf, V. 1978. *The Waves*. New York: Harcourt, Brace and Jovanovich.

INDEX